Throwing Plates at the Moon

Kelvin Bowers

SUMMERSDALE

Summersdale Publishers Ltd
46 West Street
Chichester
West Sussex
PO19 1RP
UK

www.summersdale.com

Printed and bound in Great Britain.

ISBN: 184024 261 2

Front cover design copyright © Kelvin Bowers 2002
Note: Place names are spelt as they were at the time of travel.

For Zhenka

Introduction

I decided to run across the earth instead of the moon because it seemed the least crazy option. Besides, I could look up along the way and bathe my face in moonlight anytime I wanted. When we were kids chasing across the pot bank tips in search of cups that still had their handles, we'd thrown crockery at the moon and taken great chunks out of it. Anything seemed possible then.

Ever since I could reach to lift the latch of our front gate and step outside, distance had a mesmerising effect on me. There were cast-iron gas lamps in the street in those days – converted to electric before they were uprooted – and I'd taken big strides between them, seriously marching off somewhere or other with my head held high.

The very same impulse that would take me away from home when I grew older ...

I wore a pair of spiked running shoes to my wedding. They had once belonged to a ginger-haired rat-catcher who became the cross-country champion of Europe. I removed the sharp spikes and dyed the leather uppers to match my velvet burgundy flares. It was the tail-end of the sixties.

A blanket of snow covered the pavements on the night before our wedding. Next morning I slid towards the registrars. My father-in-law to be was a driving instructor. The L-plates were still firmly attached to his vehicle as he pulled into the car park to deposit my bride.

Existing photographs show family and friends obscured by a flurry of snowflakes; the results of a hastily processed roll of film rather than the inclement weather. Through the grey flecks I can barely detect the man who changed my life. But he is there. And his signature is on our marriage certificate.

His name was Kris Hemensley, and he was the first poet I ever encountered. We met in 1966, when I left home to immigrate to Australia. I had a job awaiting me at the end of the voyage. The advertisement in our local newspaper read: *Come to the land of sun, sea and sand – work for the Melbourne Metropolitan Tramways.*

So there I was. For just ten pounds. Sailing across the world to become a tram conductor.

At Southampton Docks my father gripped my hand firmly. We had never shaken hands before. Afterwards, from a crowded deck aboard the *Fairsky*, I watched my parents wave a tearful goodbye through a flickering wall of ticker tape and balloons. A few days later I was already homesick. I sat in the quietest lounge of the ship scribbling letters on thin blue notepaper to the people I had left behind.

This is how the poet found me.

If it disappointed him to learn that I was a middle-distance runner and not a writer, he didn't show it. Instead he recited the names of all the athletes he'd heard of. Landy, Zatopek, Ibbotson and Pirie … the list was endless and included a good few heroes of mine.

I had once beaten Derek Ibbotson in a mile race on a grass track at Huddersfield and quickly recounted the win. Kris raised his eyebrows.

'It was a few years after his world record,' I owned up. 'He was overweight by that time.'

He nodded, but in a way that nonetheless signalled some acknowledgement of an impressive encounter.

'That's the reason I'm going to Australia. To become a better runner.'

I explained how in recent years a new crop of athletes had emerged from the southern hemisphere and begun to dominate the distance events.

'There's a man out there – must be in his seventies now. He was Herb Elliott's coach,' I said.

Elliott had demolished a world class field in the 1,500-metre final of the 1960 Rome Olympics. Film of this event included shots of a wiry old man nimbly vaulting the spectators' barrier to wave a yellow towel furiously above his head as his protégé strode around the final bend.

This was Percy Wells Cerutty. The man I was going halfway around the world to meet.

'Waving the towel meant that a world record was on the cards,' I told Kris. 'It was their pre-arranged signal. Angry officials bundled Cerutty out of the arena but Elliott broke the record.'

'Is he approachable then, this Cerutty chap?' asked Kris. 'How will you get to meet him?'

'I don't know yet,' I admitted. It had never crossed my mind that this might pose a problem.

Our voyage to a new land was not as I imagined. The *Fairsky* was no luxury liner. Even if it had been I would have felt no less restricted. My limbs were used to early morning runs along canal towpaths. They resented being confined to the rise and fall of wooden decks. Assisted passengers were relegated to the very bottom of the ship, four to a cabin. Here, it was even more claustrophobic. There was a constant hum from the engine room nearby, where the ship's pulse ticked over as her bow made shuddering progress through the waves.

Ports of call, which had sounded so exciting when I first learned of the itinerary, were in reality few and far between. They were, however, to provide my first steps on foreign soil and I relished an opportunity to properly stretch my legs.

When the *Fairsky* entered the Suez Canal I rode a camel to the pyramids. This expedition lasted all of five minutes and cost a fortune. My trousers reeked for days afterwards but I was pleased with the snapshot I posted home.

At Cairo, Kris informed me that he was half-Egyptian, his mother having been born in Alexandria. Thirty years later, I met her in Weymouth, still missing the sun and talking with a strong accent.

'She uses it like an Arab, to jump queues!' Kris laughed.

Kris had a beard, the bushiest I had ever seen, and a bit of a belly too. Arabs shouted: 'Hey Castro, Castro!' and grinned at him when we took the launch ashore to Aden.

Between these short stopovers I filled my days by reading. This was where the poet came into his own. He possessed more books than I thought had been printed. Most of these were stashed inside two large naval kit bags. Many more occupied the remainder of his luggage.

Since leaving school I had read less and less; the occasional biography of an athlete perhaps. But I do recall listening to the classics that were read out aloud to me. As a young boy, rather than face school dinners, I opted for visits to my grandparents' terraced house in Oldfield Street. There, my gran would have a hot meal waiting for me, which I'd eat whilst listening to *The Archers* on the radio, or Grandfather's latest passage from Dickens.

My grandfather was blind. His white stick hung from a coat-hook behind a heavy green door. It swung to and fro like a frosty pendulum whenever anyone entered or left the room. When he was not reading to my gran from the cumbersome volumes of Braille, or shuffling a set of dominoes which had tiny raised dots upon them, my grandfather sat astride a labyrinth of willow and made baskets for a living.

In winter, when it grew dark early or the smoking pot bank chimneys were further wreathed in fog, I would stand on tiptoes to help my gran light the gas mantle. At first, the sound the hissing gas made scared me. But then I would quickly raise a match to the fragile white gauze and wait for the mantle's soft warm glow to fill the room.

The yellow light illuminated a coalscuttle in the corner and Gran's empty Mackeson bottles on a shelf behind it. Each night she dipped a red-hot poker into her dark glass of stout until it too hissed like the delicate mantle overhead.

'Iron is good for you,' she would whisper to me in a conspiratorial tone.

If I owed a slender knowledge of literature to my grandfather, then perhaps I also inherited a certain endurance from him too.

Once, he pressed small silver medal into my palm and asked me to read the inscription engraved upon the back of it. I did so to myself at first, and then loudly repeated what I had read.

'National League for the Blind. T. Broadhurst, 7 April, 1920, Stoke to London.'

Grandfather, whose first name was Thomas, had once taken part in a protest march to draw attention to the meagre wages and poor working conditions of the blind. He marched from his birthplace in the Potteries to London, and delivered a speech to the Prime Minister when he got there. Women wept along the way and tossed money into his path.

Afterwards, with little improvements forthcoming, someone less articulate set alight the local workshops for the blind.

'The fire brigade pumped water from the canal and hundreds of fish rained down onto the flames. But the building burned to the ground and we all stood and cheered.' Grandfather puffed at a pipe between chuckles. 'They nabbed a chap called Chicko for it and he got eighteen months!'

Sometimes, when his pipe went out, his hand would pat-pat the tabletop until he found his box of matches. The picture on my grandfather's matchbox depicted a man wearing an old-fashioned swimsuit whose name was Captain Webb. He was the first person to swim the English Channel. I was astonished by this. I could not swim one stroke and always begged my mother to write notes detailing various skin ailments that would prohibit my entry into the school swimming pool.

Sports day was different. There was no way I'd ever miss that. I was tall and skinny – just the right size for loping over the mown grass or sprinting fast when I needed to. Running was my thing, it was as simple as that.

2

As our ship gently heaved and rolled towards a new continent, Kris and I reminisced and gleaned fragments about each other's backgrounds.

One day he handed me a paperback. It was called *On the Road* and from it I learned all about the beat generation who shouted poetry from the open boxcars of freight trains trundling across America. These were fascinating tales of unpredictable people sharing crazy adventures and getting by on next to nothing.

By the time we stood squinting in the strong sunlight at the distant land mass that was to be our new home, my journey had somehow altered course.

A smartly dressed representative from the Melbourne Metropolitan Tramways came aboard when the ship docked in Port Melbourne. There were a few other employees besides myself and once through customs we were whisked away to our allotted lodging houses.

Mrs Crispin was to be my landlady. She lived in a bungalow with a rusty tin roof, an untidy garden and a flea-ridden dog called Rolf. There was also a lodger, Danny, who drove container wagons into the outback and disappeared for days on end. Whenever he was home the pile of lager cans in the cluttered front porch mushroomed and threatened to topple.

All anyone talked about was horse racing and this often resulted in my having to loan someone a few dollars after 'a bad day at the trots'. Danny would then disappear into the bush, along with his memory of any outstanding debts. He returned only to resume losing more money, my money, on another diabolical selection of horses. I never knew him to win any of his bets, which must have been quite difficult to accomplish week after week. Our landlady was much the same.

Mrs Crispin's house was situated just across the street from Hawthorn railway station, only a couple of steps from the square mile city centre. It was in a scruffy nondescript suburb redeemed only by a healthy outcrop of odd characters and misfits.

I met a couple of these that very first night when I strolled to the nearest hotel a few paces down the road. Rain was making mud puddles out of small piles of dust heaped on the pavement. In a side street under a lamp stood a man wearing a kilt. I heard him long before I saw him. He was playing the bagpipes.

At the bar of the hotel a cracked brown leather suitcase of a face hauled itself towards me.

'Interested?' the square jaw demanded, pointing to a bulging sack at his feet and shooing the flies away.

'What's inside?'

'A pig.'

Kris's passage through Immigration Control had been altogether more traumatic. His hefty canvas kit bags had been emptied out and several items confiscated and labelled pornographic. He was then given a lecture on the Australian authorities' unwillingness to allow such suspect literature into the country. Later he was given directions to a Salvation Army hostel. It was not the welcome he'd anticipated.

We met up the next day and I took him along to Mrs Crispin who had one empty room remaining. Soon after Kris moved in he found a job as a ticket collector on the railway platform opposite and for a couple of weeks we both left for work each morning dressed in uniforms.

Once out of the house on Hawthorn Road there seemed distinctly more likelihood of our experiencing that healthy lifestyle predicted by Australia House in London. Back inside though, at mealtimes, whenever our landlady screamed abuse at her trusty mongrel, Kris and I would grimace. When Rolf was in trouble he was usually in the kitchen and because cigarettes were rarely out of Mrs Crispin's mouth long enough for her to draw breath, this inevitably caused a shower of ash to erupt over whatever tasty morsel was being greasily concocted for our supper.

My career as a tram conductor clattered downhill from the start. I was hopelessly inept at dealing with the new coinage. Worse still was the very real prospect of my spilling the entire collection of fares from my leather satchel when attempting to inch along the running boards outside the tram as it rumbled in and out of the city.

I had seen more experienced conductors take shortcuts in this manner to get from one end of a crowded tram to the other during rush hour. But the bag was heavy and swung out away from me over the lines, scattering coins onto the road below while I gripped the rail in sheer terror.

When all miscalculated fares were accounted for, my weekly wage was considerably reduced.

I handed back my uniform and telephoned Percy Wells Cerutty.

'And what would a Pom want in Portsea?'

I was speaking to the man himself now but it was hard work.

'I want to improve my best time for the mile.'

'And what would that be?'

I held my breath. 'Four minutes, twelve seconds.'

There was a staccato explosion on the other end of the telephone. Percy slowly repeated what I had just told him and added, 'Have you any idea how far behind you'd be when Elliott crossed the line?'

'That's why I have to improve,' I persisted.

A short silence followed.

'No harm in your paying a visit I suppose. Tell me, have you ever seen a sand dune?'

I explained how badly off we were for sand dunes in the Midlands where I came from.

'Perhaps the Pom will wish he'd never seen one,' laughed Percy.

Portsea lies at the narrow entrance to Port Philip Bay some sixty miles from Melbourne. It is the poorer neighbour of Sorrento, a fashionable beach resort frequented by the wealthy. Prime Minister Holt had a holiday home there at the time but was later to vanish without trace whilst swimming offshore.

3

I alighted from the carriage at the near deserted railway station to find Percy sitting behind the wheel of an open-top sports car. He wore a yellow shirt and a lilac scarf which the wind tugged alarmingly once my bag was in the boot and we were underway.

The road was narrow before it became a dirt track and snaked high above the ocean. Within seconds it became clear that Percy's zest for life included dicing with death.

It was difficult to indulge in conversation above the roar of the engine, but I was grateful for this as the odd prayer could have slipped out inadvertently mid-sentence.

Somehow we reached our destination intact.

Nancy, his wife, stood on the veranda of a single-storey building that had been much extended over the years.

'What kept ya?' she enquired.

'Ah, the bloody car was playing up again. Brake trouble, so I kept the speed down.'

'Grab yourself a glass of water, love.'

I followed Nancy into the kitchen.

'We never touch tea even when there's a Pom a-visitin'.' She winked at Percy who by now had his eyes fixed on my arms.

'We'll have to work on that upper body,' he told me. 'But I'd better fix the brakes first.'

There was only one other athlete living at Portsea and within a few minutes we were introduced.

'Vesty, show the Pom here where everything is,' shouted Nancy.

Sylvester Stack looked stocky for a runner. He had severely cropped blond hair and serious blue eyes that always appeared to be fixed intently on a finishing tape he alone could see. I never once saw him run.

Vesty led me to the bunkhouse. On the way there we passed a small square shack.

'Percy built that when he first found the place years back. Wanta see?'

I nodded and he lifted the latch to the door. The little room had been patched up many times and was empty but for a very small bunk occupying the end wall.

'Landy slept in that in the fifties, and Murray Halberg when he was over from New Zealand.' Vesty spoke in a hushed reverential manner, for these men were both gods in our eyes.

'Halberg was a lanky guy wasn't he? He would have had to have curled up some.' I climbed into the high bunk and lay my head on the pillow.

Our sleeping quarters were in a larger wooden shack a little further from the main house. Vesty appeared to have few possessions, mostly consisting of a pile of scratched vinyl records leaning precariously beside his bed.

'Perce gave me this.' He puffed out his chest, and for a split second I thought, *Oh yes, a new upper body*. But then I saw that he was pointing to a wind-up gramophone.

'Do you like Joan Baez?'

I nodded. However, my fondness for the purity of her voice was not to last. Vesty saw to that. 'We Shall Overcome' became what I had to overcome whenever he reached out to crank up his beloved gift from Percy.

The Australian army were fighting in Vietnam and Vesty was paranoid about receiving his call up papers. Each morning before we collected our mail he would psyche himself up by playing 'We Shall Overcome.'

The psychological damage this did to me was immense.

I spent many hours with Vesty pretending, at his request, to be an interrogation officer firing questions at him in an attempt to undermine the pleas of a conscientious objector. He had rehearsed this role countless times and seemed to me to be utterly convincing. Less convincing was the violent aggressive streak that occasionally got the better of him when unrehearsed sentences such as 'I'll kill the fucker!' echoed about the camp due to some minor dispute with one of his workmates on a building site down the track.

The sand dunes at Portsea are very steep. I ran up and down them until my legs buckled or I retched – whichever occurred first. At that point I'd sink into a miserable heap or roll downhill gasping for air. Perce would observe my discomfort from the top of the dune, arms folded.

One day when I was taking a shower there was a noisy rap on the bathroom door and his voice bellowed out: 'Real men wash in the sea!'

And he did, too. Plunging into the waves each morning whilst I pretended to measure my stride length in wet sand at the shore's edge. Of course, I'd not dared to admit to being a non-swimmer and so was always nervous that he would have a heart attack in the water or suddenly get cramp and wave to me for help.

When we were not at the beach I'd run barefoot on the soft tracks that wound through the ti-tree and scrub surrounding his property. Sometimes these were timed runs that Percy duly recorded in a red canvas-bound book which he kept in his office.

Often I was called upon to saw logs for the woodburner or help weed Nancy's vegetable patch.

'Never forget what you are about,' Perce instructed. 'Whether it's feeding the chooks or cutting down a tree, concentrate, observe, practise your breathing.'

There were lighter sides to his strict regime. When friends arrived with lively children at weekends, Perce would join them on a trampoline and pretend to be a clown. He was very good at this. He loved dancing too and would suddenly grab his protesting wife, who would be in the middle of preparing a meal, and whirl her screaming around the kitchen during television pop shows.

We ate splendidly. I tasted lobster for the first time, and long before everyone began eating muesli for breakfast Perce devised his very own version. There were giant sacks of raw rolled oats and different nuts and raisins which we'd scoop together into large bowls. No one was allowed to add any milk so it took a long time to digest.

Although I did put on a little weight I doubt if my torso ever gained the proportions Perce was aiming for, despite hours heaving dumbells and doing sit-ups under a corrugated lean-to we called the Muscle Hut.

Kris came to visit me at Portsea once. I was nervous about him meeting Percy. Smoking was banned for a start. Also, anyone apart from Nancy who was overweight was directed either to the door or the sand dune.

I need not have worried. The two of them spent half the night chatting about the great tradition of storytelling in Australia. At one point Perce even recited lines from Banjo Patterson and Henry Lawson.

My favourite time during these weeks was in the evenings after the dishes had been washed and stacked away. We'd all sit beside the woodstove in a partitioned corner of the kitchen and talk. Here Perce taught me the true value of yarns around a campfire in the company of friends.

Many of his tales were linked to the famous athletes he'd befriended. But he also spoke of overcoming a difficult upbringing and about a nervous breakdown from which he recovered by slowly gaining the confidence to jump from the topmost diving board at St Kilda Baths in Melbourne.

That and giving up smoking he considered to be the two hardest things he'd ever had to tackle.

My contributions were short and sparse by comparison, having much less experience to draw upon. He was surprised however, to hear that I came from a town in the Potteries – the one that Arnold Bennett omitted when he wrote *Anna of the Five Towns*. Perce named his son Arnold after reading this novel because the grim lives it portrayed affected him so deeply.

When he asked how I came to be an athlete I confessed that to begin with it was no more than a ruse to avoid arithmetic lessons.

'Jesus, don't give this fella the shopping money, Nance!' he grinned.

Then I told him all about the marathon I'd run; round and round a football field in the local park. I showed him the newsclipping I'd kept: 'Kelvin does his own Olympic Marathon. Fourteen-year-old's 26 miles in under four hours.'

After this I was known as the Boy Marathon Runner and I was invited to join the local harriers.

The harriers met at weekends in the boat shed of a country estate and raced over the surrounding parkland. Jackets and trousers were draped over the hulls of upturned rowing boats. Horse liniment was slapped onto shivering thighs. Sometimes startled deer would cross our path in the park. And afterwards the athletes stood three at a time in tin baths of tepid water, rinsing mud from their aching muscles.

On harsh winter nights my father would put on a long grey raincoat, tug down his flat cap and stand with a stopwatch under the streetlights as I ran lap after lap around the block.

Percy was intrigued by the marathon. I could tell. But some time went by before he properly let on.

'I ran a lot of marathons in my day as you well know. Fifty miles too a good few times. Once or twice even a hundred miles without stopping. But there was one special run I dreamed of making and never did. Know what that was?'

I shook my head. Perce leaned forward as if no one else must ever know.

'From here to England. Ten thousand miles. Now that's a marathon!'

4

Percy's neighbour was a builder who offered to take me on. I was given a job chipping mortar off a stack of used bricks. Then I was sent up a ladder with Vesty to rip off the tin roof. The bricks were freezing before the sun warmed them. Later in the day, the crêpe soles of my desert boots grew tacky from the heat of the corrugated roofing. We ate our lunch down on the jetty, where I soothed my hot feet in the sea.

Percy's stable of would-be world-beaters had dwindled since Elliott's day. Now it was down to just a couple – a failed tram conductor and a galloping Gippslander whose khaki-coloured nightmares kept me awake at night.

I stayed there for three months. But my heart wasn't in it. Finally I took a train back to Melbourne and moved into a small flat with Kris the poet. Then I found myself a proper job packing bras and pants into cardboard cartons labelled Parramatta and Wollongong. There were smoky jazz clubs in the city. Folk singers in the coffee bars. The *Sergeant Pepper* album had just been released. And one blustery afternoon I walked past an open window hidden behind a lemon tree in the garden of the house next door, and heard the first few lines of 'A Whiter Shade of Pale'.

When the job got me down I caught a ship to Tasmania and travelled south by bus to Hobart. There I found a worse job still – at the end of a conveyor belt in a paper mill stacking more cardboard cartons. Each weekend I headed for the bush, where well-marked tracks led up to Mount Wellington. Often, I began these solitary hikes with a leisurely stroll uphill along Cascade Road, past the oldest brewery in Australia.

The mountain, although high, was not wild enough to be without a café. Halfway up, for the price of a Coke, I'd sit at one of the tables overlooking the wide estuary of the River Derwent. On my second visit the owner of the café sat beside me and talked. Far below us the bay was blue. Racing yachts pricked up their silvery white ears like ghostly hares and went skimming across the water in droves.

'Peaceful spot, eh?'

'It's beautiful,' I said.

'I came here a long time ago from Austria. I had lost my family already you see. I was looking for this. The quiet, these views of the little boats down there, just specks …'

The man smoothed out the wrinkles in the tablecloth where I'd rested my elbows.

'Poms come here when they're homesick,' he said. 'They come here to read road maps that have familiar-sounding names running through them. And to see the apple orchards and drink the cider.'

'Yes, I can see how they would be reminded of home,' I agreed.

'But,' he stressed, 'some of us have no past worth returning to. So we stay, and really it is not so bad.'

I was back on the mainland by Christmas, working in the warehouse again on Dorcas Street, when news broke about the bushfires.

'Hobart's on fire!' my workmates shouted. 'The whole bladdy mountain's gone up. Strong winds from the Antarctic are fanning the flames. Reckon Mount Wellington's just a cinder heap by now.'

I think I'd always known that I would return home to England when the two-year term stipulated by the assisted passage was up. England's football team had won the World Cup in my absence. And the streets seemed to have shrunk in the wash.

I had given up running and was trying to write. I wrote poems and a story in verse for children about a dustman who emptied the sky. I showed my story to a friend who lived in London. Afterwards, we walked to Hyde Park and sat on the grass, and watched Mick Jagger fill the air with butterflies.

That same year I hitch-hiked to Morocco and back.

In the following spring I found employment at a nursery. The boss let me drive the tractor providing I stayed off the road. I would daydream behind the wheel when the trays of seedlings had been unloaded, and every so often think of Percy – and that one run he never made. I even began to recite aloud to myself the lines John Donne wrote: 'To live in one land, is captivity, To runne all countries, a wild roguery.'

But running had become that shadowy lost domain for me – something akin to Alaine-Fournier's *Le Grand Meaulnes*; a magical time that I would forever associate with my youth but perhaps never be able to enter into again. At school I had won my first mile race in stockinged feet, and then played chasing games around the tram shed at the bottom of our street. Once I lapped the block a hundred times without reason or reward. I would also regularly run as fast as I could between two towns a mile apart, setting off beneath an iron-girded railway bridge shaped like a coathanger at a place we called Neck End. There was a sports outfitters under the bridge, with white running shoes made of kangaroo hide in a window displaying silver trophies.

I suppose these were my first 'journey runs', although I didn't know what a 'journey run' was at the time. The Greeks and Romans did. They had to run carrying messages between towns and cities. And 'Fotemen that runnen' were used in the fifteenth century to race ahead of slow-moving coaches and prepare for their master's arrival at the inn. Endurance jaunts with a purpose these, unlike that of Ib'n Battutah, the indefatigable Moroccan who strode from Tangiers to China and back in the fourteenth century, just for the hell of it.

One morning when I was still working at the nursery, I found myself hunting for an old pair of trainers. The next day they were on my feet.

Ten pairs of Adidas Gazelles were packed into a metal box on the roof rack. I ticked the list and closed the lid. I had estimated a thousand miles for each pair of running shoes. After that the heels would begin to wear down at the edges and I was prone to ankle injuries.

Almost two years of planning had brought me to the brink of the real journey. The same distance as Percy's marathon. Same dangers too. But the opposite direction.

Information from the meteorological office had determined periods of the year best avoided when passing through certain parts of the world. And the Automobile Association had put me in touch with Mike Artus, a New Zealander who had recently driven his granny overland to Asia. En route he had compiled an intricate dossier outlining the different road conditions and difficulties we could expect to meet.

I returned to my checklist. Four camp beds. Mosquito netting. Two and a half thousand water purification tablets. A child's potty ...

A long time had elapsed since I warmed my hands over the cast iron woodburner in the bright little kitchen at Portsea. I was twenty-seven years old and married now. Leona was five years younger than me. Our son Zhenka was two years old. His name came from a Russian poet whose verse we both admired.

Leona had long brown hair and played the guitar. She wore a fur mini skirt to the Isle of Wight rock festival and we rented the gardener's cottage of a large house built by one of the Wedgwood family.

People set out for Australia every day. Some jet back and forth so frequently they regard themselves as long-distance commuters.

My own journey out and back had been across the ocean on both occasions, aboard the *Fairsky* and the *Fairsea*, Italian ships from the Sitmar Line. But I had been anxious to see something more of the world and for a time toyed with the idea of an organised overland holiday trip back to England. The colourful brochures I collected from the travel agents showed photographs of a luxury coach cruising smoothly across desert wastes. But there the dream ended. I didn't have the courage to take it any further.

People change. Acquire new skills. Gain confidence, or become foolhardy enough to attempt almost anything. How does it happen? Do we meet a chain of people who gently, without our even realising it, steer us back towards some hitherto disregarded path?

If so I had met those people. A migrating poet with his portable library. The silver moustachioed Aussie who waved a yellow towel. And here by my side a woman who had pencilled in red the route we would take.

There were other people too, at different times, and those more directly involved in helping propel my legs along this particular road. A bookmaker called Fred Berrisford, the original one-armed bandit. He had one arm and one leg but more energy than an octopus. And the England goalkeeper Gordon Banks who lost the sight in one eye as the result of a car accident. People dealing with adversities of one description or another; those who recognised and responded to a challenge. They each helped in various ways; writing letters, attending functions and raising funds.

Two friends were to accompany us: Jeff and Sue Walters. I met Jeff in the foyer of a theatre one night, handing out flyers about a music event. He was tall and bespectacled with a brown tinged beard that elongated his narrow face. He wore tight corduroy trousers that did the same for his height. Sue was an inch or two taller, with long brown hair like Lea's. Together we looked like a family of Quakers.

Jeff and I hit it off immediately. We were both fervent armchair travellers with a mutual passion for mountaineering exploits. This was despite an acute fear of heights which he attempted to alleviate by placing all his climbing books on the topmost shelf of a high bookcase. Even then, balanced on a chair, he became pale and wobbly. Sue, on the other hand, was unfazed at the edge of clifftops but nervous about my impending trek across terra firma.

This was our plan. Each day I would set off running whilst the others drove ahead in a support vehicle. They would arrange food and drinks along the way and I would aim to cover between 25 and 30 miles a day. It would be a journey of fourteen months duration that would take us through Belgium, Holland, Germany, Austria, Yugoslavia, Bulgaria, Turkey, Iran, Afghanistan, Pakistan, India and Australia.

On 21 January, 1974, a group of businessmen were invited to attend an informal function hosted by Gordon Banks and the Lord Mayor at Stoke town hall. The event was staged to announce 'the longest run in history' to the press, and hopefully to gain support from prospective sponsors. Until this time only a handful of people were aware of our intentions and they had been sworn to secrecy.

I borrowed a jacket for the do from my best mate Barry Bowler, and put on a flash gold-striped tie for luck because it was a gift from Australia. Lea wore her new white cheesecloth dress with wide sleeves, and she arranged her long hair like a Native American squaw. We arrived at the reception to find several large maps pinned to an exhibition stand in the centre of the room.

After a brief introduction by Don Edwards, the Lord Mayor's secretary, Jeff was called upon to make his speech. He stood in front of the maps with a ruler tucked under his arm and when he spoke he sounded confident.

'The existing accepted record for the longest distance ever run is 3,686 miles. But one of the longest runs in the record books is from Istanbul to Calcutta and back in 1836, by a man named Ernst Mensen. However, the authenticity of this 6,984-mile run is very much open to doubt, as the Norwegian courier claimed to have covered more than 90 miles a day, swimming across thirteen rivers on the way.

'Kelvin …' Jeff paused momentarily, raised his ruler and swept it dramatically from one end of the maps to the other, 'intends to run from England to Australia: a staggering distance of over 10,000 miles. He is likely to face extremes of temperature in the mountains of Eastern Turkey. Between Ankara and Samsun the route lies through the Bolu Pass with a climb of almost eight miles through a region of snow. Between Erzurum and Maku the winding mountain road stays at 8,000 feet for 14 miles at one stage, and between Sari and Mashad in Iran, there are fourteen tunnels, all unlit, and one of them a mile long.'

Jeff continued to tap the maps with the ruler as he reeled off statistics and pinpointed a variety of terrifying obstacles. I tried to detach myself from the close involvement, pretending that I was hearing it all for the first time and wondering what on earth the businessmen would make of it. The 'run that would eclipse all others' sounded such a tantalising prospect. I sensed a concentrated hush among the group of people standing beside me. It seemed impossible not to be gripped by the excitement of it all.

'In Iran, the temperature will top 100 degrees and when Kelvin reaches Afghanistan he will have to cross the Desert of Death on his way to Kandahar and the halfway stage at Kabul. Next, he must negotiate the infamous Khyber Pass in the North West Frontier. And then the long haul through Pakistan and the jungles of India.'

Jeff took a sip from a glass of water before resuming.

'Finally, he has to cross his third continent, Australia, from west to east, where the great trek will come to an end in Sydney. If Kelvin succeeds he will almost have trebled the existing recognised long-distance mark.'

The room fell silent. Everything depended on the next few minutes. Our dreams hinged on the reactions to Jeff's spurring words. But he had done his homework well; a lion's share of organising already. Someone at the back of the room began to clap their hands. Soon there was wholehearted applause from the rest of the group.

Next came the questions. We braced ourselves for a rough ride. Whatever lay ahead, whether in the Khyber Pass or the Australian desert, could not be any more formidable.

'What about wild dogs? Rabies? Are any of you qualified in medicine?'

'How will you get by in the trouble spots of the world? What precautions have our embassies advised you to take?'

'And your young child? How old did you say he was? Two? Isn't that asking for trouble?'

We answered the questions as honestly as we could. Sue's first-aid certificate wouldn't be much use if she were required to stitch up any dog bites. But Lea was adamant that it was the right time to take our son with us. There would be greater problems if he were still in nappies, and in a year or so the journey would interfere with his education.

When someone asked what made me think I was capable of running such vast stretches, Brian Calvert spoke up for me. He was the newspaper reporter who'd covered the story of my marathon run when I was just fourteen. He described how he had not expected me to get much further than five miles round a 410-yard grass track with no company.

'I was very wrong,' he said. 'Kelvin ran on and on until he was exhausted, then he walked a little, then ran again. Eventually he was down to a shambling trot and collapsed several times, but he would not give up.

'When he passed the 20-mile mark I suggested that he had proved his point and should stop before he did himself harm, but Kelvin had set out to run 26 miles, 385 yards and that was what he was going to do. When he could run no more he walked, and when he couldn't walk he crawled, but he made it in the end, and earned the headlines the next day. If that doesn't show you how determined he can be, I don't know what will.'

There was a murmur of approval. Then a director of Stoke City Football Club strode forward with a cheque. More contributions were swiftly handed over and in the euphoria that followed several people got carried away.

'One vehicle isn't enough for this kind of expedition: they must have two.'

'Land Rovers, that's what they need for the desert.'

'And walkie-talkies to keep in close contact with each other in the wildest regions.'

Everyone suddenly became very positive. By the end of the evening all my running kit had been donated and plans were afoot to use the run to raise funds for a local boys' club. Snooker star Ray Reardon even offered to play an exhibition match with Gordon Banks to help boost the finances.

Jeff and I were amazed. So were Lea and Sue. After the 'run launch' was over we headed for an Indian restaurant around the corner to celebrate. There, we promptly left behind Jeff's briefcase containing all the maps and the facts and figures he'd so diligently compiled. Everything was retrieved the next morning but we came to regard the incident as an omen, and sure enough our project took a nosedive a few weeks later.

Britain was in the throes of an industrial crisis. That winter, power cuts became the norm and when the nights closed in both department stores and cornershops were lit by candles. The nail in the coffin came when the working week was cut to a mere three days. Money was scarce and finding further sponsors grew increasingly difficult.

Turf accountant Fred Berrisford had been appointed coordinator of the record attempt. He and his secretary, Elaine, worked tirelessly to drum up fresh support. On my twenty-eighth birthday, Fred drove me to a nearby garage and told me to climb inside a brand new British Leyland J4 van that was parked on the forecourt. Then the owner of the garage, Bill Bell, appeared and handed me the keys. To speed things up, Bill even gave up the registration number he'd been saving for his new Jaguar: OVT 100M.

With the donation of this vehicle and also a small trailer, further sponsors came forward. The people of Stoke-on-Trent rallied round and a departure date was fixed. In the meantime, my own preparation had suffered because of the uncertainty. On the night before we left I went jogging along the canal towpath one last time.

'He's running to Australia tomorrow,' observed a man to his son as they moved aside to let me pass.

The enormity of what I'd taken on suddenly hit me and my legs began to wobble. Too late now, I thought …

April 7 was the date inscribed on the medal awarded to my grandfather when he marched to London. We chose it by chance and the day dawned cloudless.

5

A civic send-off had been organised. We were all ushered into the Mayor's parlour at the town hall in Stoke. Glass-fronted cabinets displayed a choice selection of Wedgwood and Royal Doulton.

The Mayor was short and shabby, his dark hair slicked back. He seemed weighed down by his official chain which interfered with the flow of his signature as he leaned forward over our leather-bound logbook. This accomplished, he stubbed out a cigarette on the marble fireplace and directed us outside onto the town hall steps. He handed me a letter addressed to his counterpart in Sydney and we posed for photographs.

Friends had gathered to wave us off. A few members of the running clubs joined me for the first ten miles. We strode out briskly along the A34 before they turned back to their homes, hot showers and Sunday lunches.

When there was only one shadow left soundlessly trailing my footsteps I studied the tarmac unwinding into the distance. I knew the road led to London. I had travelled this road often enough in the past. But as for it leading on to anywhere beyond that? Wild tribal territories for instance. Or the Desert of Death. It seemed impossible to comprehend.

More comforting perhaps to think of things closer to home. Already the Duke of Sutherland's estate lay behind me. A tall stone monument stood on a rounded hill thick with ferns. This was the rough parkland through which we once raced.

As a youth I had won the county cross-country championships at the foot of those hills. The course was snowbound and very undulating but I negotiated the icy ruts along the wide paths through the woods without difficulty and led from start to finish. When I crossed the line Roy Fowler dashed towards me.

'Quick, can I try on your shoes?'

Roy ran for England. On the continent he was known as the Red Fox. He trained in pit boots and flew racing pigeons that had won just as many prizes. He was clear favourite to win the men's race that afternoon but had forgotten his running shoes. That is how the pair of spikes I owned won both races.

All week long my father had applied Dubbin to those shoes, working his rough fingers into the stiff leather until it grew soft and supple as a second skin. They became Roy's lucky shoes and he ran his fastest races in them.

I was given a brand new pair instead.

Before long I reached the glassblowing factory where I had first worked upon leaving school. It was Sunday and the offices overlooking the road were empty. Colleagues there had presented me with ten crisp new pound notes in 1966 as a farewell gift to cover the cost of that first journey down under.

There were newborn lambs in the fields. Narrow-boats sat in the canals with names like *The Blackthorn Rose* and *The Milky Way*. Sometimes passengers in overtaking vehicles would spot the destination in black lettering upon my singlet and wind down their windows to shout encouragement or exercise their wit.

By mid-afternoon I could feel a troublesome blister on the big toe of my right foot. It was unexpectedly hot and the elation of finally being underway, coupled with the camaraderie of my clubmates, had prompted me to push the pace along a fraction too quickly.

That night, behind some farming machinery beside a barn, I peeled off my damp running kit and stood in a small plastic bowl to bathe my feet. Our new home on wheels was parked in a lay-by. The white British Leyland J4 was no spacious campervan, but we had kitted it out as best we could and with the bulk of our luggage housed in a small two-wheeled trailer at the rear, there was just enough room for us all to sleep inside.

Earlier I had arrived to find Zhenka already tearful. The sixth member of our intrepid party – his favourite teddy bear – had been left behind.

This first night we learned which corner of our cramped quarters was handiest for the kettle, and also how quickly Zhenka's potty would spill over if left on the lid of either bunk.

We tucked into chicken and cake before preparing for bed. Each of us felt relaxed and optimistic about the days ahead.

Next morning I got lost in Lichfield.

Looking back, it seems odd not to have imagined ever getting lost. But I didn't. However, getting lost became part and parcel of our daily routine. It was not until I reached Afghanistan, where there was only one road to choose from, that my course seemed safely plotted.

The day after we set out, the road I had invested all my hopes on began to branch in many different directions. Only then did I realise that I had not even discussed with Jeff how we each intended to make our way through busy city centres. Ring roads and bypasses, although less problematic, would greatly increase the mileage. Keeping that to a minimum was my first priority as I pressed on into the centre.

Normally, I would not have hesitated to ask directions. But something – perhaps the sign 'ENGLAND TO AUSTRALIA' a foot high on each side of our white van, or those same names neatly stitched to my singlet – prevented even the most timid of enquiries.

I strode purposefully along the pavement. Briefly jogged on the spot at a junction. And then all too quickly headed off anywhere.

Soon it became obvious that I had made the wrong choice. Shamefaced, I quickly executed an about-turn and embarked on the same pitiful charade. I repeated this humiliating procedure three or four times before a kindly voice stopped me in my tracks.

'Saw you on the telly last night.'

I winced as the butcher beckoned me inside his shop, where we stood amongst a pile of sawdust on the tiled floor he was sweeping.

'Here comes your van now. They must be looking for you.'

He winked, wiped his palms on an apron that resembled a frost-bound sunset, and firmly clasped my hand.

'All the best, my boy. All the best.'

The butcher's name was Blaze. And he duly wrote it into our logbook: Basil Blaze. He had red mutton-chop whiskers that crept up his ample cheeks like small curling flames.

As the days proceeded we settled down to a different kind of life. I got lost less and made good progress despite the blister.

We split up on the edge of London, agreeing to meet before nightfall at Blackheath. By the time I reached the cricket ground at Lords, rain had set in for the day. The map I clutched was soggy and my feet splashed through deepening puddles. Dripping brollies grew menacing and hostile.

I crossed the Thames at Vauxhall Bridge, sat down at a table outside an Italian café, and ate spotted dick in the pouring rain. My last meal out on English soil.

It was six hours before I saw the others. The van looked in a sorry state. There were newspapers covered in mud laid down on the floor inside, and the cushions all felt damp. Soon enough though, the kettle was boiling on the camping stove.

I put on a dry set of clothes, settled back and told them all about the greasy spoon I had found beside the river.

'Mouthwatering, Jeff. No other word for it.'

6

From Dover we caught a ferry to Ostende. I thought of Captain Webb in his striped swimsuit slamming shut the door of his bathing hut at the foot of the white cliffs and striding confidently towards the choppy grey waves.

Once across the Channel, the entire journey seemed somehow more valid. From these drab docklands I could travel on foot, unimpeded by oceans, all the way to Southern India.

Sue though grew increasingly nervous now that we were in foreign parts, and took to sleeping with a knife under her pillow. Zhenka sensed her discomfort, as only children can, and plagued her mercilessly whenever an opportunity arose.

Boredom was one obstacle entirely overlooked. Yet for Jeff and Sue it posed a serious threat. Lea busied herself each day with all manner of tasks, not least that of seeing to the welfare and safety of a lively two-year-old. And my time was filled in the simplest way of all: purely by placing one foot in front of the other, over and over again.

In both cases a sense of achievement – hardly apparent, but sufficient enough to sustain us – turned into a wall that divided us from our two best friends.

Jeff was dumbfounded. All the attention to detail he had paid when compiling facts and figures to satisfy our sponsors had not prepared him for the drudgery of his own role behind the steering wheel.

Time spent in the van, overnight and during rest stops each day, grew increasingly oppressive. Out on the road, in a flat landscape, my slow footsteps echoed across a grey expanse of cobblestones.

It was not easy running slowly and it did not come naturally to me. I much preferred striding out at a good fast lick, but of course that was no way to attempt a run of this kind. In a vehicle, bridges come at you like low-flying aircraft. On foot they could take an eternity to reach. All my preparatory runs had been over circular courses: not even out and back because that would have been too boring. Now, our route to the Orient lay in one direction only and the road seemed to stretch interminably because I'd never been along it before.

To begin with, I divided each day's running into three or four different stints on the road. The distances I covered varied, depending on how many built-up areas I had to pass through. But most days I was on the move for at least four hours. Occasionally I would take a short walk between runs and Lea would join me, pushing Zhenka in his baby buggy. It was my wife's first journey overseas and she was so determined to see it through that she talked of us both walking the rest of the way if Jeff and Sue decided to turn back with the van.

'We'd need a new baby buggy,' she said, 'and a couple of decent rucksacks, and a lighter tent than the one we've got. But we could do it if we kept everything down to an absolute minimum. I'm sure we could. Did you read those lines of Herman Hesse that Barry quoted in the letter he sent? He wrote that "self-realisation is not attained by clinging to a world of repose, paradise and islands of happiness. There must be new experiences to carry one forward." I think we are far more aligned in our thoughts than we have been for a long time, don't you? In the past we've neglected our horizons and dwelt too much on the daily grind. I may not have found that out if I hadn't come on this journey. Now, even after such a short time, everything seems limitless.'

'You're right,' I said, 'but I'm hoping Sue's worries are just teething troubles and that she'll begin to enjoy it given a few more weeks. The worst thing is when Zhenka throws one of his tantrums – but they've experienced that lots of times in the past. Whatever they decide, I've no intention of abandoning the van. If things get worse and they do both go home, someone else will have to fly out and take over the driving.'

Later, when I replied to Baz Bowler's letter, I told him how much Lea and I wished he was with us, because in all my running life I never got closer to anyone or enjoyed sharing the experience of a run in the same way that I did with him. And I signed off with the words: *If you ever want to chuck in your job and join us, there are planes to deliver you here in a few hours and we'd gladly hang around until you showed up.*

At the small town of Borgloon I met a marathon runner: the Belgian champion Karel Lismont. He took me to his father's terraced café and placed a jug of wine on to one of the formica-topped tables. We sat down and his father joined us with three glasses. He too was of athletic build but none of the trophies on the shelves lining the room bore his name.

'Was your father a sportsman?' I asked.

'No,' replied Karel. 'But he does the dancing. He does the dancing still.'

The old man fussed with a beer mat and awkwardly fingered his crumpled collar whilst his son tried to explain how far I was running. At the mention of the word 'marathon', Monsieur Lismont nodded and pointed towards the bar. In pride of place above a colourful range of liqueur bottles, hung a large framed photograph with three signatures scrawled across it. An Olympic flag flew at the top of the picture, and in the foreground, on the second step of a dais, stood Lismont in his tracksuit, stooping forward slightly to receive his award.

'Two years ago in Munich.'

'I watched it on television,' I said.

Lismont relayed this to his father and the man beamed with pride, then scraped the legs of his chair over the red tiled floor and rose to leave the room.

'I know where he goes to,' the athlete smiled.

We drank another glass of wine, emptying the jug. Lismont asked after the Red Fox, whom he had often raced against in Europe.

By this time his father had reappeared, brushing aside the colourful plastic strips of the fly curtain as he came towards us.

A red leather box the size of a travel clock was in his hand. He cradled it like some delicate butterfly. Then he slid it, still gently, across the table.

'He says for you to touch it. For luck. For this Percy. This Percy's marathon.'

I fumbled with the catch, then flipped the lid open and slowly ran my fingers over the silver medal.

For a few days the atmosphere seemed relaxed both in and out of the van. The running was going well too, although the lack of hot baths meant that I suffered from more niggling aches and pains than usual, and my ankle joints tended to stiffen overnight. Even so, the early morning runs continued to be the ones I enjoyed the most. I would rise with the sun. Put on my running kit outside the vehicle, so as not to disturb the others. Then jog off alone down the empty road. After half an hour or so, Jeff would drive by on the way to set up breakfast somewhere ahead.

We had reached Germany and were passing through a heavily forested region. Deer grazed in clearings. Pine-plank tables had been positioned on the grass for picnickers. It felt healthier to be eating outdoors and everyone's appetite had increased accordingly.

In the short period before the locals set off for work each morning, there was a wonderful stillness in the woodlands bordering the hard strip of asphalt. I heard cuckoos. Other birdsong too. Otherwise nothing but the sound of my padding feet.

The forests stretched for miles and took hours to run through. The road led to the Rhine Valley, where there were tiny bent figures working in the steep slanting rows of vines dotted above me.

At Rudesheim, the caretaker of a newly built sports stadium insisted that we sleep in the heated changing rooms and make use of the hot showers. We often stayed in the meadows of nearby farms, where Zhenka chased black-faced lambs in and out of haystacks and hid from chickens in barns.

One night I lay in my sleeping bag in someone's garden shed. Another was spent in a carpenter's workshop, where a huge stove was lit for us to dry our clothes after hours of unrelenting rain. Jeff climbed a stepladder to toss logs down into the flames, and Lea accidentally set a towel on fire. Sometimes we were handed pitchers of fresh milk or long necked bottles of homemade apple wine.

The highway which ran beside the Rhine did not stay peaceful for long. As traffic built up I nervously threaded my way along its edges. Quite apart from the discomfort caused by fumes from the car exhausts, there could be no let up in concentration now. And this in itself taxed my nerves to the limit.

The road remained busy all week until I turned off at the Neckar Valley and found a near deserted stretch which wound beside a smaller river. Here it was possible to relax and enjoy the countryside again.

I took deep breaths, filled my lungs with clean air and looked about me at the wooden boats on the far side of the water. No sooner had my attention wandered when I stumbled against a narrow kerb and turned my ankle. I fell heavily onto the gritty surface of the road. I lay there for a minute or two, then painfully attempted to haul myself upright. I half succeeded by standing on one leg but lost my balance and pitched forward again. Unable to put any pressure on the injured foot, I cursed loudly, slewed back onto the grass verge and waited for the others to find me.

For a few uncomfortable days I seldom ventured outside our tent. Then heavy rain swamped the groundsheet and I was forced to endure the confines of the van.

This was an entirely different environment and already the others were far more accomplished at the art of living in it than I was. Even the simple act of making a cup of tea involved unforseen obstacles. Zhenka's Dinky cars had first to be removed from the top lid of the bunk, not always gaining a sympathetic response from my son. A frantic search for enamel mugs and the kettle would follow. Next came the cooking stove and gas cylinder, both stowed in the trailer. Last of all but most essential ... where was the water?

'Did anyone refill the water containers last night?'

I soon realised that Jeff and Sue's disillusionment with close living at a slow pace was not without grounds.

My ankle was tightly bound when I resumed running, but I ran in short stints with many rests and trod down as lightly as possible until the sprain eased.

After crossing the Austrian border our route from Salzburg took us higher and the temperature fell. Every day brought grey skies and thunderstorms.

To dampen our spirits still further, Sue's despondency returned and she began to talk of going home. It seemed unlikely that Jeff would continue without her, and so we made frantic telephone calls to try and find a new driver.

Within days we learned that a complete stranger named Chris Baxter, aged twenty, was giving up his job in a bank to join us. Our friend Baz Bowler had also handed in his notice at the engineering company where he worked. They intended to fly out to Istanbul in the first week of July.

To reassure us, my mother sent a photograph of Chris from one of the newspapers covering the story. It showed a remarkably innocent and friendly face, peering through National Health spectacles and clutching a small suitcase.

'He looks a bit lost doesn't he?' said Lea, showing real concern.

I nodded. He reminded us of Paddington Bear. But without the padding of his duffel coat. We scrutinised the photograph at greater length to see if there was a label attached to him.

'If I was doing a bank job his till would be the one I'd go for,' I groaned.

'But don't you think it takes something to team up with total strangers?'

Lea was right. It did. The sort of complete blind faith more commonly found in lemmings.

One morning I glimpsed a reflection of my long legs in a row of shining milk churns awaiting collection at the edge of a village. I was no longer limping.

Halfway across Austria, I met John and Nora Doyle. Their small cream campervan was parked in a manicured lay-by beside a wide lake. John had on a red and white chequered shirt, tucked into faded blue denims that matched his eyes. The man was woefully thin and his shirt billowed out like a sail whenever gusts of wind rippled the water. He had seen me coming from a long way off.

'Can you stop? I guess you must. At times that is. It wouldn't be non-stop, your run. Now that would be the most far-fetched thing.'

'Like walking on water,' I grinned.

'Nora!' he raised his voice and hammered the nearside of the campervan with the flat of his hand.

'Jonathan, you'll have the jug over!'

'The fella on the high pass, day afore yesterday, I knew it. I told yer he'd be a-catching us.' He turned to me. 'Nora was set on climbing him,' he pointed to a high mountain on the other side of the lake. 'I ask you. Look at it! I doubt we got halfway. But guts is that lady's middle name. Nora!'

The door of the van opened wider. His wife wore orange slacks. She was beaming, but felt the cold and eased the neat cuffs of a windcheater down over both wrists when the mugs of steaming coffee had been handed to us.

'Brr!' she clapped her muffled hands together while I told them who I was and what I was doing.

'This is the fella we drove by,' he turned to me and looked angry.

'I wanted to stop there and then. I would have slammed my brakes on. They shouldn't steer their poxy noses up your rear now should they?' He indicated the traffic zipping by. Then he paused to gulp down his hot coffee and watched to see if I did the same.

'It's OK I suppose. For you to take coffee I mean. Liquids must be awful essential. I would have thought.'

Nora put her hand on his shoulder and looked as though she were about to say something. But the moment passed and John continued.

'I have a camera. Super 8. No big shakes. I make little movies. It's a hobby of mine. But I do it properly with captions and all.'

'He even adds music,' Nora interrupted.

'That's right,' said John. 'And what was that tune? The minute we saw him. I told you.'

'"The Long and Winding Road",' Nora beamed again.

'"The Long and Winding Road",' echoed John.

I made as if to leave when I handed back my empty mug, but John went off to get his camera.

Nora chatted to me while he was gone, not looking at me but down at her feet.

'I always associate marathons with getting married,' she said. 'Jonathan and I are from Toronto. We were honeymooning in Vancouver. We married in 1954. Anyway, he had to get tickets – a surprise, a total surprise it was – for the final day's events at the Empire Games. We followed the sprinting. That was our favourite. My dad had been a sprinter. But the marathon is what I'll always remember about that day.'

John had returned. He gave her a hug and took up the story.

'Well, the Englishman, Peters. You couldn't tell. He looked OK. OK when he reached the track. To tell the truth you couldn't see for Union Jacks.'

'And the noise,' said Nora, excited now. 'We were yelling. Everyone was yelling.'

'Then it all went quiet. Real quiet. And we couldn't see why at first. I lifted Nora up above the heads in front of us but she just burst into tears,' John swallowed hard. 'Then the man's legs

buckled. He didn't know where he was, but would he give in?'
There was a long pause. 'Do you know who won that race? Who
entered the stadium after they'd carried him off? No, neither do I.
Nor anyone.'

Then he thought to lighten the conversation. 'Nora and me
though, we've lasted the distance. Haven't we just?' Another hug.
'After that we took to following the marathons. Even arranged our
holidays around the different races. I was in plumbing. Those
winters in Toronto, they are most definitely something else. I was
a busy man. Nora, she worked in a florists. You still help out there,
don't you honey? Nora likes to keep busy. Me, I've got my filming.
Now that I'm retired we get along to most of the races.'

'I especially like to see all the strange little hats they wear when
it's hot,' Nora enthused. 'There was one man. He was tall. Now
Jonathan's tall, but not nearly so tall. He wore a lace doily fastened
with hairgrips. Jonathan filmed him, didn't you dear? He did very
well too. Remember?'

'He could run alright. Used to raise his knees high like one of
those thoroughbreds pulling the gigs. But that headgear. Now that
was something else. Sure I filmed him.'

'In an Easter bonnet …' Nora threw all caution to the wind and
began to sing. She had a good soprano voice. It was like briefly
stepping into a musical. John looked embarrassed though and made
an excuse to hush her.

'That's what I chose. The music. I fitted it all together seamless.'

They were giggling at each other when I left them. It had been
a good morning.

That afternoon the clouds cleared and I fished out my sunhat
for the first time. Lea had sewn a white handkerchief to the cap's
brim at the back. Nora would have loved it.

8

The first few villages I came to on the morning we crossed into Yugoslavia were empty. Their occupants were already busy working in the fields beyond. A cluster of heads were just visible between mounds of hay parallel to the spot at the roadside where a row of heavy black bicycles lay. Blue cornflowers and red poppies poked between the dusty spokes of the wheels.

Movement down this road consisted more of animals than motor traffic. Bullocks hitched to long creaking wagons. Horse-drawn carts. And cows, whose thin dusty flanks were regularly thumped by the young boys guiding them from one sparse patch of grass to the next.

On market days, even before first light, the road was full of jolting carriages. Sometimes, horses were reined in for a brief halt they clearly resented. And whilst new passengers clambered up to join those already huddled together inside the carts, a hoof would strike the stony surface below and a spark would fly past the iron-rimmed wheels.

Once or twice a light-hearted race developed as I drew alongside. This caused great commotion if the cart was full and the poor horse was unable to match my pace. Then, amid much hilarity, the driver would be urged to flick the reins harder, and even to use a whip.

Sentry boxes stood behind wrought-iron fencing, and chunks of fallen plaster lay at the foot of many of Varazdin's crumbling buildings. My footsteps raised pastel clouds of dust and disturbed a sleeping black dog, who shook his fur coat ferociously and deposited the same shades of grey into the gritty air.

In Vukovar I watched a man carry a many-tiered wedding cake over the cobblestones of a deserted square. A waitress dressed in black emptied a white tablecloth of breadcrumbs into my path. On the way out of town I saw a woman peg sheepskins onto her washing line. Another fished the trotters of a wild boar from a tin vat of broth on the doorstep. And on the road itself, occupying its entire width, there gathered other women who shouldered scythes and hoes before making for the fields.

One clear morning I overtook them under the faintest of sickle moons.

Jeff had taken to asking at smallholdings for permission to camp overnight. This was largely to dispel Sue's fears when there were no campsites within reach. But after a certain date, I noticed that TV coverage of the World Cup also featured in his reasoning. So much so, that on days when my last run ended in the middle of a village, I would first scan the rooftops and then simply make my way to the house with the most imposing TV aerial. Often as not I peered through the flimsy wooden gates of its entrance to discover our van.

'I was just coming to get you. How on earth did you find us?' Jeff would greet me with a glass of plum brandy.

One such overnight stay developed into a party after the national football team won their match. The village schoolmaster was sent for, but spoke only a smattering of Italian. One man though, knew an English song and climbed onto a box of rusting tractor parts to sing it. 'Rudolph the Red-nosed Reindeer', in a deep baritone voice, floated over the Danube.

I fell asleep in a wooden bus shelter the next morning and woke to find that a shower of rain had fallen. The wet roads were steaming, and I couldn't remember which country I was in.

David Bursac was building his own house. It was half-finished, and he sat on a neatly stacked pile of concrete breezeblocks in a large ramshackle garden. Jeff, Sue and Lea were grouped around him and as I approached I could see that they were all eating strawberries. Zhenka had wandered away to look for David's two small children who were hiding.

We were invited to stop over. Our host provided drinks, and Sue and Lea prepared a meal. Halfway through the meal a violent storm blew up and David urged everyone inside his half-built home. Lightning lit up an orange sky as we rushed back and forth to collect our plates and cutlery from the table outside. There was a chicken coop in the garden, midway between the table and the building materials. A clothes-line had been strung up inside it. Washing hung to dry there flapped wildly, like the wings of strange birds grown tired of their captivity.

Later, when the thunder rolled elsewhere and the children were tucked up in their makeshift beds, Lea asked David where their mother was. He showed us a photograph, smudged many times over at the edges where he had held it. Then he fumbled in a box looking to find a match that had not already been struck. When he found one, he dragged it sharply down across the rough concrete block supporting the fireplace.

The match flared up, and for an instant I caught a reflection of the flame in his grey watery eyes before he pinched it out between the blackened tips of his finger and thumb.

'You see how it is?'

Outside, abandoned strawberries lay scattered in the mud.

9

The road that led to Belgrade became difficult to run along as soon as it entered the industrial suburbs. High-sided container trucks thundered dangerously close. Polythene sheeting and empty plastic bags spiralled high into the air. Buffeted like a shuttlecock in the slipstream of each overtaking wagon I fought to keep my balance and tried hard not to stray too far out into the road.

Closer still to the city, where sombre blocks of flats stood, men and women in overalls converged on workshops and warehouses with their heads bent low against the driving gale. Some stopped momentarily to cluster around news-stands, or to catch their breath. A small girl weaved between them with a loaf of bread tucked under her arm.

On our way through the capital, Lea discovered a toyshop. It was Zhenka's third birthday. He chose a green tin boat with a bright red deck. When a candle was lit, steam propelled the small boat up and down a puddle in the gutter outside the shop. Jeff and I were fascinated.

Beyond Belgrade, the road serpentined away from the Slavonica Plain up into the low rounded hills above it. The afternoon was hot but enjoyable. Wide observation bays had been landscaped into the bends along this scenic route. Best of all though, the road seemed free of heavy goods vehicles.

Some little way beyond the town of Mladenovac, I came to a turn-off. I stopped to consult a small piece of paper on which Jeff had written the names of places I was due to pass through.

As I did so, a black car braked, then reversed at speed towards me. A policeman swung open the nearside door and jumped out to confront me.

'Kragujevac?' I pointed to the name at the bottom of my crumpled list. Without hesitation the man indicated the direction I should take.

'Thank you,' I mumbled my gratitude and turned to face the road to Kragujevac.

A heavy hand made its presence felt on my shoulder. The officer steered me back, away from the road to Kragujevac, and gestured towards his car.

Foreigners have a nasty habit of raising their voices when trying to make themselves understood. I proved no exception. The officer beckoned to his colleague. Together they insisted I climb into the back of the car. I looked for help from passers-by, but no one was looking. As my voice wavered marginally short of screaming, my left arm was twisted behind my back and someone's knee thrust me onto the rear seat of the car. When I shut up they allowed me to sit upright.

The car was speeding back into the market town of Mladenovac. Our van was already parked inside the compound of the police headquarters there. Behind the windscreen, Jeff, Sue and Lea looked worried. Zhenka had hold of his birthday boat. He giggled as his dad was dragged off for questioning.

I was frog-marched into a corridor and told to sit on a low wooden bench. A guard looked on from the doorway, periodically tapping the black leather holster around his hips. Whenever I made as if to move, he slid his fingers around a long wooden baton and gave me an unconvincing grin.

An hour passed. Uniformed men strutted to and fro along the narrow passage. Keys jangled. A man entered the building carrying our logbook. He pushed open the door of an office with the toecap of his dusty boot.

A second man followed him inside. He wore a trilby hat and a light coloured raincoat with wide lapels. In the pocket of his raincoat was a rolled up Yugoslav newspaper which carried a report of the journey I was making.

Thirty minutes more passed. Overhead, a florescent tube lined with charred insects stammered on and off before bathing me in a sickly yellow light. Suddenly, an attack of cramp brought me awkwardly to my feet. I stretched out my leg and the back of the wooden bench slammed hard against the wall.

The guard turned and glared at me. His hand glided over the polished wooden truncheon. His grin widened. Then a smaller man in a dark suit appeared at my side and patted me on the back.

'Football?' he looked down at my shorts and running shoes, and swung his leg back and forth. 'Bobby Charlton?'

I nodded.

'Georgie Best?'

I nodded.

'Gordon Banks?'

By now I was already guiding him past the guard and out to the van.

'Quick Jeff, find that photograph of us all on the town hall steps with Banksie!'

Jeff squeezed out of the driver's seat and shuffled through a cardboard box in the back of the van. When he found what he was looking for he wound down the window and handed it over.

The man at my side instantly recognised the England goalkeeper and pressed the photograph to his heart. Next, he dashed up the steps of the building and hurried past the guard – whose grin capsized.

In a few minutes, he was back and the police inspector was with him. Together they hugged me. Zhenka was handed a policeman's peaked hat.

'Kragujevac!' I told them, with a solemn look on my face.

'Kragujevac!' They both agreed.

10

A mural depicting spanner-brandishing workmen dwarfed the square in the centre of Slivnica. The town lay just off the main highway to Sofia, Bulgaria's chief city.

We were there to replenish food supplies. A young man who spoke English showed us where to change our money and where to purchase bread. The man had once worked in Poland, but his recent request for travel permits had been met with refusal, and he was bitter.

'Only three per cent of a population of eight and a half million are allowed out,' he told us. 'And I am not a red spider, so for me it is not so easy.'

He ran two nicotine-stained fingers across the plywood lid of our trailer and laughed. 'Red spiders! It is our name for these people. Tell me, do you have Solzhenitsyn? Or cosmetics? I will buy cosmetics from you for my sister. I will buy Solzhenitsyn also. You can bring them to my flat but do not park in my street or the streets near to me.'

'I think we have Solzhenitsyn,' I pointed to the roof rack. 'We have a box of books up there.'

He drew a map to show us where he lived and where to park.

'Your travels,' he sighed, 'how you step beyond the frontiers with every permission.' Again he sighed, and looked over his shoulder. 'We may exchange the books but not the legs ... pity!'

It was raining in Sofia. A steady drizzle. Lea elected to join me on my walk through the city. We took turns to push Zhenka in his buggy. The wet cobblestones played havoc with the small plastic wheels, and one of the tubular struts snapped in half.

Zhenka was not overfond of walking. He dawdled as much as he could until one of us gave in and picked him up. By this time the streets had filled. Trams overtook us, packed with people dressed in their Sunday best. In the centre of the city the streets were lined with flag-waving citizens. Zhenka climbed onto my shoulders for a better view.

'It's an Arab delegation,' whispered an old woman. She clung to my arm and stared up at me. Her eyes were like two pale green marbles come to rest in a tiny oval face, much powdered and pinched tight. Rain dripped from her headscarf whenever she shook her head. And she shook it after each sentence.

'One day Bulgaria will have the same problem with the Arabs as America has with the negroes. Everything you see here is show – for the tourists. You have to live here to understand.'

The grey headscarf was frayed at the edges. The wet cotton strands looked like thin wisps of hair plastered to her brow.

'In the villages people are afraid to be seen going to church. Can you imagine?'

There was a roar from the crowd as the motorcade sped by. Zhenka saw the flags waving and did the same with his hands. Then hailstones clattered against the shopfronts and the people began to disperse. We huddled together in the middle of a cobbled square and looked up over the bedraggled hammer and sickle banners. Red stars topped the spires of the dark grey buildings. Chandeliers blazed in the windows of a hotel ballroom where people were dancing.

The old woman took hold of Lea's hand and gripped it tightly. 'Watch yourselves … and keep freedom!' she shouted into the storm.

I left Sofia a day later by way of Lenin Road. It joined a four-laned highway heading for the Ihtiman Hills. The road was busy. Women in blue bib and brace workclothes were repairing it.

I kept taking liquids and salt tablets because the weather was much warmer. But it was worrying to find that the heat was affecting me so soon, and the first few doubts began to niggle inside. The long straight roads were the worst and to pass the time I took to reading number plates – D, NL, F, GB – as the traffic zipped by. Soon my head would be buzzing from the heat and my stomach would begin to feel peculiar due to all the salt tablets I had swallowed.

On the flat pastoral land of the Bulgarian Thrace I passed large cooperative farms and market gardens. Workers lunching outside a hydroplant waved to me. Engine drivers sounded their hooters. There were strange butterfly-shaped designs in black silk, draped over gates and pinned to trees, and black-edged photographs were pasted to noticeboards and posts wherever fatal accidents had occurred.

Some days the stiffness in my ankles did not go away. So rather than calcualte how far I had still to run before I could expect to see the van, I would close my eyes each time I shuffled past a kilometre sign. At other times my watch became like a magnet and I would sneak my wrist further across my chest as I ran, and turn my knuckles to the sun – yet still somehow avoid seeing how many minutes I had been on the road. These were the long spells that hurt the most. Those I tried to blank out.

Some mornings I achieved this by inventing silly advertising slogans like *Go to Turkey on an egg*, or else I'd make lists inside my head of all the things I planned to do when I reached the van. *First I'll have a mug of water, probably two, then I'd better shake the grit from my shoes and smooth out the irritating ruck in my sock, or I'll have another blister to burst. Next, I'll read a few lines of* Watership Down *to Zhenka and pay him with pebbles for the last of the cherries.*

A man offered Jeff petrol coupons for his wristwatch at a place called Pazardzik. Jeff shook his head. But the man persisted and thrust the coupons at him through the open window of the van.

'Have them, have them!' he shouted – unaware that he was being watched by two men on the other side of the road. They were well-built men, dressed in smart dark suits and they approached him from behind. By the time he spotted them it was too late. Nothing was said by anyone. He was led off towards a waiting car and Jeff's intervention was ignored.

In Plovdiv a drunk with one arm scuffled with me outside a cemetery. On the outskirts of the same city a young lad standing on the back of a moving truck threw an empty beer bottle at me.

In the countryside life was different. A woman dug up five cabbages for us and carried them to Lea in her apron. Another presented Sue with a tiny bouquet of wild flowers she had picked.

I was making good headway at last, settling into a rhythm on the road I hoped I could maintain. It was the ideal time to meet Franz and Sylvia. They cycled by me on a flat stretch of road just before the border. Franz was in front. He braked to slow down, then waved and shouted, 'Hi!'

Sylvia caught up some minutes after. *'Bonjour Monsieur.'* She glanced towards me and, breathing hard, pedalled on.

They were both resting at the foot of a tree when I next saw them. Franz patted the shaded tufts of grass where they sat and offered me a tomato, first sprinkling it with sugar 'for energy'. Sylvia uncorked an aluminium flask and I took a few swigs of water.

'There was a tap set into the wall back there, just before we saw you. We refilled our carriers. It should still be cool.'

It was. I nodded. 'I missed it,' I said, biting into the tomato. 'This tastes good, with the sugar. I've not eaten them this way before.'

'Why not? It's a fruit after all,' said Franz.

'Where are you cycling to?'

'India,' Sylvia told me. She dug her fingers into the calf muscles of her legs. 'That's if I don't seize up this side of Turkey.' She gave Franz a guarded look.

'You won't!' he grinned back. 'What about you? How far are you running?'

'Australia. I'm running to Australia.'

His grin widened. 'What?'

Franz, Sylvia and I spent the following few days on the road together. They were so intrigued by my marathon they asked if they could help pace me to Istanbul.

Franz was Dutch. Sylvia came from France. They had been travelling for two months, averaging 65 miles a day. But they agreed to halve this for my benefit.

Overnight my shadow sprouted wheels. Franz rode immediately ahead of me; Sylvia a few yards behind. I had to run faster but their company was well worth it.

A wedding procession crossed our path in one village. An accordian player and a fiddler led the bride and groom along the dusty street. A man danced beside them and swung a live chicken by its legs in time to the music.

11

Across the border, in Turkey, the road was lined with sunflowers. The traffic was noisier. There was also a faint trace of salt and seaweed in the air. I began to look for the Sea of Marmara.

At Babaeski, a number of men jumped from a lorry and stood to applaud as I passed. A young boy handed me a peach from his basket. A policeman stepped out of the crowd and pleaded with me to have a drink with him.

It was a roller-coaster of a road. Franz, Sylvia and I strained forward at the top of each rise. We could see further ahead now, but the edge of the continent was a long time coming. When, at last, a deep blue horizon floated into view, Sylvia tinkled the bell on her bicycle. I threw my hat in the air.

The AA route guide described the section as 'flat sandy coastal plain.' We estimated that it was no more than 32 miles to the Mo Camp, where we had arranged to meet Chris Baxter and Barry Bowler. Jeff decided to drive straight there.

The two cyclists and myself would make our own way and see them later in the day.

It was hotter than ever and the AA guide was hopelessly inaccurate. Perhaps a motorist could be excused for describing the route as 'flat', but as far as we were concerned, it was 'bloody hilly!'

We bought fruit and bottles of Coca-Cola from roadside stalls. I sucked peach stones dry as I ran. And whenever we halted to rest for short spells, Franz would delve into a deep nylon saddlebag and hand us each a tomato.

After about 20 miles I slowed to a walk and Franz and Sylvia cycled on. In front of me the road rose sharply and the tarmac felt slippery at its edges in the heat. The closer I got to the city, the wider the road became. Trucks and coaches thundered by. My ears buzzed.

Over the brow of a hill our van suddenly hove into sight. Sunlight lit up the windscreen and hid the occupants even when they sailed by with headlamps flashing. Once a safe turning point had been found, the van swung around and came back towards me. The passenger door slid open and Baz let out a wild Samurai yell.

Behind the wheel sat a bemused stranger. Baz introduced me to Chris Baxter and we grasped hands firmly. Chris looked even younger than the photograph I had seen. He was taking on what amounted to one of the most tedious four-wheeled journeys of all time. A lot would depend on his patience.

Baz was already in his shorts, raring to go. He tucked in behind me until it was safe to run alongside. He had on a baseball cap with a wide beak to shield his eyes, and a purple singlet with a Mickey Mouse motif. We looked at each other and giggled. He'd had a haircut too, and he took off his cap to show me.

'Chris reckoned it's a brillo pad!'

'What's he like?'

'He's a good bloke, Kel. He'll be fine.'

It was ten miles to the campsite and we talked all the way. Our pace was brisk despite the heat and we began to make inroads on the two cyclists ahead.

'They're going to India,' I told him. 'Sylvia couldn't ride a bike until a couple of weeks before they set out.'

'How far have you come today?'

'It's going to be over forty miles.'

'Christ, in this heat too.'

'What about India?'

'Yeah, fuckin' hell!'

We broke off talking to help a fruit-seller who was struggling to right an overturned handcart he'd been pushing. The cart slid part way down an embankment. We hauled it back up to the roadside for him, whilst he ran about retrieving the fruit. The man gave us both a melon for our trouble and we carried them into the camping ground like trophies.

'All sorts happen along the way,' I told him. 'A week ago some idiot tried to hit me with a bottle.'

'Shit!'

'It rolled across the road without breaking,' I laughed. 'But it's good Baz, the running is good. You'll love it, you see if you don't. Remember last Christmas?'

'Yeah, I've been thinking about that. When you first told me about how you wanted to run to Australia.'

It was Boxing Day and we were running hard. I have never run harder. But we were talking still, even as we ran. That was all part of it. Like Zatopek in the Olympic marathon, turning to ask his opponents if the pace was fast enough.

On the previous day we had run in the woods. Up and down the hills through the ferns. Many laps of a small circuit. Ran and ran to see who cracked first, whose legs buckled. And Baz had broken me that day. He was truly flying.

We went back to the cottage, where Lea had prepared Christmas dinner, and we put on paper hats and pulled crackers and played games with Zhenka. But all the while Baz and I were still in the woods …

The next day it was my turn. A long 20-mile run on the roads, with Baz pressing on in front until the very last hill. I overtook him on my toes and left him for dead.

'It was at the bottom of that long fucker leading up to the nurseries and the cricket ground,' Baz continued. 'I said I wouldn't mind running across Europe. But Asia? You had to be fucking joking!'

At the Mo Camp Baz pointed to a tent.

'That one's ours.'

The sun was low in the sky now and a slight breeze blew inland off the sea. The tent wobbled like an orange jelly. It looked less sturdy than a toddler's wigwam.

'Who put it up?'

'Chris did. He knows more about camping than I do.'

'I think there may be some poles missing,' I said.

Baz considered the tent again but said nothing.

'Did you bring the pressure cooker?'

'We did,' there was a slight pause, 'as far as Heathrow. Chris thought it was in my hand luggage. I thought it was in his.'

'Oh well, you're both here now. That's what counts.'

12

After a few days in Istanbul reorganising ourselves and buying a pressure cooker, it was time for Jeff and Sue to catch their train back to England. From now on they would be following our progress through letters and the occasional telephone call.

There was an acute sense of failure that we had not managed to live together in a small space. Running was only part of the challenge; we could all see that now. We hugged each other. Then they climbed into the van for the last time, and Chris drove off to the railway station.

I had an appointment with the consulate press officer that afternoon. He was to arrange news coverage of our departure.

'Take a seat Kevin. How are your feet?' He pulled out a chair for me, and I told him they were fine.

I unfolded a map and he spread it out across an empty table.

'The coach drivers Kevin. Always a hazard. More so for your support group than you though. Still, your driver got everyone this far. Bugger of a journey isn't it? Drove down myself last year. Never again. Feet alright?'

The telephone rang and he walked back across the room to answer it.

'Good grief! Is he alive? Of course I will.' He put down the receiver and looked at me with a serious expression on his face. 'Kevin, I'm sorry. Have to dash. Archbishop Makarios has been overthrown by the Greeks. Bloody serious stuff this. Could mean war. Bugger of a thing to happen when you're running across the country, what with those bloody coach drivers. Look after those feet Kevin.'

At five in the morning, on 19 July, Baz and I set off along the dusty highway leading to the old city walls. Except for a few stray cats near Topkapi Gate and a man bent double beneath a roped consignment of shoeboxes, the road was deserted.

We ran through the still-sleeping metropolis towards a horizon blistered with mosques. Loudspeakers dangled from minarets. 'Stamboul's inhabitants were already being called to prayer.

People began to appear at windows and in doorways. As dawn broke they came out into the streets. Hoofs clattered over broken cobblestones. Horns blared from gaily decorated minibuses. The silence had been unreal. Bells, whistles, hooters and sirens now vied with each other to fill it.

We jogged along a leafy avenue beside the remains of a grand Roman hippodrome. On our right towered the azure-tiled mosque of Sultan Ahmet and beyond it the vast dome of Hagia Sophia, the famous church of the Holy Wisdom.

At the waterfront we crossed a footbridge to Eminonu Square and found ourselves engulfed by ferry commuters. The Galata Bridge vibrated with rush-hour traffic. Red slivers of sunlight lapped the huge pontoons beneath it. Cruisers, trawlers and warships were moored close by.

Out in the hazy distance over the Golden Horn, lay the Asian settlement of Uskudar. A coffee-seller who had read of our journey in his morning newspaper ran with us and pointed to a faint outline of buildings on the opposite shore.

'Uskudar is Persian for "runner" or "courier" – just like you!' He was breathing hard and waved us on. But then he thought of something else we should know, and turned back and chased after us.

'Your Nightingale woman! She nursed at the barracks there.'

In the sixth century BC, King Darius the Great linked the two continents of Europe and Asia with a bridge of boats. Nowadays, the Bosphorus is spanned by one of the longest suspension bridges in the world. Pedestrians are not allowed to cross it, but the Vice-Consul had obtained permission from the Mayor for us to do so. That was before the sudden threat of war.

Even in peacetime such a strategic crossing was heavily guarded. Now, rumours that Greek saboteurs intended to destroy it had led to the armed guards being doubled.

Unfortunately we missed the approach road and found ourselves a hundred feet below the massive concrete structure. Half-hidden by giant shadows, we began to scramble up a rocky bluff towards it.

Meanwhile, Chris displayed for the first time his uncanny knack of getting us in and out of tricky situations by deciding to wait midway across the bridge. Turkish troops rushed to surround him, whilst Baz and I vaulted a parapet onto the road and sprinted along the 3,542-foot span.

With a polite wave, we raced past the group of soldiers still in conversation around the van, and headed for the Asian side of the bridge.

'Did you know Kel, that the only other person to have crossed the bridge on foot died of a stroke on the other side?'

Chris volunteered this information a few days later, when we were all flat on our backs suffering from a mysterious illness.

'A chap in the British Council Library told me all about it. It was after someone's birthday party apparently. He was an American and a few of the English contingent were giving him a lift home. When he asked them to stop the car, they thought he was going to throw up. Instead, he took off across the bridge as fast as he could. He was overweight too. Totally out of shape. Anyway, he just keeled over. There was hell to pay and it was all hushed up.' Chris could be counted on to provide the most curious tales. His timing was impeccable.

Too ill to run, we spent the day camped on a hill overlooking Istanbul. At the roadside an old man was selling peaches from a cabin made of plywood scraps. Truck drivers sat cross-legged in the dust, anxiously listening to his small transistor radio. Half-hourly reports of the fighting in Cyprus were interposed with stirring military marches. A state of emergency had been declared. And martial law was now in force.

That night, from our high vantage point, we watched hundreds of vehicles moving slowly out of the city and up into the hills. Blue paper was pasted over everyone's headlamps to comply with blackout regulations. Under cover of darkness, less than a hundred yards away, a group of soldiers were camouflaging an anti-aircraft gun with bales of straw.

We had a fitful night's sleep. Each sound, from a mosquito to a moped, resembled the drone of a Greek bomber.

13

Whatever it was that struck us down vanished without trace after a day's rest. But when the muzzle of a big gun swung over the maize field where we were recuperating, Chris and Baz must have harboured misgivings.

When we did break camp we found that the coastal route to Izmit was congested. Burnt-out wrecks of trucks and coaches lay in grim twisted heaps where they had demolished the trees from the peach orchards adjoining the road. We could find no alternative pathway to avoid the oncoming vehicles. And to make matters worse, the sun shone directly into our eyes.

'Did you expect this?' I asked.

'I don't know what I imagined,' said Baz. 'I suppose I just concentrated on the idea of running a marathon each day.' He drew breath, 'I never thought about the fucking traffic!'

'I overlooked it too, Baz, but at the end of the day it's what drains you the most.'

'Overlook it now and you're a dead man Kel.'

He was right. Only a few days earlier, two speeding buses had collided here, killing twenty passengers.

Ismail Kirikel had studied in Bournemouth. He was visiting his family at a small mud-bricked village some distance from the main road. He stood among a circle of admiring friends who had just met him at the bus station. His fashionable clothes indicated to them how much he had achieved and how far he had travelled.

The bus that had brought him from Istanbul overtook Baz and me at a place called Duzce. Ismail had watched us from the rear window. Now, as we approached the group of people gathered around him, he handed us two cans, left over from his journey.

'If you have the time you are most welcome to come with me to my family home.' He slung a jacket over his shoulder and his sister offered to carry it for him.

We followed the car driven out to collect him along twisting dirt lanes. When we reached the village, Ismail instructed a group of men to heave two heavy wooden gates from their hinges so that our van could scrape through into a cobbled backyard. Here we met his father, squatting in shadows and surrounded by dried sheafs of corn.

'He's a brushmaker,' explained Ismail, presenting Zhenka with a small besom to sweep out our van.

'My grandfather was a basketmaker,' I told him.

We removed our shoes and entered the house. Ismail and his brothers led us to an upstairs room. We sat on a thick handwoven rug around a low table and drank hot sugared milk from tiny glasses. The meal was served by his sisters and much to Zhenka's amusement we ate it with our fingers from large communal bowls.

Ismail wanted to make films. He lit a large oil lamp that looked very old, and projected shadows onto the walls with his hands. Zhenka waved the besom.

When we had eaten, everyone assembled in a dark adjoining room. More oil lamps were lit. More visitors arrived. The women sat together in a far corner until they were all told to go downstairs. Lea followed them out.

Meanwhile the men formed a circle to play a game. They each held out their hands and clenched their fists. Then someone stood in the middle of the circle and hunted among them for a gold ring. The wrong choice meant a punishment by the flick of a knotted red handkerchief.

'This is what I will film one day,' Ismail assured us.

Back on the road, Baz ran a little further every day. Sometimes we chatted for mile upon mile. But there were also days when we would jog together without speaking, tongue-tied and miserable. This usually happened when the road became too dangerous to run on, or whenever petrol fumes from overtaking trucks caused us to hold our breath.

Cornfields smoothed the wide skyline. There were gypsy wagons in tall reeds beside a lake and a half-rotted horse in a ditch, with an anchor branded on its rump.

Amongst the mountains between the Bolu Pass and Ankara were small plains where abandoned log-cabin settlements stood. Convoys of tanks and armoured vehicles shook leaves from the trees as they rumbled towards the Greek border.

The campsite on the edge of the Turkish capital was set in a dust bowl next to a vast military airbase. Chris went looking for a garage to replace a jack which had snapped in half in Yugoslavia. I spent the whole day with him, meandering between pyramids of worn tyres and lifeless beat-up trucks, in a shantytown of used car parts. Samovars were on the boil wherever we stopped.

Beyond the spacious city boulevards we encountered a lunar landscape. The road zigzagged through hot barren hillsides and outcrops of mauve-coloured rock. Stark Anatolian surroundings – grand but oppressive.

There were roadworks five miles from Cerikli. Chunks of tarmac lay in dull powdery heaps beside abandoned pickaxes and orange bulldozers. Here, the surface of the highway was nothing more than an ochre-coloured marl, studded with hoofprints and caterpillar tracks. After a steep and dusty downhill run we took a turn signposted for Samsun, and left behind the remains of the major overland artery.

For a short distance the hills were less rugged. But by the time we descended on Delice, high mountains surrounded us again. White goats negotiated tricky boulder-strewn escarpments in a veil of dust and the sun broke through the dark clouds like the golden beak of a bird.

Out in the eroded hills there were crimson-tinted stones and cliffs like clenched knuckles. In the fields the women wore dresses the colour of sunflowers and melons. The soil beneath their feet was red.

There is a black and white striped minaret in Sungurlu. Chris pulled up on a spare patch of ground there, next to the town's rubbish tip, to wait for us.

'You speak Ingiliz mister? Ingiliz?'

The metal sides of the van reverberated from the blows of a dozen grubby fists.

'Can my brother offer his guidance? He is small. Small guide, small price?'

'You have cigarettes madam? My brother is even smaller. He will charge you only two cigarettes, and bubblegum perhaps.'

Inside the van, the patience of all three occupants was sorely tried, particularly when Zhenka hammered back defiantly.

When Baz and I loped into view the local children were distracted for a short time and directed their questions at us. I looked towards Lea. She put her hands over her ears and screamed. Chris lit a cigarette and laid his arms across the steering wheel. Zhenka gave up hammering and burst into tears.

Stops such as this were brief indeed. Baz and I were back on the road in no time. The children followed hard on our heels, until one by one they drifted away to plague others.

Dark mountains lay on a plain like half-submerged water buffalo. When we reached them, dry-stonewalled shacks stood close to the road, with tin pipes rigged up to collect rainwater from the steep hillsides. Cows and donkeys drew creaking wooden sleighs past them, round and round the flattened cornfields.

Some days sapped our energy and spirit more than others. This was one of them.

At nightfall Chris parked the van on the forecourt of a petrol station adjacent to a noisy café. We rinsed the dust from our arms and legs. Chris went off to refill our water butts. Lea tucked Zhenka into his bed and made for a dilapidated concrete toilet block on the far side of the garage.

None of us saw anyone leave the café but she was followed. A few minutes later she came back in tears.

'Some bloke just kicked open the door and started unbuttoning his flies. I had to punch him and slam the door shut. Didn't you hear me screaming?'

Without thinking, I grabbed one of the wooden boards we used for the base of a bed, and hurled it into a group of truck drivers sitting outside the café. They pushed back their chairs angrily and stood up to face us. One man snatched a knife from the table, but his friend gripped him by the arm. He spat at us instead and grinned.

By now Chris had his key in the ignition. The van rocketed forward between a line of blue and yellow petrol pumps, its rear doors swinging open. Pots, pans and potato peelings flew into the air. We jumped inside and drove away.

14

We spent the rest of the night outside a large bus terminus. Lea blamed her attack at the petrol station on all the media attention we had been getting. In addition to our TV appearance in Ankara, the leading Turkish daily, *Günaydin*, had printed a full-colour spread on their front page.

'It's that stupid woman from the press,' she sobbed. 'She insisted I put on a bikini for those photos even though she had to borrow one for me.'

The pictures showed Lea bending forward in a red bikini to pour water over my bare feet. Soon the copy of the newspaper we'd saved lay in a crumpled ball on the floor of the van.

I strode past the garage at the crack of dawn. Tall cypress trees lined the road. Herds of water buffalo waded through rivers of corn stubble.

On the outskirts of a village I was overtaken by a wagon full of young lads perched on top of swaying bales of hay. They waved and tossed the huge head of a sunflower to me. It landed with a thud in the middle of the road.

I reached the industrial town of Corum as the night shift workers filed out through the gates of a cement factory. A sudden wind powdered my hair and beard with dust. The wind blew the lid of our trailer over a hedge. Chris's watch vanished in the dust storm too. A small boy grabbed it from the dashboard when his back was turned.

At a roadside café near the Black Sea coast, an elderly gentleman in a cane chair translated the headlines from a newspaper he was reading.

'This is not good news for you my friends.'

He tapped the ivory handle of his walking stick over the newsprint.

'It tells us that Britain are supplying war planes to Greece.'

He took a fob watch from a narrow breast pocket and paused to look at it. 'This was made in London. In Clerkenwell. It was a gift from my son. All my grandchildren live there. Next year I will make a visit. If I am not too old.'

He tapped the newspaper again. 'I think it would be better for you to be outside Turkey, don't you agree?'

Later we opened out our map. Baz estimated that we were 700 miles from the Iranian border.

'A month away at least.' He sighed.

We ran with a sense of urgency now, unsure of our reception in the towns and villages along the way. When it became evident that the crisis had worsened, Chris peeled off the GB stickers from the van, and Baz and I put on plain white T-shirts. We also decided to stay well away from the local inhabitants.

One night when the time came to camp, Chris drove off the main road, along a dirt lane that led to the hills. He stopped the van where a dried-up riverbed cut across our path to form a three-foot deep gully. Everyone was grateful for the solitude.

'This is more like it.' Baz lit a hurricane lamp and climbed onto the roof rack to find a new book to read. He fished out *The Records of a Weather Exposed Skeleton*, a series of haikus about the pilgrimages of a seventeenth-century Japanese poet named Basho. We all relaxed and turned in early.

Sometimes Chris and Baz slept under the stars on campbeds. But the wind picked up and they came inside. Chris chose his alternative spot – curled up on the front seats, with his head on a pillow under the steering wheel. There was a full moon, and he draped a large cotton sheet across the windscreen to stop the light shining in his eyes. Within a short while we were all asleep.

Bang! Bang! Bang!

Baz, Lea and I sprang upright. Chris remained inside his sleeping bag.

Bang! Bang! Bang!

Still he slept on. Baz reached over the back of the seats and shook him awake. 'Someone's hammering on the bloody windscreen, Chris! Take a look will you, for God's sake!'

Startled to see us all staring at him, Chris raised a hand to the top of the dashboard and fumbled for his glasses. Then he drew the cotton sheet back a few inches and peered outside.

'Christ! There are six of them! They want me to open the door!'

'No!' we all yelled at once.

'Don't be bloody daft: they've got guns! They can blast their way in if they want to!'

His response stunned us. We watched, open-mouthed, as he wound down the window of the door and stuck his head outside.

The men were clad in the mottled green uniform of the Turkish army – a simple fact that our heroic driver failed to mention. The moonlight shone on their tin helmets as they peered in at us. One of the men stepped closer and began to speak. Chris shrugged his shoulders.

The soldier drew a bayonet out of its sheath. Steel glinted as he slid it a few inches from his throat. He pointed into the darkness and beckoned us to follow him in our van.

There were bandits in the vicinity. We were being given an armed escort back to the nearest town.

15

At the large tobacco port of Samsun, grave-faced men and women stood in groups on street corners. A radio broadcast from the crackling tannoy system of a nearby mosque announced that Turkey was recalling all overseas-based citizens in preparation for enlistment. The country was on the brink of a full-scale war.

Zhenka was excited to be at the seaside. He clutched a yellow plastic bucket in one hand and a sky-blue spade in the other. Lea had promised him the Black Sea and he pictured waves of liquorice curling between his toes. But the sea was no different than any other. Except that this one had the bloated body of a dead horse floating in it.

A gang of boys dragged the horse ashore and began to prise the iron shoes from its hoofs. This accomplished, they threw them jangling onto the beach. Four rusty moons half-buried in a grey volcanic sand. Zhenka tugged at his mother's hand and together they both turned around and walked back to the van.

When Baz and I set off along the coastline, it rained so hard that we lost sight of the Black Sea. But we knew it to be out there still by the sound the stones and shells made when the tide came in – rattling like dice rolled across teahouse gaming boards.

There were more gangs of children to contend with, some armed with evil-looking catapults. If the stones missed, the mosquitoes didn't. We slid into our sleeping bags covered in a mixture of sweat and insect repellent.

On fine days, oblong patches of hazelnuts were laid out at the roadside to dry in the sun, and large green tobacco leaves hung from racks in the fields. The fernhills between Samsun and Trabzon were separated by thicket-covered ravines. Waterfalls plummeted down them into the sea. Women carrying metal jars parted the waist-high ferns on their way to and from the village wells. Their sons and daughters toiled on the beach in youthful road-mending teams, filling straw baskets with sand and pebbles to empty into the potholes.

There were fishermen with moustaches mending their nets at

the village of Bolaman. Beyond the village, the mountains dropped close to the sea and the road disappeared into a series of tunnels cut into the rock face.

A couple of bored soldiers were guarding the entrance to the first tunnel. One of them pointed his rifle at us and laughed. The other kicked Baz hard up the backside. He was the meaner looking of the two and it would take more to relieve his boredom. But they waved us on anyway.

The tunnels were short and unlit. We ran through them quickly. When we reached the others, Chris showed us the propaganda leaflets handed out by the soldiers. Baz turned around and pointed to a dusty boot mark on the back of his shorts.

Ever optimistic, Chris stopped the van a stone's throw from Giresun. But he attracted such a large crowd of onlookers that I almost missed him. A group of small children jumped up and down on top of our trailer. Their elder brothers and sisters pressed forward for a better view inside the vehicle. They asked for souvenirs and cigarettes and they spilled out across the road.

Two boys pushed hard to create a gap through to the rear doors of the van and when these were opened they emptied a football jersey full of hazelnuts inside onto the floor. Just as quickly they retreated, back into a maniacal bagatelle of heaving skin and bones.

A few days later we entered the historic trading port of Trabzon. The red-roofed Trebizond of old; a favourite haunt of soothsayers and magicians who once mixed their strange potions in the narrow back streets.

There was a letter awaiting collection at the post office. It was from a friend of ours named Keith Bartlam. Keith was just out of university and killing time before taking up a teaching post at Hull. He had two months to spare and would dearly love to run through the Khyber Pass. If there were no problems he intended to fly out to Baghdad and then catch up with us by train somewhere in Iran.

Lea and I were reading the letter in a café, when two cockneys walked over to us. One was tall and silent, the other short and boisterous. John and Dennis could not have been more different. But they were good mates.

They were on their way to the Himalayas in a VW campervan. Dennis hoped to study Buddhism in a Nepalese monastery. We never found out what John was going to do.

'Had a fuckin' party and a half before we left, didn't we Dennis?'

Dennis nodded, then withdrew into long a silence punctuated by impromptu spells of meditation.

'The folks had fucked off for the weekend. First time I'd had that fuckin' house to myself for years. Party and a half, eh Dennis?'

We looked at Dennis, but there was just a blank look in his eyes.

'We built a fire in the garden. This youth's a dab hand at making fires. Outdoor stuff, that sort of thing. Hash pancakes big as dustbin lids, eh Dennis?'

He was warming to his tale now, rekindling it all for us until we could almost inhale the dope.

'Tossed the fuckers with the old man's spade I did.'

'That's how the greenhouse went up,' Dennis interrupted. We all stared his way.

Then John banged on the table and upset our glasses of chai.

'Nobody knows how the fuckin' greenhouse went up.' For a split second he was angry but then he paused and burst out laughing.

'All that glass exploding in the heat. Fuckin' amazing Dennis, wasn't it? The dog ate a pancake when we was trying to douse the fucker. Wolfed it down and then threw up all over me mum's pillow. When I shoved the fucker in the washing machine the feathers came out. What a party and a half, eh Dennis?'

I tried to imagine their party. A greenhouse in flames at the bottom of a suburban garden. And the leaves of the tomato plants shrivelling into white ash and floating into the darkness like those feathers in the wash.

'I miss the dog,' said John.

16

We left the Black Sea coast the next day. At the town of Maçka, the narrow road was dynamited to clear a landslide. During the delay this caused, Chris quoted extracts from New Zealander Mike Artus's itinerary covering the next stage of the journey.

'*A steep climb from Trabzon reaching 6,627 feet at 46 miles with winding mountain roads up to Gumusane, then bare and rocky. Great care is necessary on all bends. Use horn frequently because of heavy truck traffic.*'

'The road seems quiet enough at the moment.' Lea had just returned. There was a smell of freshly-baked bread in the canvas bag she stowed in the food safe.

A sudden explosion rocked the van. Zhenka's full potty wobbled alarmingly, and we reeled around to see a gaping hole in the tarmac ahead. Chris made himself more comfortable. He turned a page and continued reading to us.

'*Very tortuous section. Road second-class except for last forty miles to Erzurum … includes two passes … the Zigana being the most arduous and definitely not to be undertaken at night, as the road is very narrow with sheer drops. Gravel sections of fifteen miles at the top of each pass.*'

Steamrollers slowly began to crush the rubble that had tumbled onto the road after the blasts. They flattened a way through for our van and a few trucks queuing behind us. Baz and I watched the vehicles pull away and when the dust settled we followed on in single file, up the narrow road over the mountains.

From now on Baz intended to run every step of the way. Almost 8,000 miles, from the Black Sea to the Pacific Ocean.

We took it in turns to make the pace. And on the hairpin bends we heeded the cautionary advice read out to us earlier. Water came cascading down between rocks and rhododendrons as the road snaked higher. There were only a few trucks lumbering uphill that morning; less still rattling downhill towards us. But the mountains were far from deserted.

There were several women standing on boulders in the wooded heights. When they caught sight of us they screamed and spat.

Those who stood closer to the road rushed off to hide until we'd passed. When they reappeared they shook their fists.

Halfway up the pass, Zhenka ran from the van as we approached.

'Listen to the mountains! Listen to the mountains!'

I stopped and cupped a hand behind my ear. Baz knelt down in the road and pressed his ear to the ground. The silence was overwhelming. There was just a faint tinkling of small bells from the necks of goats between the trees on the opposite slopes.

'The mountains sound happy Zhen.'

It was the only breather we took during the 10-mile run to the summit. At the top, a thick line of cloud divided the highest peaks like the white paw of a polar bear. We ate our breakfast and looked down at the road below. Sometimes we could make out its path. Then it would disappear in a great jumble of rocks and we would be hard pressed to pinpoint where it re-emerged.

'Any good at jigsaw puzzles Baz?'

'Naw ... we'll find our way down there soon enough.'

There was a ramshackle teahouse in a small village called Ikisu. An English-speaking schoolmaster in a scarlet cloth cap invited us to have a drink. His companion was a stocky lorry driver whose truck had broken down outside. The man's hands were covered in grease and he rubbed them up and down on the knees of his baggy brown overalls.

'This place. Of all places for you to meet. Ikisu. It means *where two rivers meet*. And this man at my side? Who is he? My friend here, who is a good friend always. Well gentlemen, I will tell you that he is the kayak champion of all our country!'

The man's greasy hand shot out like a piston rod and lodged in my palm for a few brief seconds. Each time he heard the word 'kayak' he glanced up at the schoolmaster and pretended to paddle furiously. The schoolmaster waved his scarlet cap when the time came for us to depart, and the lorry driver waved his imaginary paddle.

Chris and Lea set up camp halfway down the mountainside. It was a well-chosen spot, overlooking the galvanised roofs of Gumushane, yet hidden away from its occupants. The moon was bright and round in the chilly air. When we brushed our teeth our elbows cast shadows that moved to and fro over the iron rooftops like the violin section of an orchestra. And I thought of the man without a paddle a little further up the mountain.

Forked lightning hacked into the black clouds above the battlements of Bayburt. We had crossed another 6,000-foot pass to reach this fortress town renowned for its large silver mine in the days of Marco Polo.

A straggling line of soldiers were returning to their barracks trailed by eagles. They chanted in unison and yet were hopelessly out of step. For a time we fell in line behind them, then jauntily broke ranks.

There were blanketed donkeys tethered to a stone monument on top of the Kop Dagi Pass. It was a bare windswept summit, almost 8,000 feet high. Lea pegged out washing to dry while Baz and I opened a tin of sardines.

Climbing the pass had not been without incident. First of all we encountered a cackling old woman in black. She sat on a rocky ledge above us and used her feet to roll a large stone directly down into our path. The stone shattered when it landed at our feet and the sharp pieces careered down the mountain. Chris and Lea heard the sound echo some way off and thought it was a gunshot.

A few bends further up the road, a battered minibus hurtled from nowhere and deliberately swerved towards us. Neither Baz nor I saw the driver's face. We were already close to the edge of the tarmac and were both aware of the sheer drop that lay beyond it. At the very last moment the driver slammed on his brakes and the minibus slew back across the road. A cloud of dust and ricocheting pebbles was the last we saw of it.

That evening, Lea was cooking by torchlight when we jogged to a halt. It had been difficult for Chris to find a safe spot to stop on the narrow mountain road, and even when they did there had been problems.

'I had the trailer top full of sliced vegetables and cooking stuff when some old man came along and started waving his arms about, telling us to move on. So I pretended I didn't understand him and after a few minutes he went away. Next thing I know, a small boy – hardly bigger than Zhenka – wants to give him a ride on his donkey for a toothbrush he'd seen.'

Lea had set up the stove between two narrow mounds of earth that formed a handy windbreak. She had just taken the lid off the pressure cooker and was about to ladle out the vegetables when Zhenka cried for her to come and see what he'd found. Our son had been busy excavating one of the mounds with his plastic spade. Now he unclenched his grimy fist and thrust the palm of his hand under the beam of the torch.

'Kel!' screamed Lea. 'Zhenka's got someone's tooth in his hand! I think I've just cooked supper on top of a grave.'

17

A Mr Rumbell from Kent was at the wheel of the first container lorry that passed us when the road from the coast joined the central route across Turkey. He mistook us for army personnel doing a spot of early morning PE and his truck thundered by without slowing. Chris had stopped in a wide lay-by a few miles on. When Mr Rumbell reached the spot, he pulled in and climbed down from his cab. Lea was preparing breakfast on the trailer top. Chris and Zhenka were kicking a brightly coloured ball about on a grassy mound. Each time Zhenka struck the ball with his foot he giggled with delight.

Mr Rumbell scrutinised the sign 'England to Australia' in blue lettering on the sides of the van, and introduced himself.

'I take it that was him I saw back there?' he said.

'Probably.'

'My word, they was goin' at a fair lick. Tell you what, I'll bet a few goodies wouldn't go amiss?' He walked back to his truck and returned a few minutes later carrying a cardboard box. There were tins of condensed milk and packets of ginger biscuits inside.

'My son loves sport. He's into everything. He loves his running. Loves roller skating too. But there's no money in it is there? Best stick to soccer I told him. Buy his old dad a nice little semi then.' Mr Rumbell had a hearty laugh which began deep down inside and shook his belly. It went with his name. He lived in Bromley with Anita, who was not his wife. And he wished he saw more of his son than he did.

'Driving trucks though. It's no life for a married bloke is it? Short hauls maybe, but not this bloody lark. Anyhow Mrs Bowers, give the old man a kick up the backside from me won't you? Good luck now.' His belly shook some more as he climbed back up into the cab.

It was late afternoon when we ran into Erzurum. A fine coating of snow still lay on the bonnets of the cars parked up in the shade. The altitude of the town is 6,398 feet and when the sun dipped, the canvas tarpaulin on our roof rack grew taut and stiff with frost.

John Buchan based part of his famous novel *Greenmantle* on this garrison town, recounting in fiction the intrigue behind a real-life Russian advance of 80,000 troops during the winter of 1916. Besides being a strategic stronghold, positioned to fend off any military approaches on Constantinople, Erzurum lay slap-bang in the middle of an earthquake zone. And, if that was not off-putting enough, the locals frequently reported seeing wolves padding through the suburbs, scavenging for food in temperatures that plummeted 30 °C below zero.

We left the town on the first day of September. The road crossed a plateau ringed by mountains 11,000 feet high. Soldiers of the Frontier Field Army were engaged in early morning manoeuvres. A few of the grey-coated sentries waved to us and stamped their feet on the hard frozen earth to keep warm. They guarded military installations alongside the road. Chris unintentionally cluttered up an officer's car park with cooking utensils as he and Lea prepared breakfast. The officers rubbed sleep from their eyes in disbelief and pleaded with him to remove himself before the General's inspection.

Rain threatened to cause floods of biblical proportions outside Pasinler. Inside it was even worse. The women wore rough hessian garments and carried sacks on their backs. They spat at us whenever we were not looking and sometimes when we were. If we turned to face them they hurried away, swinging down the back streets like shabby canvas buckets. The men were playing backgammon in the cafés, sheltering from the storm.

On the way out of Pasinler, a small Fiat piled high with rucksacks and mountaineering equipment had come to a standstill in the middle of the road. I had only seen two cars in the town but the horns of both were blaring. We helped the driver and his companion push their car closer to the kerbside.

When the driver got out to thank us he was so tall I didn't think he would fit back inside. The two men were Polish and they were on their way to climb a mountain near Lake Van. The tall man did the talking. They had driven from Gdansk.

'We are saying the jokes when the engine stalls. But do you

know what we are saying?' He patted his friend's shoulder. 'Piotri here comes from a small fishing hamlet near the city of Sopot. It lies on the narrow peninsular that is hugging the Baltic. It is so small but it is famous because the name of it is "Hell". I am joking with Piotri when the power cuts out – Piotri how can you live in Hell, here is hell!'

A push start in the pouring rain got the little Fiat moving. The two climbers waved but didn't want to risk their vehicle stalling a second time, and the car splut-spluttered out of Pasinler.

Eastern Turkey seemed inundated with travellers. Over the course of the next few days we met two Italians racing back from Nepal; then a delightful couple from Leicester with their two small daughters, who were slowly making their way to India in a battered Bedford van; and, halfway up a mountain, we met the low-budget bus to Delhi carrying an enthusiastic group of Aussies on the overland trail home.

Stiff-legged, they clambered out of the dusty coach to take photographs. Their driver looked like Hemingway. His open shirt revealed a tattooed chest. A happy lad with freckles, whose tousled hair flared like a bushfire in the sunlight, promised to shout us beers when we reached Melbourne. He lived in the Dandenong Hills not far from the city and his neighbours turned out to be people I had once spent Christmas with.

'Yeah, I've ridden on Puffing Billy,' I told him, recalling the narrow-gauge railway up to Ferntree Gully, in the heart of the Dandenongs.

'Small world, eh?' he smiled, and the bushfire on his head blew out of control.

'Not if you're bladdy well running across it mate!' Baz had everyone grinning with his loud Aussie accent.

The Tahir Pass led us to high cold pastures where workmen were erecting pylons. Television was on its way to Eastern Turkey and an icy wind whistled through a tangle of steel cables.

In the town of Taslıçay we were allowed to camp at a small gendarme post. Sentry boxes tilted at odd angles on the hard uneven ground inside the quadrangle where Chris pulled up next to a jeep.

A mechanic manoeuvred himself from under its chassis and rolled down the sleeves of his grey woollen shirt against the biting wind. As he strode towards the corridor of the barracks room, Zhenka bounced a ball to him and a lively kickabout ensued.

The soldier was shaking dust and grit from a doormat when we left the next morning. Zhenka stood on the passenger seat and saluted him as the van rolled by.

Large herds of sheep and goats were grazing beside the road leading to Dogubayazit. Baz and I pushed on towards the border town.

By noon the bandaged knee of Ararat was visible. By late afternoon it was bloody. A red sun dripped through grey woollen clouds like the marking dye daubed on a sheep's fleece.

18

Children pushed toy trucks made of wire along the dirt streets of Dogubayazit. The thin wheels of these little trucks left erratic trails in the dust like the intuitive calligraphy of tyre-marks created by their fathers and elder brothers on the icy roads which led from the mountains down to the town.

Butchers stood in one street sharpening long knives. At the bread shop a small boy moistened dough with one sweep of a wide brush that he hid behind when I looked in. His father, the baker, clutched the hem of a grey apron and stooped to wipe the sweat from his brow.

The bread was still hot and I hugged it to my chest. The dough had risen long before the sun in Dogubayazit and the air was crisp and clear.

A metal sign pointed directions back to the motel car park where we had camped overnight. Above it hung the white conical mantle of Mount Ararat. The rusting sign was riddled with bullet holes. Standing where the marksman must have stood, I could see the outline of a boat.

Kurdish families were on the move near the 'Mountain of Noah'. Their camels were laden with goatskin tents and hefty wooden stakes. We watched them from the pot-holed road that led to the border and listened to their fierce dogs barking long after they were out of sight.

On the Iranian side of the border, a smooth-surfaced highway led to the frontier town of Maku. The town boasted flowerbeds and electric streetlights. Two letters awaited our collection at the local post office, tucked behind a wall calendar that was six years out of date.

'You guys been on the road in all that time?' Jim was an American prankster with lots of money who bought expensive carpets and played chess.

Later, at the Maku Inn, we drank ice-cold lagers together while he told us all about the carpets he collected; how their patterns and colours varied throughout the provinces, and how one merchant had been so desperate to make a sale that he had rolled up his eldest daughter in his most valuable carpet.

Jim laughed when he described how the girl spun out at his feet when the carpet was unrolled for inspection.

'We were both in a state of shock but she was the one who screamed!'

A mule train loaded with wooden tubs of water jolted into Maku's main street on the morning we set out for Tehran. A 580-mile journey lay ahead across the dry uplands between the Zagros and Elburz mountains, 4,000 feet above sea level.

Many flocks of sheep moved in single file, dividing the open spaces like moorland walls. Lush ribbons of emerald lay in pockets amongst the bare brown hills, revealing hidden river courses and shallow streams.

Soldiers were playing volleyball on a dusty makeshift pitch outside a gendarmerie post at Tazeh Kend. Lea purchased flour by the apronful from a mud-walled house on the edge of the village. Afterwards she baked a cake in the biscuit-tin oven, whilst Chris and I watched the soldiers finish their game in the fading light.

Behind us we could still make out Mount Ararat glinting like an arrowhead in a purple bank of cloud. On the lower slopes, much nearer, we saw the lamps from an Armenian settlement flicker into life. Two women were approaching the village from this direction. They wore crimson dresses and were riding camels. Lea shouted for Zhenka to come and look.

'Now that's one way we could have got here without a vehicle, isn't it Zhen?'

'I'd get camel-sick.'

'No you wouldn't. You'd get used to it, just like you got used to sleeping in the van. I'd love to have ridden camels instead of ponies when I was a little girl.'

'They're too high.'

'They kneel down for you when you want to get on and off – if you know the right words to say.'

'Magic words?'

Lea laughed. 'I suppose so. Your dad didn't know any when he rode a camel and so he couldn't get off until he paid the man more money.'

19

The weather was bad on the way to Tabriz. Brown floodwater swept across the road. When the rain stopped, other storms blanketed the sky in dust.

One day I saw a lamb ripped in half by three vultures. On another day, the driver of an open-topped wagon took a slippery bend too fast. The truck overturned, throwing its cargo of bleating sheep onto the road. The driver and his mate were shaken. We gave them mugs of hot tea, then they staggered back to slit the throats of the injured animals. Oil gushed from the battered engine of their truck and pools of blood flowed across the white road.

Mr Rumbell of Bromley stopped by. He was on his way home from Tehran. He gave one of the men a lift to the nearest town while the other remained with the sheep and the damaged wagon.

A few days later Keith Bartlam met up with us in Tabriz. He had travelled out by train and looked totally exhausted. Not many people would want to spend their summer holidays running across Iran and Afghanistan. Keith was a resilient and determined character, if a little serious and overcautious at times. He had already called in at the local gendarmerie to ask if the road was safe between Tabriz and Tehran, and seemed shocked at their complete indifference.

'I showed them the civic letter addressed to the Mayor of Tehran, but that only made things worse. I don't think they like him.'

Lea, Zhenka and I had cholera booster jabs at the local hospital in Tabriz. Afterwards we went to the cinema to see *Bedknobs and Broomsticks* dubbed in a strange mixture of Farsi and English.

When we left town there was a high pass to climb. Keith was eager to play the role of pacemaker but set off too quickly. Baz and I held back.

'No racing,' I warned.

'No racing,' he nodded.

The Shebli Pass was 6,890 feet above sea level. We enjoyed the climb but were anxious about the onset of desolation.

'How much fucking wilder does it get?' grunted Baz.

I had never seen anything remotely as barren. There were round-winds too on the high plains. Distant spirals of dust drifting across the empty landscape. One of them caught up with us just below the top of the pass. One minute we could see the road ahead, and the next it had vanished under a tarpaulin of sand.

We crouched in a ditch and shielded our eyes from the stinging grit. When the wind abated and the dust settled, the three of us stared in disbelief. There was Chris, in the van, just a few feet away from us.

'How long have you been there?' Baz shouted as he shook the sand from his hair.

'Never saw you. Never saw a thing.'

There were small pyramids of dung baking in the sun outside some mud dwellings on the banks of the river Qezel Owzan. Women from the village pounded their washing onto the smooth boulders at the riverside.

With the aid of a Super 8 cinecamera, Lea was recording segments of our journey on film. Washday seemed a good subject. She took her camera down to the edge of the water and slowly focused on the wet piles of clothes at her feet.

One old man with a stubbly white beard and baggy patched-up trousers took exception to this intrusion. He picked a pebble out of the water and threw it with all his force. The pebble landed short but Lea got the message. She quickly put away the camera and scrambled over the rocks back up to the van.

The old man was clearly of some importance in the village. Others followed his example. Suddenly the air was full of stones raining down from different directions. One of them hit Chris on the leg before he had time to slide the van door shut. He had driven off before we arrived, but when the villagers saw us they picked up more stones.

Five minutes later, the owner of a matchworks in Tabriz stopped his jeep and invited us to join him for lunch at his friend's house. This turned out to be a large salmon-pink building visible from a sharp bend a few miles down the road. We reached it along a well-maintained drive bordered by freshly clipped bushes.

Our host was a silver-haired man in a thin powder-blue cotton suit. He stood waiting for us on a tiled veranda under the shade of a wide bamboo porch. It was midday. The heat was intense.

'So!' he said, as he held out his hands. 'You cross this country of ours by foot? Well, you are most welcome. Come now please.'

The mud walls were painted white on the inside. On one of them hung a thick grey rug with a sparse abstract stripe in the same salmon-pink colour as the smooth outer walls. The man from the matchworks stood up as we entered and he too clasped our hands. The room was cool and pleasant to be in.

The man whose home it was shook his head when we explained what had happened earlier at the riverside.

'With or without your cameras, there are many more who may throw stones at you. And what can we do about this?' He stroked his chin where a beard had once grown, but could find no solution. Instead he shrugged his shoulders and frowned hard.

'Nothing, nothing is to be done …'

By the time we had eaten and talked, and showed the man where we had come from and where we were going to with the help of his daughter's globe, the sun was much lower in the sky.

'It will be cooler out there now, for the last few miles of the day,' I told him.

He nodded. We all filed out onto the yellow tiles of the veranda. The shadows were long. They had crept under the slats of the bamboo awning and were spilling across the floor towards the lower half of the pink mud walls.

'Davidan be Salamati!' He spoke the words softly and very slowly, and everyone inched forward to listen. When he signed our logbook he added a translation. 'Run safely my friends!' it read.

That night Chris rolled up his trouser leg to reveal a graze where the stone had nicked his shin.

'Davidan be Salamati!' he said, and gave a little grin.

20

Keith ran with us most mornings. The afternoons were too hot for him. He was used to running faster and covering fewer miles. Baz sometimes followed close on his heels. I tended to drift back and let them press on ahead.

We ran out across the plains. The bone-dry plains led to fertile valleys. And the valleys became shadowy gorges.

Tunnels had been blasted through giant spread-eagled fingers of rock. Some of the tunnels were long and all of them unlit. We entered their black gaping mouths with trepidation. Ahead of me, Baz carried a torch. The beam from it swung to and fro and picked out Keith's pink arms, relentlessly pumping up and down.

At the exit of each tunnel we had to shield our eyes against the blinding sunlight. The temperature was in the nineties. Lizards scuttled from under our feet into clumps of weeds at the roadside.

The road skirted a grey mountain called Jahan Dagh. A new oil pipeline had recently been laid alongside this road. The pipeliners were following our progress. One of them caught up with us at a town called Khorram Darreh.

'Any of you guys speak my lingo?'

A youthful suntanned figure waved his canvas hat and pushed his way towards us through the crowd gathered around the van. He had long blond hair which the sun must have bleached. He looked and spoke like a surfer.

'Australian?' asked Keith.

'Near enough I guess. Kiwi! I'm from a place called Rotorua, on the North Island. Ever heard of it? Where the hot sulphur burns your nostrils when you sniff the air?' He laughed. 'Anyhowz, my mates must have seen youz three running. Said I was to ask youz back for a bite and a beer.'

'Can't be bad,' said Chris.

'One of our lads comes from your neck of the woods. Always going on about that soccer player. Stanley someone or other. Calls him the Wizard of the Dribble.'

The Kiwi thrust his way back to a dark blue dodge truck and

jumped inside. He pulled away in a cloud of dust and Chris set off in pursuit. The two vehicles rattled along a wide dirt track for a few miles and came to a sign nailed to a creosoted wooden stave, freshly hammered into the sandy earth. The words 'Camp Five, Takestan' were scrawled upon it, and there was an arrow pointing to a metal hoarding beside a high barbed wire fence. The larger sign, in bold red letters, read: 'Neil Price International Construction.'

The gate was open. The Kiwi parked up outside a large prefabricated cabin, one of a dozen huts dotted about the site.

The boss was a balding stocky man wearing sunglasses, with no fat on him. When we shook hands his grip emphasised the nature of his work.

The boss led us to the shower room and we stayed under the showers for a long time, marvelling at the jets of hot water. Afterwards we met the rest of the gang in the games room of an air-conditioned cabin shipped over from Houston. All the men were bigger than we were. Matlock John was enormous. They all shook hands like the boss too, and they thought we needed fattening up. Roast beef and Yorkshire pudding was on the menu. We ate more than they did.

The man from Stoke was called Harry Bone and as soon as I sat beside him he wanted to talk about Stanley Matthews.

'Ever see him play?'

'I remember his benefit match,' I said. 'I saw it with my father.'

'So did I. All them names, eh? Puskas, DiStefano ... I thought the old man's ticker would go. All night he kept muttering "Is this heaven or the Victoria bloody ground?"'

Harry's pulse was racing. He was passionate about his football. The others had heard it all before and they were preoccupied with their darts.

Harry Bone was a hard drinker. They all were. They worked hard and played hard. After a few more drinks I was the only one left with him. He leaned over to me. He was so close now I thought he was about to whisper something in confidence, but he spoke with the same loud booming voice.

'When I asked if you'd ever seen him play, I meant when he was the best bloody player in the world, not when he was past it!' He took another long swig of beer and nudged me. 'Even then he could send them the wrong way, eh!'

A dart missed the board and bounced off the wall. It slid across the grey flecked lino and came to rest at our feet under the table.

'Each time I get home from this shit hole I look at my front door and think of shuffling Stan, out on the wing wearing number seven.' Harry dribbled with pleasure and wiped the beer from his cracked lips with the back of his hand. His palm was big and sunburnt, and the lines that criss-crossed it reminded me of the canyons we had run through.

'Never any player to touch him since. Well, we know that, you and me. I don't suppose those fuckers do.'

He bent down under the table to retrieve the dart, and then spun around and threw it at the dartboard. It was a difficult angle and he was too far away. But when I heard the soft thud as the arrow hit the target, I knew where it had landed.

21

The pipeliners had a black mongrel mascot named Moose. Zhenka fed the dog crisps and missed him when we left Camp Five.

'Can I have a dog when we get back to England?'

'I suppose you can,' said Lea.

'Good, then I'll be able to take it for walks around the petrol stations won't I?'

The track left by the construction workers laying the oil pipe between Tabriz and Tehran was some fifty yards from the main highway. For much of the distance it ran in a straight line. There were no trucks using this track and for our purpose it was infinitely preferable to the harder surface of the road. Baz and I took our time. We walked instead of ran and read an English newspaper on the way.

When we did have to leave the track at a town called Qazvin, an overweight coach driver hopped down from his cab to lob a stone into my stomach. The notorious 'Valley of the Assassins' was close by. Tehran was even closer.

At the British Embassy in Ferdowsi Avenue we met Corporal Mick Morrison from Swindon. He was a newcomer to the Embassy staff and a long-distance runner himself. Mick introduced us to another runner: Commander John Butterfield, the US Naval Attaché.

John had founded the Iran Roadrunners. He was a busy man but took his exercise seriously and wanted to know all about our run. He asked if I would present the prizes at the International School cross-country race he was helping to organise that coming weekend.

Before the race took place we saw our first ever game of American football. The children were kitted out in helmets and had thick padded shoulders. There were even cheerleaders on the sidelines and Zhenka was handed a paper streamer to wave.

Afterwards, John invited us home to meet his family, and we sat around a floodlit swimming pool eating sirloin steaks and peanut paste. Earlier in the year his wife Priscilla had taken part in the

Boston marathon. Priscilla was tall, lean and pretty. Everyone in the family was the same. When her young daughter produced the family album and pointed to the photographs of her grandparents, aunts and uncles, they were all the same too.

The Butterfields sipped orange juice and offered us beers or something stronger. They told us about a jogging boom that was sweeping the States.

'Like Beatlemania, Kelvin. My Ma wears trackpants to the shop and no one bats an eyelid.'

Priscilla was a picture of health. She tried hard not to fidget when Chris struck a match to light his cigarette.

We went jogging with them one Sunday. It was a club run for fun. I had never heard the term before. We jogged along dusty tracks and tree-lined boulevards near the Shah's palace. There were mums, dads, sons and daughters. They were clad in everything from shorts and singlets to cut-off jeans and tennis shirts.

Most of the joggers were Americans but there were a few English and French among them too. Chris joined us but could not pace himself properly. Seven miles later, he came in at the tail-end chatting to a large Parisienne whose bra strap had broken.

'Run for fun,' I overheard him telling her.

'Walk to talk, and ...' as he produced a packet of Players from his shorts, 'Smoke to joke!'

'*Merci Monsieur Christopher*,' she laughed and quickly took a cigarette from the packet.

John Butterfield described the next leg of our journey as the most breathtaking he had ever undertaken.

'Nailbiting stuff, Kel. The air on those mountaintops must be intoxicating but all I could smell was burning rubber. Believe you me, a cab ride to the Caspian borders on pure science fiction!'

The kamikaze cab drivers were not out in force on the morning we left. But the commander was right. The route over the rugged mountains was an extraordinary feat of engineering.

A river flowed beside the road. Yellowing leaves spun across the top of the water. There were beehives between the trees high on the riverbank. And the pale green canvas of the beekeepers' tents flapped in the wind further up the slope.

The road from Karaj to Chalus zigzagged between rocks and disappeared in and out of tunnels all the way up the mountainside. Many of the tunnels were unlit and Chris drove close behind with the headlights full on to make it easier for us to see.

The longest tunnel stretched for over a mile, straight through the summit of the 10,000-foot high mountain. A guard operated traffic signals from a small glass-fronted cabin at its entrance. Inside, it was only wide enough for a single stream of traffic, but we were allowed extra time to enable us to charge through to the other side.

Once through the Kandavan tunnel, the road dipped alarmingly. Autumn was approaching. Chris had to scrape ice from the windscreen of the van. The steep descent down the switchback tarmac caused a constant jarring of knee-joints already stiffened by the cold air of the high places.

The altitude brought on headaches too. Zhenka demanded cornflakes to cure his. Baz settled for an aspirin. And although the rarefied air had no direct effect on me I took a tumble on a sharp bend that left me winded and hugging a metal road barrier above the sheer drop of a few hundred feet.

I was bending down with my head between my knees when Spencer Lippincott drove up. There was a large unseemly dent in the offside wing of his shiny blue car.

'Fifteen times usually does the trick,' the man called out to me from the half open door. He struggled into a thick fleece-lined jacket, before making his way across the road to us.

I shook hands with the tall thin-faced Englishman and then continued dipping my head low until the stitch in my side went away.

Spencer looked puzzled. 'Strange highway to choose for a spot of running.'

'Baz and I are on our way to Australia,' I told him. 'We don't have a lot of choice as far as less dangerous options go.'

Spencer placed his hands on his hips and stared up at the sky.

The mountains shouldered billowing clouds which buffeted snow-filled gullies whenever the wind picked up.

'I've been contracted out here to help improve the traffic system in Tehran,' he explained. 'Now you lads, tell me which of us is more likely to be successful?'

It was Spencer's day off. Hurtling around the tight bends over the mountains was his idea of relaxation.

'I went to school with Bruce Tulloh. You know, the chap who runs barefoot. He ran across America a few years ago.'

'That's right,' I nodded.

'He wrote a book about it too,' said Baz, '*Four Million Footsteps.*'

We had all read the book. Spencer had a signed copy. It was part of the reading I had primed myself with when preparing for the journey. Other books included Dervla Murphy's account of her bicycle ride to India, *Full Tilt*, and Eric Newby's hilarious *Short Walk in the Hindu Kush*.

'Well lads,' Spencer got back into his car and began to remove his sheepskin coat. 'Mad dogs and Englishmen, eh!'

The tyres spun over the dirt before they gripped the tarmac. With an exaggerated wave, the Englishman assigned to cope with the horrendous traffic congestion back in the Iranian capital skidded out of sight.

The stitch in my side returned as soon as I resumed running. We walked part way down the mountain talking about the races we had watched Bruce Tulloh run.

'The last time I saw him was at Parliament Hill Fields,' I said, 'in the National cross-country championships. He was rounding a tight bend, covered in mud, with his arms outstretched like a tightrope walker.'

'Yeah, he ran like a stick insect didn't he?' said Baz, 'with his elbows jabbing out sideways. Tell you what though Kel, four million footsteps is a cockstride.'

22

The village of Goch Sar lay hidden somewhere amongst the hills. Two children who lived there were playing in a roofless ruin not far from the road. By balancing a wooden floorboard on what remained of a window ledge, they had created an ingenious see-saw and were now happily bobbing up and down on each side of a stone wall.

Further down the mountainside the grey walls of the gorge lessened, and wherever the valley widened there were vast plantations of small conifers.

Much taller trees grew on the lower slopes. Donkeys dragged slender lengths of felled timber between them along cart tracks through the forest.

As the road fell it became warmer. Hayricks on stilts rose above the open pastureland. At the bottom of the Elburz range of mountains we found ourselves 85 feet below sea level.

Closer still to the Caspian coastline we ran past tea plantations and cotton fields. Whenever we left the road to run along the grassy paths beside it, our footsteps ignited a firework display of frogs.

Russian ships were unloading their cargo at the port of Now Shahr. A few miles along the shoreline we came to a makeshift sign on a piece of cardboard taped to an oil can. The message in black ink spelt out my name followed by the words 'this way' above a wide arrow filled in with a light-blue marker pen.

The arrow directed us down a long overgrown driveway to a tumbledown house facing the beach. It was a large house full of Americans, two of whom we had already met in Tehran.

'We sneaked past you in our hired minibus at the entrance to the Kandavan tunnel,' Ted Smith told us. 'You were talking to the guard and it was a dangerous place to stop. Anyway, Vicky wanted to surprise you with her sign.'

Ted and Vicky were two of Commander Butterfield's fun runners. Indeed, Ted could easily lay claim to being the fastest among them. He had run for America in his younger days and clocked 46.6 seconds for 400 metres. Now in his late thirties he still looked in tremendous shape: every bit the all-American athlete.

Vicky wanted us to meet two friends of theirs, Bill and Shirley. They were joggers too but had been visiting the mountains during our stay in Tehran. Bill had a college-boy haircut that made him look meaner than he was. He had broad shoulders and his small head sat upon them like a baseball. The couple came from Santa Fe, the artists' colony in New Mexico.

'Bill's a sculptor,' Shirley told us.

'And a runner,' added her husband, visibly struggling to keep a straight face.

Vicky breezed over with a plate of spaghetti. 'There's more movement in those sculptures of yours Bill.' She laughed and prodded his paunch.

Later we all went down to the beach. Keith and Ted had built a bonfire out of driftwood and a few of us rolled a heavy log across the sand to sit on. Someone produced an icebox full of bottles of wine and port, and Zhenka was given his first taste of an American fizzy drink called Kool Aid.

The sky was cloudless and yet so full of different constellations and shooting stars that it appeared busy and crowded. On the beach the waves tumbled and frothed, and sparks from the bonfire blew low across the incoming tide. We hugged our arms around our knees; but for the flames it would have grown chilly.

'And what do you reckon Barry?' asked Bill. 'Now that you've run from the Black Sea to the Caspian. Is this marathon of yours fun?'

Baz pushed the branch he'd been holding into the heart of the fire and began to recite a page from one of Zhenka's Dr Seuss books.

'Here are some who run for fun, they run for fun in the hot, hot sun!'

'The hot, hot sun,' joined in Zhenka, practising the echoes he'd heard on the mountains.

'It's our particular kind of fun, yes,' added Baz. 'And rock climbers and pot-holers, they have their own version too.'

Bill looked at him. 'Even though at the very least there is a damn lot of discomfort and sometimes very real danger?'

'Yes, despite all that. But of course you have to be a runner, or a climber.'

'I am a runner,' Bill interrupted, and the firelight revealed a few grinning faces, while Vicky laughed out loud.

'Or, you have to be simply passionate about whatever provides the buzz to even begin to understand all this,' went on Baz.

Ted nodded. 'When you're so devoted to something it can't be explained in a rational way.'

'That's exactly what my mom said,' cried Vicky, 'and she was talking about my father!'

Bill glanced in my direction. 'Now don't get me wrong. I think what you guys are doing is incredible – crossing mountains, deserts and what have you. Real mind-bending stuff. I mean it's a goddamn link across the millennia. We're in the realm of Greek gods and Pheidippides here …'

'But …?' smiled Shirley.

'Well, take Rimbaud, the French poet. He set out to explore his soul. Now that is a nigh on impossible journey for anyone to undertake. In fact it forced him to backtrack into the real world where he ended up mapping out trade routes in a very hostile environment.' Bill poured out more glasses of port and carried on talking.

'What I'm saying is, there are artists who seldom venture beyond their studios but who still skirt these nightmare realms. It is a very isolating experience.'

'All runners are lonely,' I said, 'and in many ways they are like painters and sculptors too. Running is a most solitary occupation and yet it can lead us to feel at one with everything.'

Vicky laughed and spilled her drink. She was always laughing. 'Five grown-ups and a toddler crammed inside a little van. That's your real achievement!'

Lea nodded. 'A few nights ago I stayed up until the early hours writing letters home. I was sitting on my pillow with my feet tucked inside my sleeping bag. Everyone else was asleep. Baz, Keith and Kel were wedged tight beside me, hardly able to turn over. Zhenka snug behind them, and Chris lying across the front seats in the most cramped space of all. There was just a faint glow from the light above the passenger seat, but I wrote for hours. It seemed so private compared with my life in the van during the daytime.'

23

We ate pancakes with maple syrup for breakfast, when the sun was no more than a wave's height from the sea. Bill dished them up for us and joined in when we set off running an hour later, along the wet sands.

'You are a runner, Bill,' I grinned.

'No, I'm a jogger. There's a big difference. If there wasn't I'd want to go all the way to Australia with you.'

After a couple of miles Bill stopped and Baz and I shook hands with him.

'You guys are runners sure enough. But you're dreamers too. I like that.'

He set off back, sprinting down the beach for a short stretch, waving as he ran.

'How can he do that,' Baz laughed, 'with all those pancakes inside him?'

There were fewer villas overlooking this part of the coastline. No gardens full of exotic shrubs. The people looked poorer too. It was more like what we had become accustomed to.

'I was just getting used to the port,' said Baz.

'In the bottle?' I asked.

'Yeah, in the bottle and out of it.' He patted his stomach where his singlet was stretched taut. 'Our appetites are fucking embarrassing aren't they? No one else gets a look in do they? Poor Chris, he's no more than a skeleton in that driver's seat!'

As we ran we recounted all the food we had eaten beside the campfire under the stars. The dirt path we were on meandered below the level of the road. Dead horses had somehow been shunted into a ditch beside it and flies buzzed around the protruding bones. The stench was sickening.

'When people make their big trip overland they don't necessarily smell much of it do they?'

'If they do they can just wind up the windows,' agreed Baz. 'But they also miss out on the smell of the earth and the trees.'

We turned inland two days later, exchanging deserted beaches for sprawling towns. At Amol, where the coastal route rejoined the main road between Tehran and Mashad, we met a man from Yorkshire named Errol.

Errol was busy changing the wheel of a green Bedford van. Both he and it had seen better days. Chris had stopped to offer help and then perhaps wished he hadn't. At any rate he seemed relieved when I arrived.

'Yer mate here was telling me that you once lived in Melbourne.'

'That's right; Domain Street in South Yarra.'

'Never, which end?'

'By the botanical gardens,' I told him, 'overlooking Melbourne High School's cricket field. It was a single storey building with wrought-iron fencing painted white.'

'And don't tell me,' he interrupted, 'yer landlord was a bit of a poofter who played the lead in all the local Gilbert and Sullivan productions.'

I nodded.

The Yorkshireman's face lit up. It was weatherbeaten to the point of gale force. Despite being unable to find the wheel nuts which he had just unscrewed, he proceeded to tell me his story.

'Ma never liked it there. She was always hankering for the Dales. Dad was Italian though and his family had settled in Melbourne. But we emigrated. Dad sold ice cream but things didn't work out. Ma ran out on us. She met this bloke and they just drove off into the bush. In my Dad's ice cream van too. They lived in the outback in a fucking ice cream van. I went there once. They were living like Abbos. Corrugated tin fencing all around the damn van and my Dad's sign *Carlo's Cornets* fading in the sun. Soon as I was old enough I wanted to see the old country. When I got to Blighty I stayed. Years now it's been. This is my first journey back.'

We left Errol scrabbling about in the dust, cursing his wheel nuts. We were back in the land of horn-blowing taxi cabs and excitable shopkeepers now. On the edge of town a young man in an ill-fitting striped suit rode his motorcycle along the pavement and over my right foot.

Several schoolchildren began hurling stones at us in an untidy village called Neka. Keith and I stopped running and attempted to reason with them. Baz however, charged on ahead. He was hit three times before the blazer-clad mob withdrew to collect more ammunition. Then, as the youngsters moved towards us, a small shepherd lad suddenly rushed into their midst, wielding a whip. No sooner had he lashed out at them than they were gone, dodging down the side streets in an unruly rush of heads.

It was market day in Gorgan. We were overtaken by Turkomans on their way from the Steppelands beyond the Russian border to trade horses at a nearby bazaar. Outside the town, cottonfields occupied a vast plain and turbaned tractor drivers ferried the cotton pickers to and from their stints under the sun.

As we proceeded, the forested foothills of the Elburz mountains drew nearer. Soon the trees on their slopes overhung the road and gusts of wind pelted us with acorns. Just beyond the Shah's hunting park there was a signpost written in Farsi pointing to a leper colony on one side of the road. On the other side a sign in English advertised 'HOT TEA!'

An American ex-serviceman wearing a woolly skullcap stood cradling a chipped mug of coffee. He was working on the communication towers that had recently been erected high in the mountains.

'After ten years in Vietnam I thought I'd seen it all, but these Iranians beat everything. Can't rely on any of them. Do it yourself and it gets done, that's what I say. What about a coffee, boys?'

Sam Fischer rocked back and forth on thick-soled boots that gave him the added inches he clearly coveted. They enabled him to look down on most of the people he moved among and he eyed the Iranians like Texan steers and verbally branded them useless, or worse, whenever an opportunity arose.

He took off the grey woollen cap inside the café, looked at it forlornly and patted his bare head.

'Been out of a Stetson too long boys. Ain't no amount of money worth not wearing a real man's hat!'

Since leaving the Caspian coast we had covered 249 miles.

Neither Baz nor I had ever run that far before in any one week. Most days had been hot and humid. But the temperature fell rapidly when the sun set; so much so that in the mornings Chris often awoke to find the lenses of his glasses iced over. We'd leave him breathing hotly on them whilst we wobbled stiffly towards a new day.

In view of our aching limbs it was a fortuitous time to meet an Iranian whose father owned a Turkish baths in Bojnurd, sixty miles down the road.

Ali was studying in England at Brighton University. He had returned home to attend the burial of a relative. He passed on his address to Chris and promised to look after us when we arrived.

'Hot water Chris. How long is it since you turned on a tap and scalded yourself. I can hardly wait!' said Baz.

'How come we never saw a Turkish baths in Turkey?' asked Chris.

Bojnurd turned out to be an apt name for the jumbled network of mud-walled streets we entered two days later. Chris set about locating the address he'd been given, helped by noisy directions from Zhenka.

'Left Chris, left, left. Chris look …' he tapped excitedly on the windscreen and pointed outside. The chopped-off head of an oxen was propped up against an empty Pepsi crate, its wide dry nostrils spread flat upon the pavement.

All hopes of the hot water we had been promised slowly began to evaporate. We could find neither Ali nor his father's Turkish baths. Instead he found us.

'There is commotion. Which I hear. And I appear at this commotion. And there you are!' Ali explained as we followed him through the busy streets to the Turkish baths.

Once inside the brick building, the sound of running water led us to quicken our pace along the ornately tiled corridors. Ali grinned and pushed open a wide door.

The hot clammy air swirled around us and we could see no further than a few feet ahead. Our arrival however, had not gone unnoticed. A man draped in a towel, whose hairy chest only partly concealed his glistening rolls of flesh, loomed out of the steam like a listing battleship.

The man confronted Ali and pointed a chubby finger in our direction. A thick black moustache clung to his upper lip like a bat hanging from the roof of a cave. Whenever he scowled his eyebrows met in the middle. He was scowling now as Ali quietly led us away from him.

Much later, when we had bathed and had reached the home of his parents, Ali told us the reasons behind the man's behaviour.

'Foreign visitors are regarded with suspicion and required to register with the police. The man asked if you were my guests and for how long.' Ali looked uncomfortable. 'We must do that now. I will take your passports and perhaps one of you should come with me.'

Keith decided to accompany Ali to the local police station. In the meantime, Ali's father agreed to show us around.

The house was built of sun-baked clay laced with straw and tamarisk twigs. Inside each room the floors and walls were adorned with splendid carpets, some of which had been two years in the making. Zhenka was more impressed by a large silver samovar. Lea told him that it was the FA cup.

Ali looked relieved when he and Keith returned from the police station.

'Have you warned them yet about Savak, father?'

'There is an ancient Persian proverb,' said his father, 'which tells of the king having many ears and many eyes. Savak are the Shah's secret police and they have informers everywhere. My son believes you met such a one at the baths earlier.'

'The Shah is not a popular man,' said Ali. 'Recently there was a strike at a brick factory in Tehran. The dispute was shortlived. A large group of Savak agents entered the plant and beat fourteen workers to death with clubs.'

24

Camels were grazing in the playground of the local school at Shirvan. Lea and Zhenka sat close by shelling pistachio nuts. A group of women stood watching them from across the other side of the road. All the women were dressed in chadors and their dark eyes were invisible from even a short distance away. But they laughed and clapped their hands when Zhenka pulled down his shorts to pee. They had taken him for a girl with such long blond hair. Not that he minded. It often happened. And anyway, he did not understand why a boy should be praised just for not being a girl.

At first he had been fascinated by the clothes the women wore, how they hid themselves from head to foot inside a silken cloak that allowed only a brief glimpse of their big eyes through the narrow slits. He was used to the chadors now, just as he had grown accustomed to the camels.

Sometimes a hand with a sweet in it would emerge from a chador, and then he would have to try and remember the words his mother had taught him to say. Often, he couldn't and so on the whole he thought he preferred the camels to the chadors.

'Camels are funny creatures aren't they Chris?'

'They're knock-kneed Zhen, watch when they run.'

The school employed two teachers and one of them was a peace corps worker from the States, called Dan Calegari. Dan was walking home with a pile of books under his arm when Baz and I approached. All three of us were coated in a fine layer of dust: chalk from the blackboard in his case; and in ours, sand thrown up by trucks delivering sugarbeet to a local factory.

Dan and his wife Susan lived in a large mud house not far from the school. They invited us for a meal and insisted we stay for the night.

'I've never found teaching a particularly easy occupation in this country,' Dan told us, 'but I've never experienced such overcrowded classrooms before. The kids are crammed together six to a desk here which makes discipline something of a joke. It took me years to learn Farsi and at the end of the day all they seem to understand is a good whack behind the ears.'

Dan was exhausted and disillusioned, but his eyes still registered an enthusiastic twinkle. Next morning he looked happier. It was a public holiday for the Shah's birthday. We left them wrapping national flags around the lamp-posts in readiness for the celebrations.

We reached the holy city of Mashad on 27 October. Chris met us on the outskirts after collecting mail from the British Consulate. He and Lea had found a good campsite and we remained there for the next two days.

Zhenka was pleased to stay put for so long. He had befriended a sandy coloured Labrador with a litter of five puppies. One night Lea overheard him talking to them. 'Come into my bunk and come travelling, puppy dogs.'

Much of the time in Mashad was spent preparing for the coming trek across Afghanistan, refilling gas cylinders and obtaining tourist visas.

The name Mashad means 'place of martyrdom'. In the ninth century, the eighth patriarch of the Shia sect, Imam Reza, was fatally poisoned. The resulting gold-domed shrine above his tomb became the holiest place of worship in the country.

Lea and I wandered around the outer perimeter of the mosque with Zhenka. The building was encircled by the bazaar and our path was often blocked by crowds of people on their way to pray or to barter with the stallholders. We made slow progress until I hoisted Zhenka onto my shoulders.

'Are those helter-skelters?' He sounded excited.

'No, they're minarets.'

'They look like helter-skelters!'

When we got back to the campsite we found the others bent over our map of Afghanistan. The map's pristine condition indicated how infrequently it had been used. Perhaps deep down we never really thought that we would make it this far. Baz readily admitted he hadn't a clue where Afghanistan was before joining us in Istanbul.

'The frontier is about 170 miles from here,' Keith told us.

'Less than a week away,' added Chris.

'What does Mike Artus say about it all?' I asked.

Keith eased the pink elastic band from a bulging cardboard folder and sifted through a pile of papers. 'Here's something compiled by the British Consulate that applies to us,' he said. We gathered around to listen.

'Afghanistan is a strictly and sincerely Muslim country in which extreme modesty is customary. Generally speaking neither men nor women will expose any bare skin except for their hands, feet and faces, and in most districts women, even if not veiled, will hide their faces from strangers.' Keith paused before adopting an appropriately solemn tone. 'Neither men nor women should wear shorts.'

Baz adopted an earthy grunt. 'Shit!'

25

The road between Mashad and Islam Qala ran close to the Great Salt Desert. A grey green scrubland fringed the desert on one side of the road. On the other, mountains the colour of rainclouds met the sky in a murky haze.

Abandoned mud forts were dotted along the length of this ancient highway. Positioned a day's journey apart, they had long ago provided safety and shelter for the trading caravans on the old silk route.

'Just think Baz, Marco Polo wrote about these very same caravanserai. They once played an essential role in the Great Khan's postal system,' I told him.

'To tell you the truth Kel, I'd rather not know what they were used for or how long they've been around. What I like most about these ruins is that there are no informative signs. But …' he paused, grinning, 'I wouldn't mind being a postman.'

'Talking of communications,' Keith gestured towards the foot of a slope far off to our left, 'look over there.'

We both looked and could just make out the carriages of a train rattling in a wide loop around a small settlement.

'They're the rail tracks from Tehran,' said Keith. 'That must be Sang Bast, the end of the line.'

'So there's not even a railroad across Afghanistan?' asked Baz.

'No, there never has been. Next time we see a train will be in the Khyber Pass,' Keith told us.

It was late in the day and the copper telegraph wires beside the road bisected a pale moon low in the sky. Usually by this time we would all be relaxing in the van, but a delayed start that morning meant that we would not now reach our 40-mile target before dark. Somewhere ahead, dogs barked at the dusk, as if to settle some dispute with a sullen intruder.

At my side Baz limped to a halt and removed a shoe.

'Clobbered a dirt pile,' he said, and shook out the grit, whilst Keith and I took a breather.

The road was empty. When we resumed running we focused intently on the white line neatly painted down its middle.

The white unbroken line led us through the wilderness to a small army outpost where a dusty arena was lit up by swinging oil lamps. Inside the dirt square a group of turbaned recruits were being instructed in the art of wrestling.

Under one of the lamps sat Chris, engrossed in an *Observer* colour supplement sent out to us at Mashad.

'Ever heard of a chap named Sebastian Snow?' he asked.

'I've read articles of his I think. Isn't he a travel writer?'

'Well this isn't written by him but it's all about him. He's halfway through a long-distance walk from the tip of South America to the top of North America.'

Chris handed me the magazine. The report had been written by the mountaineer Chris Bonnington. In it, he described Snow's strict routine of one hour's walking followed by ten minutes break. All alone, with a pack on his back.

There were photographs with the text. From these it seemed clear that the long-distance walker had already lost a lot of weight. I gave back the colour supplement to Chris, and watched the men wrestling in the dust. They were not as skinny as Sebastian Snow but they had that same determined look in their eyes and it made me feel a little uncomfortable.

Row upon row of hand-painted Bedford trucks were parked outside the prefabricated customs buildings at Taybad, on the Iranian side of the border. Even at a standstill with the engines switched off, the timber sides of the big wagons vibrated with colour. The elaborate convoy artwork spilled over into the drivers' cabs too. Brightly dyed tassels of cloth dangled from the top of the windscreens, and above each dashboard an array of obscure talismatic objects vied for prominence. Promises of protection and a safe journey were evidently more highly prized than mere good visibility.

We joined a queue of truck drivers outside a barred window and waited to have our passports stamped.

Keith nudged my elbow. A young soldier was standing on top of the nearest truck grinning at us. He held a long knife in his hand which he used to slit open a hessian sack at his feet. Grain poured out of the sack and down over the side of the truck.

A man at the head of the queue cursed and spat.

It was close to midday by the time we were granted permission to continue. Spillages of diesel oil bubbled in the sun. A busload of pilgrims knelt down on the concrete to pray.

We pulled on the lightest tracksuit trousers we could find and headed for the foreboding contours of a new country. The cotton bottoms clung to our legs like long johns and I glimpsed Lea laughing in the wing mirror as they drove by.

Thirteen miles beyond Taybad, Baz thought he saw a camel. As we got closer he wasn't so sure. The camel turned out to be a plywood sign held up by two hefty posts that shimmered in the heat until we were all but upon it. It marked an invisible borderline with a terse message: 'Front of Afghanistan.'

The tilting shadow of a white pole cleaved the empty road in half at the frontier town of Islam Qala. The man responsible for raising and lowering the steel pole directed us along a grey expanse of shale to a dilapidated customs house. Lounging against its walls stood an equally dilapidated band of men with beards and turbans.

Zhenka pointed to the small badges pinned to their baggy shirts. 'What do their medals say Dad?'

Two of the men approached us.

'You need money but the bank is no good. My pocket gives a much better rate.'

His companion gave me a long wink. It was meant to be a friendly gesture to reassure us and gain our confidence. I had seen this same expression in a painting of a Pathan tribesman lining up his enemy through the sights of a rifle.

'With the money from my friend's pocket you can buy the hashish in mine,' he grinned.

By now they were close enough for me to observe what was printed on their tin badges. Customs officers.

We filed through a narrow doorway in the half-ruined building and placed our vaccination certificates on the desk labelled

'Quarantine'. The man behind the desk dusted the certificates lightly with the back of his hand, raised them to his mouth, and blew on them one by one. This done, he carefully scrutinised the dates stamped upon them and nodded his head. 'All is in order,' he said. 'Nothing deadly you are bringing with you.'

I had read somewhere of nomadic tribes who were reputed to have stolen children from towns in this locality. Back at the van I reminded Lea that now we were in Afghanistan we must never let Zhenka out of our sight. Lea was not listening. Instead she was staring over my shoulder at a giant of a man who was gently lifting up our son to sit him astride a donkey.

When the man began to lead the donkey away, she grabbed my arm and shouted.

'Quick Kel. Do something!'

I turned around just in time to see Zhenka wave to me before the donkey trotted around a corner. Lea and I dashed after him.

Seeing the look of consternation on my wife's face when we caught up with him, the tall man let go of the frayed rope around the donkey's neck and smiled down at Zhenka.

Lea tried to disguise the panic in her voice but the words tumbled out in an unfamiliar shrill tone.

'Did you enjoy your ride Zhenka?'

Zhenka looked distraught. His adventure had been abruptly curtailed. At the very least he wanted to keep the donkey.

26

We had just run across a five-mile stretch of no-man's land between the two border posts. No-man's land was appropriately devoid of people and, on first impression, Afghanistan seemed like a vast extension of an identical emptiness.

Gradually though, as the day progressed, intimations that we were not alone slowly became apparent. Not far from the road, we found a few rough circles of small stones containing the ashes of campfires. A little further away we discovered pennanted tombs and the tattered remnants of black tentcloth.

When we finally caught up with the nomads they seemed happy enough to see us. Even their wild dogs sounded less menacing in the daylight.

Dan Calegari had warned us about such animals. How a young Frenchman had recently abandoned his clapped-out Citroën in the middle of the night and started walking to the nearest village. And how he had never been seen again and was thought to have been ripped to shreds by the fierce dogs guarding the camps of the nomads.

The men wore white turbans and walked with long swaggering strides down the centre of the road. A few of them had rifles strapped across their backs, and their shadows trailed behind them like dark crucifixes.

Some of the men moved aside. Others decided it would be fun to outrun us. They were young and tall with big dark eyes cultivated from a diet of too many poppy seeds.

The Afghans giggled as they ran and Baz and I giggled with them. The dogs accompanying them were the size of huskies and the colour of the desert. They snapped and yapped at our heels and bared their teeth if we looked at them for too long.

It was a noisy and unlikely procession, along what had only a few minutes earlier been an empty highway. An assortment of leather sandals slapped down upon the concrete surface of the road and dust drifted up over our baggy-trousered escort.

It was too claustrophobic for Baz and I sensed his discomfort.

Slowly he began to pick up the pace and each time he inched ahead I quickened my stride to draw level. The animals were still yapping but the Afghans had stopped giggling. A race was on.

Within half a mile, only two of our impromptu opponents remained alongside us. Baz winked. He was enjoying himself.

'Alf Tupper would have loved this,' he chuckled.

I nodded. Tupper was the fictional hard-as-nails hero of a comic strip called *Tough of the Track*. Instantly I pictured him scoffing fish and chips prior to taking on some iron man from the East.

The man at my side looked down at me. His large eyes had narrowed. The giggles had been replaced by gasps.

Baz decided to pull out all the stops and briefly caught us unaware. For the next few strides he pulled away in front while I gathered myself to go after him.

Suddenly a hand reached out and gripped my wrist tightly. The nomad could run no further, but shaking him off was not going to be easy.

I made as if to slow down. Then I spun around and prised myself loose. By this time I was already up on my toes and sprinting away after Baz, not looking over my shoulder and accelerating for as long as I could.

'Jesus, Kel, the buggers can't handle defeat can they?'

'They're renowned for it Baz. That's why the British army never really made any inroads in this part of the world.'

'Not enough Alf Tuppers, eh?'

We passed mud villages and the camps of more nomads. There were also herds of sheep crossing the plain, and hypnotic caravans of camels lurching out of the golden dust like brittle-boned sleepwalkers.

Sometimes when the sun ran its tongue along the edge of the desert the very air would crackle and our horizon become indistinct.

We had parched throats and our lips resembled the cracked leather of our shoes, but we were slowly closing in on the oasis of Hera, and the blood was pumping around our veins.

Our first sighting of the four tall minarets on the edge of Herat came from fifteen miles out. They looked like delicate cobalt candles tapering upwards into a cloudless cobalt sky. But an oasis in the desert has all the fugitive qualities of a mirage and for a long time the minarets appeared to keep their distance. It was scorching, and we were running too fast. So, to avoid the horizon, I kept my head down and studied the geography of my shadow instead.

When we reached the mausoleum – the great Musalla complex built in the fifteenth century by Gohar Shad Begum, the wife of Tamburlaine's youngest son – I was surprised to find that each of the minarets were over a hundred feet high. Originally there were nine of them, but three had been toppled by earthquakes in 1931 and 1951. Two smaller survivors stood beside the queen's tomb. The rest of the buildings, said to have been masterpieces of Islamic art, were demolished by British troops in 1885, when making safe their defences against a Russian attack that never came.

Beyond the minarets, we jogged past a big gun perched on a hillside above the road. It had once belonged to the British and bore an emblem of King George III. The massive cannon used to announce noon each day from a spot closer to the minarets. But the loud booms were considered too much of a risk to the fragile brickwork, and so, in 1965, it was manhandled up a steep rise to its present position.

Butchers were bolting the wooden shutters of their shops when we at last walked into the city. Blood dripped like prayer beads from the tubs of sheep's heads on the patched up pavements outside. Oil lamps were already flickering and charcoal fires were being fanned alight under flimsy cotton awnings. Each narrow street we crossed smelt of woodsmoke and spices. Bells jingled. Black hooded carriages led by horses decked out in red pom-poms jolted out of nowhere and disappeared.

There was a ten o'clock curfew for Europeans in this tan-coloured city where Genghis Khan and Timur the Lame had brought down the citadel walls.

'Even at five o'clock I was told not to stray into any dimly-lit areas,' Lea told us. 'But the whole place is dimly lit. One policeman warned me off using the pavements because they were in the shadows. He said I'd be safer in the middle of the road.' Lea looped the handles of a string bag of mandarins onto a hook in the back of the van. She had begun to suspect that running was the least complicated part of this journey.

'Take this afternoon for instance. Chris doesn't think it's wise for me to go wandering into the bazaar on my own, but then he won't leave the van unattended either. So we end up with no shopping until you three arrive, by which time it's too bloody dark to see what I'm cooking.'

'We need to set off earlier in the mornings,' suggested Baz. 'Get it over with, so we have more time to sort out things like shopping and the rest.'

'Most of the women are veiled from head to foot,' said Lea. 'Perhaps I need to wear a burka so that I can just merge into the background with them. Imagine what the Afghans thought when the hippies started rolling in ten years ago!'

'The Pathans are supposed to be the worst,' said Keith. 'Just looking at one of *their* women can get you shot.'

'Maybe we should start running in the fuckers,' chuckled Baz.

No surfaced road crosses the centre of Afghanistan and so our route from Herat would have to be south to Kandahar, along a 353-mile concrete highway.

An avenue of thirty-thousand jack-pines lined the road that led out of the city. The trees shaded us from the sun. On the other side of the low mud walls which ran parallel to the road, oxen were heaving wooden ploughs across the bumpy paddocks, and men were collecting manure for the grape fields from the bases of the high pigeon towers. Snow clung to the topmost range of mountains visible far off to the north, and it was refreshingly cool in the shadows of the trees.

Baz was in high spirits. He and Keith had bought leather boots from the covered bazaar for what they considered to be a knock-down bargain. Now he juggled mandarin oranges as he ran.

'You belong in a circus Baz,' shouted Keith.

'This is a circus, mate,' replied Baz, handing us each a mandarin.

A wide plain stretched to the foot of the rugged mountains which lay ahead of us. Large dogs guarded the flocks of sheep grazing there. We watched them closely as we ran by, always slowing to a walk if they snarled or bared their teeth.

However, our concentration lapsed before we reached the mountains. Baz had been full of running all day and was twenty-five yards ahead of Keith and me. Chris drove behind us as slowly as he could. The sliding doors of the van were wide open and a Neil Young cassette was playing on the tape deck. Lea was in the back of the van kneeling over a bowl of soapy water giving Zhenka a bath.

Suddenly Chris sounded the horn and accelerated. He had spotted three bull mastiffs moving in Baz's direction and he needed to get to him before they did. As the van veered past, one of its rear doors swung open and a plastic bottle of washing-up liquid rolled into the middle of the road.

The dogs pulled up short before they reached the roadside and we all heaved a sigh of relief. I looked back over my shoulder, thinking to retrieve the errant plastic container.

A wizened old man was sitting cross-legged at the edge of the road. None of us had seen him approach, though we all fixed our eyes upon him now. He was taking long swigs from our bottle of washing-up liquid and only a cigarette from Chris could persuade him to hand it back to us.

A day later we left the plain to begin our ascent into the Parapomisus Mountains. The Mir Ali Pass rose to a height of 5,800 feet and was the bleakest spot we had ever encountered. There were no clouds in the sky and no trucks on the road. When we stopped for a bite to eat, Lea and Zhenka climbed on top of the van and looked through our binoculars.

'There's a black speck on the road ahead. Can't make out whether it's a man or an animal,' Lea shouted.

The black speck was a Baluchi tribesman. I was running ahead on my own when I drew level with him. I nodded and smiled and he did the same.

When I heard footsteps approaching from behind a few minutes later, I thought it must be Baz who had caught up with me. Instead,

I turned to find the small bearded Afghan at my side. He was wearing the predictable pair of voluminous white trousers and a long white tunic. But to keep out the cold he had also invested in a brown tweed jacket and an enormous grey-coloured overcoat. How he could stand, let alone run beneath their weight surprised me. But run he did.

After a while the Afghan removed a small silver snuffbox from the inside pocket of the tweed jacket. He had difficulty opening the clasp to the lid of the box whilst we were running and so we both slowed to a walk. Once he had taken a little snuff to chew on, and offered some to me, the man removed his heavy coat and I said I would carry it over my shoulder to make it easier for him to run.

For the next three miles he jogged at my side, not breathing unduly heavily but with his eyes firmly set on the horizon. We parted company at a tollgate close to the old town of Adraskan. It was hard to determine how far he had travelled, or if he had arrived at the place to which he was going.

27

The Russians who had assisted in the construction of the road had left behind a trail of brick bungalows which had once provided their temporary accommodation. These buildings had been padlocked since 1964 when the highway was finally paved. The Afghans were not remotely interested in them, preferring the mud-domed architecture of their own village houses. But the grounds in which they were situated made ideal overnight camping spots for us on the way to Kandahar.

One morning we rounded a bend high in the mountains and looked out over a wide valley. Down below on the plain the windows of a modern hotel flashed in the sunlight.

The Hotel Farah Rud was another example of Soviet involvement and Afghan indifference. There were flowerbeds outside the entrance and a large swimming pool at the rear. Inside the hotel the dining room was cold and draughty. Each night a noisy generator operated between the hours of six and nine. Afterwards, storm lanterns were brought out and placed upon the soiled tablecloths.

A man at reception pointed to the shining rows of unused keys. There were one hundred bedrooms. None of them were occupied. When we ordered tea, a young Afghan carried a battered teapot across the road to a stall set up opposite the hotel. This flurry of activity caused consternation and the rest of the staff looked relieved when we decided to sleep in the van.

Halfway to Kandahar a lone cyclist rode up. His name was Stan Erbrink and he came from a small town near Amsterdam. Stan had trained to be an architect in Holland but he had made his money playing bass guitar in a rock band in Canada. Now he was living off the proceeds and cycling around the world.

'I think two years will be long enough. I have targets yes, but I want to keep it flexible. If someone tells me there is something I should not miss, I will try my best to fit it in.'

The Dutchman had breakfast with us and we topped up his water canisters. He loved the idea of our running all the way to

Australia but was happy enough with the more solitary aspects of his own journey.

'I've never had so much time to myself just to think and try to work things out. People wrongly assume we must be missing out on luxuries. But the simplicity of it all is the real luxury.'

Stan was a mine of information. He had read a lot about the land he was crossing.

'Tonight I intend to make my camp in a ruined fortress at Kishk-I-Nakud,' he told us, pressing flat the concertina folds of his map on an empty corner of our trailer top and pointing to two small crossed sabres.

'Less than a hundred years ago the Afghans did away with over a thousand British troops at the battle of Maiwand. They spent their last night camped outside the castle walls. So I will put up my little nylon tent there and listen to the desert.'

Before he left, Stan picked up Zhenka and sat him down on the black leather saddle of his bicycle. He held him safe with one hand and wheeled the cycle around by the handlebars with the other.

'The horizon is our home, eh Zhenka?'

In the days that followed we met more nomads crossing the biscuit-coloured plain and more wild chases ensued. A few items of clothing were snatched from our makeshift washing line but nothing that could not be replaced.

Sand blew across the road from low dunes fringing Dasht-I-Margo – The Desert of Death.

The sand had drifted halfway up a lone petrol pump on the outskirts of Dilaram. There was a ruined caravanserai surrounded by brittle white thorns that overlooked a wide river where Zhenka filled his water pistol. Then more empty stretches of sand and scrub until we came to a craggy hill called Thief's Mountain, where Baluchi tribesmen would hide in caves after raiding caravans crossing the desert.

Sometimes the road crossed irrigation channels that formed part of the Helmand Valley reclamation project, a scheme funded by the US government in an effort to outdo the Russians. The Americans had built a huge dam to channel vast amounts of water from the Helmand River which flows from the Hindu Kush to the Arab marshlands.

In 1219, 200,000 Mongols led by Genghis Khan had swept over what was then a fertile plain. They destroyed everything in their path, including many ancient canals, leaving behind a wasteland bereft of any greenery until recent times.

Every half hour or so, clouds of dust would signal the approach of a truck. Often we would see animals tethered to their roofs: goats, sheep, a few chickens. Once, even a donkey braying loudly above the roar of the engine.

We entered the grim-looking mountains, which had once formed a natural defence of the old city of Kandahar, just before dusk on 21 November: two weeks after leaving Herat. The name Kandahar is derived from the Arabic form of Alexander's name, Iskander.

Stan had suggested we look him up at the Peace Hotel and Chris and the others drove on ahead in search of the Dutchman.

Baz and I made our way slowly along the dusty streets. Meat was cooking in the mud-domed homes. Puffs of smoke floated into the sky like lemon-coloured freckles. The moon had risen. Caged canaries were being covered and the sweat had grown cold on our backs.

The Peace Hotel meant nothing to one man we met exercising his prize-fighting hound. And a young lad trundling a pushcart loaded with tinkling bottles of soda water from the bazaar first pointed in one direction and then in another.

'Are you lost? Do you speak English?'

'Yeah,' said Baz, 'we are English.'

'Are you lost?'

There were two of them. They were backpackers. Tall and bronzed. Both Australian.

'We're looking for the Peace Hotel,' I said.

'You've passed it. It's way back there.'

The taller of the two girls held out her hand. 'My name's Wendy. This is my friend Lou. We're staying with a Mr Deveny on the other side of town. This is his card – with a little map to help you find us. Call by tomorrow and we'll cook you a meal.'

28

The UN aid camp lay on the eastern edge of Kandahar. It was once a bustling enclave for many overseas workers, with a lively dance hall, a well-stocked library and an outdoor swimming pool. Now it resembled a ghost town, and all but three of the wooden bungalows dotted around the extensive grounds were empty.

There was a light on in the porch of the second bungalow we came to. Baz climbed a couple of steps and knocked on the door. A tall, well-built man holding a can of lager opened it.

'Good job you guys could make it: there's a goose cooking in the oven and I hate wasting decent grub.'

It turned out that Ralph Deveny was responsible for Kandahar's power supply. He came from a small town in the backwoods of Alaska where his mother still lived.

'Ma shipped out the entire contents of my pantry here. She even caught the salmon we're going to be eating. Smoked it, canned it, shipped it out to me.'

Wendy and Lou popped their heads around the kitchen door. 'Who's for lagers?'

The girls had been busy all afternoon. By the end of their stay it was obvious that the stocks in Ralph's pantry would be sorely depleted.

The antipodean cookery extravaganza was a great success. Halfway through the meal Ralph's friend Victor arrived with his wife Fatima. Victor was from Italy. He was a doctor, with a soft spot for the Afghans, despite saying the most outrageous things about them.

Fatima was twice his size and deeply in love with him. She came from Zimbabwe and was dressed in a colourful sarong that she would occasionally unwrap to wind around her husband.

'Look at him. My adorable Giacometti stick insect!' she said, and laid her ample bosom on his bald head, screaming with laughter until the tears rolled down her cheeks.

Victor had brought an old projector with him and wanted us all to watch a film of a hunting trip he and Ralph had recently undertaken. Wendy and Lou pinned a white cotton sheet to the wall whilst Victor balanced the heavy projector onto a pile of books. Ralph turned off the lights and the film jerked unsteadily up and down, whilst smoke and dust particles floated across the crumpled screen.

'Is that where we stayed?' Ralph shook his head in disbelief.

'You see, I told you. The only people stupid enough to build a ruin,' cried Victor.

The shaky footage panned from a flat-roofed hunting lodge to a wooded hillside.

'There's the boar! See it Fatima?'

Fatima was in the kitchen replenishing her empty glass. 'I know where the bore is,' she laughed.

'That woman would have missed her own birth if bourbon had been in the womb!' shouted the doctor.

When the film came to an end and Ralph switched on the lights, everyone but Zhenka was fast asleep.

Fatima had not returned from the kitchen.

Ralph was doing sit-ups on the wooden deck of the veranda outside his bungalow when I climbed out of the van next morning.

'Grab yourself a coffee Kelvin. I'll be right with you.'

I sat on a high stool at the breakfast bar in the kitchen and poured myself a strong mug of coffee. Someone had already washed the dishes and cleared away the empty glasses from the previous night. Ralph followed me inside.

'I try to keep in shape,' he said. 'Yesterday, young Chris asked me if I'd ever heard of two Americans who were walking around the world a few years back.'

'That's right,' I said, 'we keep meeting people who put them up.'

'Well, they stopped here too. Nice guys. They were brothers. John and David Kunst. Twins I think. They had a small covered wagon, a dinky looking job it was, and a donkey. I pulled a few strings to secure an armed escort for them as far as Kabul. After that they were on their own.'

Ralph opened a cupboard door that squeaked and handed me a cereal packet.

'Anyway, when they left Kabul they headed down the Tangi Gharu gorge – same way you'll be going according to Chris. No one warned them off camping in the gorge overnight, so they chanced their luck.'

Ralph pulled a cord that raised the window blinds and he glanced outside. Keith and Baz had put up a tent on the lawn and someone's head was just emerging from it.

'The gorge is only twenty miles outside Kabul. But it's a god-forsaken place at the best of times. No one in their right minds would want to be there after dark.'

He reached over for the enamel coffee jug and tapped his knuckles on the windowpane. Keith looked towards us and I saw Ralph mime the word coffee. Then he walked over to the black stove and placed the jug on a hot plate.

'They were halfway down the gorge when the light started to fade. The walls are sheer there and the passage through is narrow, but it becomes even narrower as you descend down the river. So they decided to stay put. They figured that the sound of the water would keep them awake if they went any lower.'

The black coffee was bubbling over the rim of the blue and white striped jug and there was a loud hiss when it reached the hot surface of the iron stove. Ralph swore and slid the jug over to one side where the heat was less intense. Then he went back to his story. By now Baz and Keith had joined us in the kitchen and so I had to explain as briefly as I could what it was all about.

'A truck had broken down some way below the two lads,' Ralph continued, 'so they already knew that they were not alone. Maybe that's why they stayed there – for safety – who knows? In the early hours of the morning, hill tribesmen, bandits, attacked the truck and slit the driver's throat.'

'Shit!' said Baz.

Ralph nodded.

'Instead of blowing out their candles and remaining quiet, John picked up their shotgun and fired it into the air, thinking to scare them off I suppose. Next thing they knew they were in the middle of a gun battle. John was shot in the arm and David got hit in the lung. According to his brother, John fired a couple more shots before a bullet caught him smack between the eyes.'

'So one of them came out of it alive?' I asked.

'David was badly hurt, but yeah, he returned to the States and buried his brother. Soon as he'd recuperated, blow me if he didn't fly straight back to Kabul and set off all over again.'

Ralph pointed to a cork noticeboard beside a large refrigerator in the corner of the kitchen.

'Every now and then I get a postcard from him. Like I said, they were swell guys.'

29

The road out of Kandahar had been laid with assistance from the Americans. Two days earlier we had entered the city along a highway constructed entirely of short ten-foot long sections of concrete: a method of road-making much favoured by Soviet-backed ventures.

Now, Baz and I strode out over a smooth, well maintained tarmac surface that stretched for 305 miles, all the way to the capital itself.

Riding a grey Arab stallion called Vonolel (who was later awarded an Afghan war medal by Queen Victoria), General Roberts had marched a British army numbering 10,000 from Kabul to Kandahar, along this very route in 1880. 'Bobs' as he was known by his men, had decided that speed was of the essence if his troops were to relieve Kandahar and revenge one of the most crushing defeats ever suffered by a British army. They accomplished this after a gruelling march of only three weeks, although the General and many of his officers reached their goal exhausted and suffering from dysentry.

Keith was feeling unwell and had decided to stay in the van with the others.

'My pulse rate's high this morning,' he told me. 'Better not risk any running today.'

Just before setting off to follow us, Chris drove to the post office. The building had either been blown up or it was undergoing the kind of haphazard modernisation Victor had described. Either way, the prospects of finding anything addressed to us did not look good.

Chris climbed a rickety ladder and stuck his head through a wide, uneven hole in the wall. After a few minutes a hand emerged waving two crumpled airmail envelopes, and our optimistic driver gingerly descended.

He paused briefly on the bottom rung of the ladder and glanced down at the correspondence. The first envelope read 'Miss Vera Osgood'. The second, 'N. W. Bottomley'.

Chris climbed back up, only to be handed other letters. None of them were meant for us.

Clouds of dust hung over the bare earth side streets on the outskirts and clung to the backs of goats and horses. We jogged past mud teahouses and roadside shopping booths made from old timber goods wagons in a land of no railyards.

The few days at Ralph's had passed all too quickly, though we left under a cloud having overtaxed the fragile sewage system connected to the bungalow. Our congenial host from Alaska was last seen scratching his head and muttering 'Oh shit!' whilst three Afghan helpers dug up his front lawn.

The black tarmacadam road crossed the dry plains of Kandahar in a straight line. Here and there dirt tracks meandered away towards small settlements of low-roofed mud dwellings.

The sky was blue and empty and the sun felt as hot as ever. The winter migration of hundreds of nomads had already begun. They drifted down from the high mountains with their camels, goats and sheep. Sometimes they crossed our path or gravitated to the road itself, moving in long straggling lines flanked by their ever-menacing hounds.

One evening, as we approached the hill-fort of Kalat-I-Ghilzai, two men in uniform strode into the road and barred our way. The sun was setting behind the two soldiers. It burrowed into the sand like a fluorescent-backed beetle and made it difficult for us to focus on them as they waved their guns and forced us to turn around.

I felt the hot muzzle of a gun barrel poking into my back and prodding me towards a small square hut built out of concrete breezeblocks.

Baz fell, or was tripped, and went sprawling headlong through the open doorway. I was pushed inside after him. We lay in a heap on the dirt floor. The door slammed shut.

'Fuckin' hell Kel!' Baz whispered. 'What do we do now?'

I sat in the dark, shaking with fear. 'One thing we don't do is check our pulse rates.'

The walls of the room were about ten feet high. In the topmost corner of the wall opposite the door, a narrow window appeared to have been blocked up with chicken wire and cardboard.

'Let's give it half an hour,' said Baz. 'The light should have faded by then.'

'Do you think you can squeeze through that gap?' I asked.

Baz shook his head. 'No, but I think you can.'

It was the longest thirty minutes I have ever spent. Finally Baz braced himself to take my weight. I placed my right foot into his interlocked fingers, pushed hard, and scrambled onto his shoulders.

The chicken wire was easily removed and I pulled myself up and wriggled through the gap without too much difficulty. Outside it was lighter than we thought it would be. I slithered down the concrete wall as quietly as I could and nervously peered around a corner of the building.

The two young soldiers were nowhere to be seen. The place seemed deserted except for a lone camel tethered to a dark blue oil-drum a few yards from the road. I crouched low and inched along the side of the building towards the door.

It wasn't even locked. I took one more look across the road and then reached out to raise the iron latch.

Suddenly, a hand gripped my shoulder from behind and I froze.

'It's me,' Baz whispered. 'I followed you out through the hole in the wall.'

My heart pounded. I was too shaken to speak and I felt sick. Baz seemed not to notice. He was staring at the door. 'They never even locked the fucker did they? We could have walked out ages ago. Bastards!'

30

'Why is he so cheerful?' asked Keith.

'I've no idea.'

Baz was running alone some way ahead and he was laughing to himself regardless of the odd sight this presented.

Keith and I tried hard to catch up with him. We could hear his sudden outbursts of laughter and see his shoulders shaking as he sped along the road.

The morning had only just begun for us. It was an early start induced by the cold night we had spent huddled together inside the back of the van. Icicles had formed on the metal ceiling and all three of us had been eager to start running as soon as dawn broke in order to get warm.

Keith closed the gap as we reached the crest of a hill.

'What are you laughing at Baz?'

'That idiot Baxter. Did you hear him? Do you know what he called us? The Hole in the Wall Gang, that's what. The Hole in the fucking Wall Gang!'

We had evacuated our cold, damp van in favour of the open road, but that afternoon a sandstorm blew up. We closed our eyes against the flying grit and stumbled towards the spot ahead where we had last seen Chris waving us on from the rooftop of the parked vehicle.

The storm raged for the next few hours. We sat side by side choking on the orange dust. Lea read a story to Zhenka. Chris bent over a crackling radio and tried to tune into the World Service.

'Snow blizzards next, according to Ralph,' he said.

I looked at Baz and saw him bite his lip. Then he buried his head in a paperback.

Outside, when the dust storm lifted, the light was already fading. Keith helped Chris dig out the wheels. Sand had drifted over the axels.

When the top of the trailer had been scraped clear we lifted the lid and dragged out a gas cylinder. Lea assembled the small camp stove on one of bunks inside the van, connected the rubber pipe and lit the gas.

For most of the day the sun had been hidden by the storm. Now that it was sinking behind the mountaintops the temperature had already grown much cooler. We sat grouped around the kettle while we waited for it to boil.

Keith unlaced his trainers and removed his socks. Then he placed his feet closer to the small jets of flame. Baz and I did the same. Zhenka looked horrified and pinched his runny nose tightly.

'It's our toes that need warming, isn't it Zhen?' said Chris. 'The heater in this van is useless even when we're on the move. Except for stamping on the accelerator or a cold brake pedal my feet are totally redundant, and are freezing because of it.'

'This little piggy went to market, this little piggy stayed at home,' laughed Baz.

'Couldn't we afford a room in a hotel?' suggested Keith. 'Every now and then, just to see us through this cold spell?'

'Yes,' I nodded. 'If we can find a hotel.'

Chris stared out of the windscreen miserably. Heavy snow clouds were rolling across the horizon, blotting out the high peaks in the direction in which we were heading.

The blizzards Ralph mentioned swept down towards us when we were still 27 miles from the town of Ghazni. Within a very short time both the highway and the sandy contours beside it were covered with snow.

We took the lead in turns and ran in single file. An icy wind drove the irritating snowflakes directly into our faces and forced us to shield our eyes and look down at the ground.

Soon the nylon rainsuits we were wearing felt heavy and uncomfortable. Our feet began to slip back if we tried to run any faster.

When a snowplough appeared, Chris decided to follow it. They would wait for us in Ghazni and look for a hotel.

During the next few miles the snowfall ceased. As the road climbed and the visibility improved, we saw a caravan of camels padding silently below us, each one bearing spiky thorn bushes in snowy bundles across their humps.

We were able to make good progress in the wake of the yellow snow plough and were not long in reaching our destination.

The town of Ghazni lies at 7,186 feet. Legend has it that centuries ago its entire population was smothered in a tremendous snowstorm, save for a single family.

The Hotel Ghazni had a flat roof and resembled a long military barracks. Chris and Lea had been busy. Not only had they secured a room for us at the inn, but they had also got a fire going inside it in a large metal drum.

Chris met us in an empty car park outside the entrance. He was helping a young lad to drag a bulky sack of firewood over the wooden tailboard of a small wagon.

'The logs cost so little, and the room too,' he said.

'I wonder where they get the wood from?' said Keith. 'There are no trees!'

The hotel was empty but for us. The rooms and corridors were all unlit.

Five years earlier, Bruce Chatwin and Peter Levi had booked into the same hotel. In his book *The Light Garden of the Angel King*, Levi describes how he stood outside the hotel looking at the desert. A pack of wolves was howling and they woke every dog for miles. 'Never again' were the words used when he wrote about their coach trip from Kandahar to Ghazni.

'It's a replica of that place at Farah Rud,' said Baz. 'There's even a glass cabinet full of cobwebs and tinned cans of food, relics left behind by the Yankee road gangs.'

The fire was roaring when we crowded into the small square room. Logs were stacked along the foot of each wall. Lea was making hurried mud repairs to a crack in the stove's tin chimney. Nobody seemed to mind about the smoke. It was warm. Hot. Roasting.

We strung a nylon rope across the middle of the room and hung our wet running kit over it to dry.

'I can cope with life in the van when the weather is hot,' I said, 'but when it starts to get cold it's so bloody depressing.'

throwing plates at the moon

Zhenka stopped pushing his toy car along the concrete floor and looked up at me.

'Bloody pressing!' he cried.

31

We prised ourselves out of the snug square room to climb 2,000 feet on up into the mountains. At the doorway Keith paused to look back inside. The metal casing of the tall cylindrical stove was still glowing red. At its base was a gooey mess of melted black rubber stuck fast to the floor where he had left his trainers to dry.

The walled city of Ghazni reminded Baz of Gormenghast, even down to the ragged-looking inhabitants who scurried from the doorways of their adobe homes in the big castle walls. Baz was halfway through Mervyn Peake's trilogy, and later when we looked at the map there was indeed a province called Ghor in the very heart of Afghanistan.

Overnight the snow had drifted before freezing into icy ruts on each side of the road, but the highway itself had been swept and kept open. Word had it that the route ahead to Kabul was still passable – though for how much longer no one would say.

When the sky cleared the sun began to melt the snow piles and our feet splashed through widening rivulets of water. By midday, small pools had formed in the shallow dips beside the road. Some pools held the wobbly reflections of burnt brick pillars; others the bleached staves of fluttering prayer flags.

The pass over the mountains was 9,000 feet high. Beyond the pass, the road descended between rough tiers of irrigated fields. At the end of a valley, which stretched for many miles, the cold air had given the far horizon an intense clarity. Purple mountains with glistening white peaks ringed the capital and provided our first sighting of the Hindu Kush.

We arrived at Kabul on 8 December, 1974. I had run 5,482 miles, and Lea, Zhenka and myself had been away from home for eight months.

Everyone moved into the Columbus Hotel. Beds there cost very little and the hotel had a high walled garden at the rear in which we could safely park our van.

The room we chose was small, basic and, as soon as the big metal stove inside had been filled with sawdust and lit with the aid of a long spill, smoky. The electricity supply proved as sporadic as ever. Outside our room an old diesel generator was housed behind the rusty tin walls of a lean-to that rattled loudly whenever it kicked into action.

'Tell 'em to turn that fucker off Chris!' Baz shouted up from his journal. 'We'll make do with oil lamps.'

The Columbus Hotel boasted a candlelit restaurant heated by an enormous iron bowl full of glowing embers. We lounged upon piles of cushions around low carved tables, and Zhenka swayed his blond head to and fro when a blind musician struck up.

After we had eaten and returned to our room there was a faint knock at the door. Keith was nearest and got up to see who it was. For the past few weeks we had heard rumours about an Englishman with big ears who was cycling many miles behind us.

Peter Conan stood in the doorway and gave a nervous grin.

'Hello … are you the runners?'

'Come in,' said Keith. 'We've been hearing about you.'

The young cyclist hesitated before limping towards us. Baz took one look at him and hurriedly slipped a sweatshirt over his Mickey Mouse singlet.

Like us, Peter was making for Australia.

'It's my second attempt,' he told us.

'What happened the first time?' asked Chris.

Peter's face reddened. His ears were peeling and he inched a Hull City bobble hat down over the top of them. 'The first time was two years ago. I got halfway across Turkey, then some guys stole my bike. Took everything, they did. Passport, money, the lot. I had to be repatriated.'

Baz told him all about Stan. I asked if he knew of the Irish woman who had cycled to India in the sixties.

'She rode one of those heavy old-fashioned bicycles and carried a revolver with her. I can even remember the name she gave to her bicycle – Roz! She fired the revolver at wolves in Eastern Europe, and also used it to protect herself from a Turkish policeman.'

'What will you do when you get to Australia?' asked Lea.

'I'm not sure. There's an uncle in Bendigo. Maybe I'll look him up. What about you?'

'That's a point,' Lea looked at me. 'What will we do?'

What would we do? I shrugged my shoulders. 'I've no idea.'

Months later, news reached us that Peter had gone down with amoebic dysentery in Kathmandu. Worse still, his application for a tourist visa to Australia had been turned down because he could not afford a return ticket.

Wide avenues swept through Kabul. Soldiers stood guard outside the imposing façades of Embassy buildings and flags flew there. In the downtown part of the city a grey-green river flowed sluggishly between concrete apartment blocks and ancient bazaars. At the end of every street the white elbows of distant mountains pressed down upon the plain.

Most overland travellers made straight for Chicken Street. Tales of the cherry pies served at the small teahouses there had filtered back to us even before we crossed the border.

Fur pelts swung from hooks in the cluttered café. Snow was falling outside, and sawdust stuck to our wet boots. We dragged a couple of chairs across the dusty board floor and sat around a tin stove.

Tar oozed out of a fractured flue that zigzagged up through a high ceiling that was covered in soot. Chris perched on an upturned crate that had a Russian sounding name stencilled across it.

We ordered six cherry pies. The young proprietor beamed at us through a thick black beard, then disappeared behind a wooden partition at the side of the counter. A lad who looked even younger accompanied him out with our order. He too had the wispy beginnings of a beard. It was patchy and did not quite cover his chin.

The two Afghans each had soiled napkins draped over their left arms; one yellow and the other blue. A plastic-topped table was found for us and the plates set down neatly upon it.

I nudged Zhenka. 'Cherry pie, eh?'

He nodded, stuck out his tongue, and licked his lips. We all licked our lips.

When we picked up our spoons the table tilted unsteadily. Baz folded a piece of card, knelt down and slid it under the suspect leg. As he stood back up his elbow caught the edge of a plate and flipped my helping of cherry pie upside-down on the grey ashes surrounding the stove.

Everyone in the café howled with laughter. Baz asked for another portion.

32

We had been in the country now for over a month and clearly would not reach Pakistan before our tourist visas expired. On the way to the diplomatic quarter, Zhenka dug in his heels and beckoned me back a few paces.

A merchant wrapped in a long woolly blanket was folding open the tin shutters of a shop. Zhenka pointed past him to the beautiful head of a snow leopard, dangling from its skin between the furs of wolves and foxes.

Zhenka stared closer and shook his head. 'They shouldn't have killed him should they?'

'No,' I agreed.

'Do you know, when we stayed at Ralph's and I watched the pictures, I saw them take off a boar's coat with knives. Ralph did it didn't he?' Zhenka took another look inside the shop. 'They put buttons and zips on them don't they – like Mum does with Grandad Robertson's sewing machine. But they have to chop off their bottoms so they don't poo!'

The palatial Embassy flying a Union Jack was situated in the most respectable of suburbs. A vast lawn surrounded it like a moat covered in a rich green moss.

Out-of-date photographs of missing persons were pinned to a noticeboard in the information sector of the building. Whilst Chris and I sat waiting to be seen, we read the grim warnings about drug dealing and gun running that were pasted up on the wall opposite.

'Did Ralph tell you what happened when his son came out here?'

I shook my head.

'He got himself involved with some young American girl. Very young and very beautiful. She wanted to make a lot of money and she wanted him to help her do it. Anyway, he said no and loaned her some money instead. A few days later she was caught on a bus heading for the border at Quetta. Whatever the soldiers found strapped underneath her burka was enough to put her behind bars for a long time.'

'Christ!' I said. 'Prison in Afghanistan doesn't bear thinking about.'

'Ralph did what he could of course. As it happened the girl didn't spend too long in prison. She went mad! In the end they transferred her to somewhere much worse. She's still there. Totally crazy!'

A door opened. A man with gunmetal eyes dulled by all that they had witnessed dumped a sheaf of press bulletins into a wire basket on the desk and stared in our direction.

'Mr Bowers, Mr Baxter? Could you come this way please?'

Halfway along the wood-panelled corridor, the man turned around and peered over his spectacles to check that we were still in tow. When he reached his office, he gave a delicate twist on the brass doorknob and once inside selected two comfortable chairs for us to sit on.

'My secretary took your call. I understand there's a problem over visas to remain in the country and permits to get out?'

'Yes. You do know that we're running?'

'We were informed some time ago by our London office.'

'Well, obviously it takes much longer to cross a country on foot and –'

'Mr Bowers, far be it for me to raise any doubts about the merits of your journey. But the main function of our staff here is to prevent incidents occurring rather than bail people out afterwards. Do you get my drift?'

Chris and I looked at the floor. This was as bad as being in the headmaster's office.

'We must not invite trouble Mr Bowers, must we? It's only a matter of months since the King was overthrown. We all have to tread carefully.'

'I hardly think our journey is causing much political unrest.'

'Perhaps not, but the secret police here have been watching you and wondering what you are up to. Now the authorities have been in touch directly. Mr Bowers, they want you out. Can I tell them five days?'

We were, in effect, being expelled from Afghanistan.

'Yes, I suppose so. How far is it to the border anyway?'

'A hundred and forty miles.'

'We can do that,' I nodded.

'Providing we obtain the visas and permits today,' added Chris. 'Could the Embassy notify the Police Department?'

'We'd prefer you to go through the normal channels without our involvement. It's a delicate business Mr Baxter. You see, there were these two Americans ...'

'We've heard all about them,' said Chris. 'We'd better get going, it will probably take some time.'

On the way out, I hesitated and stared back at the grey eyes following our departure.

'Have you ever read *The Road to Oxiana*?' I asked.

'As it happens, I haven't. Should I?'

'I think you should,' I said, and closed the door.

'What was that about?' asked Chris.

'In the thirties, a young man called Robert Byron published a wonderful little book of diary entries documenting a journey across Afghanistan. I'll show it to you later. He wrote that the British Embassy in Kabul not only helped English visitors but also Americans – since they were highly prone to any amount of trouble.'

Chris considered this as we quietly retraced our footsteps along the passage.

Outside, on the Embassy steps, the conciliatory nature of his character got the better of him.

'I suppose he has a point,' he said. 'I'd no idea there was a coup last year.'

'Fuck off Chris, the man's an arsehole. He should never have been posted out here.'

'Listen Kel, the only sporting activity the Afghans recognise involves a horde of horsemen dragging the beheaded carcass of a sheep about. What you're doing is totally alien to them. It's downright freakish. Whenever you run past Russian workmen they line the road and clap their hands. They understand what you've accomplished. But the Afghans are likely to take a pot-shot at something so unusual. That's what the guy was getting at. Running marathons is something they have no concept of. It's not part of their culture and never has been.'

We took a taxi to the police headquarters. I sat in the passenger seat beside the driver and Chris climbed in the back. The journey passed in total silence and included a short detour to the Columbus Hotel where I collected everyone's passports, permits and visas.

At the police headquarters there was a hunchback filing his fingernails behind an iron grille where a sign read 'Visas'. His English was excellent. I outlined our predicament and asked if our visas could be extended for a period of six days. The man was happy with this and told us to return for the documents in two hours' time.

Baz was with us when we trooped back inside. The hunchback had gone for lunch and the Afghan standing in for him had no knowledge of our visas. Eventually, Chris spotted them on top of a filing cabinet and they were handed over through a cage door in the grille.

When we checked the dates we found that our visas had been extended for five days: long enough to cross into Pakistan. We turned to leave in triumph. But Baz hung about, scrutinising the dates stamped on the exit permits.

'Two days!' he shouted suddenly. 'These bits of paper are valid for the next two days and that's all!'

'He's right,' I said. 'We can stay for five days but if we do we can't get out!'

We waited for the hunchback, who was enjoying an extended lunch break. Then we waited for new exit permits to be issued.

'All bloody day it's taken. And I don't suppose there are any toilets here either.'

All three of us needed to piss somewhere soon. We scuttled outside and turned into a narrow cobbled side street. A massive wall flanked the police buildings.

'Thank God for that,' sighed Baz.

Together we watched the urine trickle down the mud wall to melt the snow at our feet.

'Aaagh! Aaagh!'

Our heads jerked from left to right – nothing. Then we looked up. Directly overhead, a group of women stood screaming at us from behind their prison bars. A man in uniform rushed out from around a corner, blowing a whistle and waving us away.

Chris was amused when he told Lea all about our visit to the Embassy.

'The place is festering with political intrigue. Secret Police, KGB, the CIA. And yet they sneak about keeping tabs on us lot! Even as we speak, Zhenka and yourself are probably in a top-secret dossier bound for Moscow!'

33

On Friday the 13th, Zhenka waved goodbye to the melting snowman we had built together in the back garden of the hotel. The time had come to leave Kabul for the Tangi Gharu Gorge.

I unlocked the padlocked gates and Chris drove away towards the mountains. There was no trace of snow in the sky but it lay in grey ridges at each side of the road and was deep and white in the foothills and over the fields adjoining the river.

The road followed the river's course through the heart of the city. It was still early and the sunlight slanted low across the murky water. Baz, Keith and myself ran into a light industrial hinterland, past a shoe factory and a large tannery where bundles of skins were being unloaded from trucks.

We proceeded out onto a high open plateau, where bare white fields flanked the road and the wind bit at our fingers and the tips of our ears.

Snow had drifted into thicket fences, softening the divisions of land. We turned around away from the wind and looked back one last time. A cock crowed. The sound of shovels scraping clear the flat rooftops of the textile factories grated on the muffled quiet.

Where the road met the craggy hills it began to drop away from the valley floor in a descent of 3,000 feet, through two narrow gorges, that would take us to Jalalabad.

The walls in the Tangi Gharu were grey and sheer. No snow lodged there or on the narrow road itself, but the river beside it was full of melted snow and already flowing faster. As the road descended steeply between the rocks, Keith began to limp. He had complained of a painful knee in the mountains outside Ghazni. Now, faced with a more severe gradient, he was forced to call it a day.

The river tumbled over boulders, roaring as it plummeted down the gorge. The road switchbacked above it through tunnels and along a concrete gallery. Baz and I ran closer together, mindful of the fate of the two American brothers.

'There must have been some reason why they camped here

overnight.' Baz tried to puzzle it out. 'I mean, you just wouldn't, would you?'

'Maybe it was late when they left Kabul,' I said. 'Besides, they had a donkey pulling a cart. It would have taken them much longer to get even this far.'

Our pace quickened. We were both running strongly. 'Anyway, they're not the only ones to have come a cropper in this gorge.'

Baz strode ahead. 'I don't want to know,' he shouted back. 'I don't want to know.' His voice echoed through the canyon, while the spray drifted up from the river.

The story that he did not want to hear concerned a retreat from Kabul by the British Army. On 13 January, 1842, a lookout on the high mud walls of the garrison fort at Jalalabad sighted a white horse. The horse appeared to be riderless, and was picking its way across a stony valley and heading for the fort. When the lookout realised that there was a red-coated figure slumped across the saddle, a patrol was hastily despatched.

At the garrison the rumours were rife. The British legation, with their wives and children, had been forced to quit the cantonment established in Kabul. If this were true, they were long overdue at Jalalabad.

The troops had marched from India to prop up an insecure puppet whom the British had deviously helped to install on the throne. Once Shah Shuja was overthrown, the Afghans were determined to rid themselves of the British and they were ordered to leave.

Promised safe passage out of the cantonment, the large contingent of evacuees were set upon in the gorges between Kabul and Jalalabad. Almost all the 4,500 retreating soldiers and 12,000 camp followers were hacked to pieces. A few were captured, buried up to their shoulders in the sand, and pissed upon by the tribeswomen before being left to die in the sun.

The lone horseman, a surgeon named Dr Brydon, was the only Englishman to survive. He told how he had refilled his tin water canister by the river's edge in the darkness, and that at first light next morning found it to be full of blood.

Eventually, the sheer walls began to slope and the narrow gorge widened into a valley lined with mulberry trees. Crops grew wherever a level shelf of ground appeared. Splayed fingers of water glistened in ditches criss-crossing the fields.

The sun, blotted out by overhanging boulders for most of our descent, now lit up the crashing veins of water below and lifted our spirits. At this point, the road climbed precipitously for a few miles until the shadows of rocky crags again veered across our path.

Then, just as suddenly, we were out, running across a plateau bathed in sunlight where the river flowed into a man-made lake. On the grassy banks of the reservoir stood the town of Sarobi. Chris had parked the van in a grove of pine trees outside the hotel Sroobi, whose prices we could not afford.

Baz and I made our way down to the water and waded in up to our knees. Keith joined us, treading carefully. He held his leg and grimaced as he came down the slippery bank.

The water in the reservoir was cold despite the sun's warmth on our backs. Keith gasped.

'It will do the knee good,' I told him. 'I've always bathed my dodgy ankles in icy streams to relieve sprains and reduce the swelling. I used to correspond with a New Zealand marathon runner named Jack Foster. Ever heard of him?'

Keith nodded. 'Everyone's heard of Jack Foster.' Foster only took up the sport to keep fit and lose his middle-age spread. He became one of the best marathon runners in the world.

'Well, Jack's doctor owned racehorses. After each ride their legs were hosed with cold water. The doctor suggested Jack try the same method and he swears by it now. The colder the water, the better.'

The night at Sarobi was a cold one, but bearable enough. When morning came, Keith looked dreadful. His leg had stiffened up completely and he could scarcely walk. He also appeared to have caught a chill.

We had seen only a handful of tribesmen in the Tangi Gharu Gorge. As far as we could tell they were all unarmed, but the poker-faced man from the embassy had predicted large movements of

Kochi nomads on the stretch between Jalalabad and the North West Frontier.

'They carry rifles, Mr Bowers, and cross-belts of cartridges,' he had scowled. 'Perhaps a smile would not go amiss when you meet them.'

Baz and I set off along the banks of the reservoir positively grinning. Snatches of wind trawled the sky for mackerel-coloured clouds.

At the far end of the reservoir the road meandered towards a cleft in the granite rocks and we entered another deep gorge. The road stalked icy torrents through the slate grey walls. This was the Tangi Abreshom, the Silk Gorge, named after the fine bolts of merchandise carried through the pass by caravans of camels on the ancient silk route.

A Japanese motorcyclist was the only person on the move in the gorge. He had a homemade box of belongings decorated with a rising sun on the back of his bike. He braked sharply when he saw us and yanked his bike up onto its stand. Then he raised the visor of his helmet and we peered inside at him. His brown eyes seemed unaccustomed to the strong light; they darted about like trapped fish. It was like looking into a goldfish bowl.

He quickly assembled a telescopic tripod and lined up his Nikon camera. He flicked the setting to automatic and the three of us waited beside his motorbike until we heard the camera click. When we asked where he was going, he waved a black leather gauntlet towards a bend in the road and said: 'Amsterdam!' He had ridden the 750 cc Yamaha through India and Pakistan.

'What was that like?' asked Baz.

'Red,' he told us.

'Pakistan too?' I queried.

'Red also.'

The riverbed was strewn with boulders where it snaked across the gravel wastes at the end of the gorge. For a time the road ran directly across the valley in a straight line. Tamarisk trees had been planted for shade. Fortified mud houses merged with the brown hillocks behind them. On the opposite side of the river lay the province of Laghman, a name derived from Lamak, the first of Noah's sons to wade ashore after the great flood.

Schoolboys were playing football in the next village we came to. A white plastic ball bounced between the trunks of two sawn-off trees on a pitch marked out with painted stones. Beyond the village was another man-made lake. Wild ducks swam in the yellow reeds at its edges and grey clouds of mist hung above the far shores. When the mist lifted we could see the pastel peaks of the Nuristan Mountains. And above the crests, a ghost of a moon tethered to the daylight.

Plantations of sunflowers and orange groves surrounded Jalalabad. We entered the 'winter resort of kings' along a wide tree-lined avenue, and stopped for breakfast in the quiet garden of a rather grand hotel.

A recent guest of the hotel had left behind a copy of *The Pakistan Times*. The newspaper was printed in English and Chris had already circled in biro a few lines he thought we should read.

'Five persons were killed when a rival group attacked them at a village near Peshawar last evening. Their attackers are alleged to have used firearms and hand grenades during the attack.'

Keith read the article twice over. Someone had told him that at least two thousand wanted men were in hiding near the Khyber Pass.

Baz leaned back against the van. The canvas seat of his foldaway stool made a sharp ripping sound. He struggled not to spill his bowl of porridge.

'Fred Berrisford was posted out here in his army days. Before we left, he warned us not to leave the road once we were in the Khyber Pass.'

'That's right,' said Chris. 'Government laws apply to the road, but have no say on either side of it. They still leave the tribesmen to sort out their own feuds.'

'Well,' I said, 'we're almost there now. We should reach the checkpoint at Torkham this afternoon. If we camp there overnight we can try and get through the Pass in one long run.'

'How far will that be?'

'It's thirty-three miles to Peshawar, but we're both running well. We should be able to do that easily if we take it steady. Besides, Chris will be right behind us in the van.'

A man with few fingers and fewer teeth was sweeping the garden clear of fallen leaves. He greeted our arrival with great expectancy, wrongly assuming that we would want to hire him as a guide. Instead, he offered to pose for a photograph in return for a can of foot deodorant.

Baz and I had eaten too much porridge to run immediately after breakfast, so Keith joined us for a leisurely walk. We walked out of Jalalabad along a dust road next to an irrigation canal, past fields of sugar cane and sesame. The valley lay on the edge of a desert that stretched to the White Mountains in the south.

In AD 632 the Chinese chronicler Hsuan-tsang had come here looking for a tooth of the Buddha. Indeed, the whole hinterland lay peppered with Buddhist ruins and shrines where Buddha himself was supposed to have shaved his head or pared his fingernails. From the second century AD the region was regarded as a must for Buddhist monks on the pilgrim trail, and for the next five centuries they came here in droves to worship and to view his staff and the robe he wore. Such an oasis took us by surprise.

Ten miles on we reached the bleak and stony landscape that we had expected to find. It looked less than inviting.

'All the more hostile for what we've left behind,' I said to Baz as we bumped elbows.

There was a long pause that would have resolved itself normally by one or other of us pressing on in front. But we remained side by side.

'I can't stand walking,' he said at last. 'And you know it fucks your feet up. Anyway, we're supposed to be running, aren't we? It buggers up the whole day when we have so much to eat for breakfast. It's too hot to walk that far. At least when we run we create a breeze.'

He was right, but it niggled me. 'Keith couldn't run, with his knee. But he wanted to exercise it and as we'd only just eaten –'

'He's not going to walk through the Khyber, is he?'

Baz accelerated and I let him go. It was no more than a few yards but we needed the distance.

Seven miles passed before Keith climbed back into the van and Baz and I took up the running again. It was noon. And it was hot. The sun lay in the sky like an ancient coin.

We jogged past small hamlets of mud houses built like fortresses, with narrow slits in their walls. Halfway through the afternoon I looked up to see a cloud of dust rising directly ahead.

'It's the nomads!' Baz shouted back to me.

The Kochi tribespeople fanned out across the road in a broad swathe of colour. Some of them wore long tweed cloaks over their baggy tunics and trousers. Their women came by on camels and on horseback. They were unveiled and sat proudly in rustling nests of skirts. Sunlight picked out their jewellery and the long rifle butts studded with camel bone.

Leather cartridge belts creaked as the men drew closer. Children laughed and raced between the legs of the animals. A few of them had catapults tucked into their belts. One had a charcoal turban and yellow pantaloons.

It was too hot and late in the day for anyone to bother with us. Even the dogs seemed reluctant to do anything other than give a half-hearted snarl as we passed.

There was a passport checkpoint at Dakka. A group of off-duty soldiers argued amongst themselves. At their feet a young boy jabbed at a scorpion with a bayonet he had borrowed from them. One man pulled himself up onto our roof rack and demanded keys to unlock the tin trunks. His search lasted longer than we thought it would. When we were given the go-ahead to proceed, our pace was brisk. The daylight was fading fast and we still had eight miles to cover.

Dust settled on the floor of the canyon like a sudden fall of soot. In the half-light Chris spotted two tribesmen positioned on rocks overlooking the road with their rifles raised to the sky. He drove alongside to shield us and we lengthened our strides and leaned in close to the van.

A few miles further on, one of a long line of donkeys laden with sugar cane stumbled on a narrow ledge high above us. An avalanche of small rocks ricocheted down the cliff face like gunfire in the dark. By now we were both jittery and had forgotten all about our feet as we pelted hard along the road.

Flames crackled in the distance when we rounded the next bend. In the firelight we were just able to make out the shapes of several large tents. This was Torkham, the last town in Afghanistan.

A steel pole had been lowered across the road. The metal sign next to it indicated that the pass was closed until morning. It read: 'Caution – all travellers are requested to cross the Khyber Pass and reach Jamrud before the hours of darkness. Please note that stopping or camping is prohibited in the Pass during the darkness. By order.'

Chris manoeuvred the van onto a bank of gravel close to a sentry box. Lea set about preparing a late supper. We all lay in our sleeping bags. Drums were beating. The sound of Pathans chanting from the crags echoed down the black valley.

34

Baz woke first. I heard him slide the lid from the trailer. There was a clank of tin mugs and shortly afterwards the sound of the kettle whistling. When I stuck my head outside, the air smelt like old parchment. A pale ochre light shed an antique lustre on the parked lorries in the compound.

The canvas ridge tents nearby were the same colour and shape as the brown hills behind them. White piles of ash lay where the campfires had blazed long into the night.

The steel pole across the road had not yet been raised, but a few Afghans were already dragging their sacks and baskets over the border. Because it was our intention not to stop on the way through the pass, we ate a light breakfast before setting off.

The sun had still to clear the higher ridges of the valley. The customs officers were shivering from the cold and did not delay us for long. We moved off when the barrier went up, and slowly ran behind the van. Less than a hundred yards down the road we were surprised to see a modern bank, and a rest house offering air-conditioned rooms. An abundance of road signs reminded Chris that he should now drive on the left again.

At the Pakistan customs headquarters a captain from the detachment of Khyber Rifles entered his name in our logbook and added an official stamp. The soldiers stood to attention at the central post and were instructed to salute when we jogged past.

Our re-entry into the twentieth century was short-lived. The road wound upwards through bare hills. Baz and I ran side by side. As the road climbed, so did the sun. The shored-up remnants of an old railway line sliced through the tawny desolation. The track crawled up the pass and crossed the road several times, vanishing into the open mouths of tunnels on the way.

British engineers riddled the scrubby mountainsides with 34 tunnels during the five years it took them to make the route passable. But the most difficult task was to cajole the tribal leaders into helping them construct a railway through their territory. Ever wily, the

Pathans reasoned that the trains would be unable to gain any speed: rendering them easy targets for looting.

We ran in single file when the traffic caught up. On one bend a clapped-out taxi full of turbaned passengers struggled to overtake us in bottom gear. The boot of the black and yellow car was open at the back and a couple of men with dusty beards sat half inside it, dangling their bare feet out over the bumpy road.

The lorries were full of noisy livestock and people and were twice as overloaded. Drivers' mates crouched astride the dented bonnets topping up water in the steaming radiators as the big trucks lurched by. Baz pointed to the blockhouses left behind by the British army.

'They look empty.'

'Well, they were put there as a safeguard against snipers,' I told him. 'Let's hope they don't need to fulfil that role any more.'

The squat look-out posts occupied most of the vantage points in the pass, but were not easy to pick out. Neither was the unlikely route up through the pockmarked valley.

'It reminds me of the slag heaps we used to race up and down when we were kids,' I said.

'It was a bloody ugly landscape to grow up in, wasn't it?'

'Remember when young lads went missing and they sent divers down into the marl holes?'

'Some of them were deep bastards weren't they? We made a raft once. Me and my brother. But just looking into the stagnant orange mire turned my stomach and I ran off and left him to it.'

After only five miles we reached the top of the rise. The railway swung away from the road like the curved blade of a knife. A donkey brayed. Dogs barked from behind a mound of earth. There was a distant hubbub that suggested habitation.

We ran into the wild frontier town as if we had stumbled upon a lost civilisation. Landi Kotal bristled with gunmetal like a medieval hedgehog.

Ahead of us, Chris was leaning against a petrol pump and shaking his head. Half a dozen men dressed in thick faded blankets thrust a variety of weapons into his arms. Someone handed over a German

Luger. Next came an Italian Beretta. Keith, who was pestering the most respectable looking man among them to sign our logbook, suddenly found himself staring into the tiny barrel of a .25 calibre pen pistol.

After the guns had been put aside, the opium and heroin were produced. When Chris pointed to the petrol pump it was the turn of the gunsmiths to shake their heads.

From Landi Kotal, the road began to descend into a small sand-coloured valley. Photography within the tribal area was frowned upon, but Lea and Keith were determined to come away with some footage. As soon as Chris pulled up they both climbed on top of the van with their cameras.

On the eastern edge of the valley, but well away from the road, was a long unbroken mud wall which appeared to enclose an entire settlement. A few children were playing in the shadows at the foot of the wall, erratically zigzagging through a yellowish dust near an open gateway.

When they saw Baz and me coming they began to shout. Their cries alerted others. Within seconds, an unruly mob surged through the gateway. Youths, toddlers and grown men charged across the open ground at full lick. Galvanised into action, Baz and I waved in an exaggerated manner and made big grinning gestures that were no help at all. Then we simply tucked our heads down and took off along the road, sprinting for all we were worth.

As we flew past I saw them stoop to pick up stones. Out of the corner of my eye I glimpsed their arms jerk back. The stones and pebbles clattered onto the road like a hailstorm. Keith and Lea lay flat and clung to the roof rack as the van accelerated away.

We ran flat out for fifty yards before glancing over our shoulders. Then we dug in and sprinted for another fifty. The sweat stung our eyes when we looked back a second time, but the chase was as good as over.

35

Black creosoted railway sleepers shook beneath the weight of an old steam engine as the Khyber Mail lumbered up-country, bound for the end of the line at Landi Kotal.

Baz was enthralled. 'Me and Mick used to watch steam engines thundering over the canal bridge when we should have been in school. Once or twice we even bobbed off to Crewe station and logged all kinds there.'

A thick white ribbon of steam billowed out of a dark tunnel and hung above the iron rails. Then the road and the railway separated and we forged on into the hills.

Chris had stopped to wait for us outside the walls of the Shagai Fort on a high spur overlooking the plains. The fort crowns the gaunt corridor of mountains at the most strategic position in the pass. It was built by the British in 1927, shortly after the Third Afghan War, and now stands as a grim reminder of our involvement in the Great Game.

Close to the fort, the melancholy cliff face was studded with regimental cap badges painted silver against a background of red or green. The Royal Engineers had served here. So too had the Gordon Highlanders and the Dorsets. Lea took her cinecamera across to the stone wall plaques. Zhenka followed, rubbing the sleep from his eyes.

'It's quite a sight, Baz,' I said. 'Pakistan and India beyond it. I wasn't sure we'd get this far.'

We stared out over the summit of the pass, far down to the V-shaped gap in the wrinkled hills where the road unravelled like a turban in a dust storm – all the way to the Khyber Gate at Jamrud.

Chris and Keith took photographs and then we moved off. There was a different dirt road for camels and mule trains winding downhill beside the paved road we were on. What little traffic there was stuck to the surfaced route.

Eight miles lay between the two forts at Shagai and Jamrud. Having already glimpsed the plains ahead, Baz and I felt less edgy on the downward side of the Khyber. We relaxed and loped forward easily, and then stretched out and ran a little harder. At the foot of the pass, where the road flattened out, many tribesmen came towards us. All of them were on foot and each one carried a rifle. They fixed their dark eyes on us briefly and then strode by without stopping.

The hot brass of the sun had dulled to a hazy circle of copper by the time we reached the tollgate at Jamrud. Whilst soldiers checked the van for vegetables at the quarantine station, Baz and I walked to the fort.

'What d'you reckon to that?' Baz stood before a stone plaque and read out the inscription on it.

'*These hillmen are men who can outpace any man in deadly, manly struggle for existence – hence their survival through the ages.*'

'It makes me think of Wilson of *The Wizard*,' I said.

'That's right; me too.'

Wilson was another hero of ours. He lived inside the pages of a comic called *The Wizard*, when he wasn't up on the high moorlands drinking spring water and running with the deer.

It was almost dark when we entered the outskirts of Peshawar. Students carried their books from college past fruit stalls lit by oil lamps. Vespa scooters rocketed from nowhere, and horse-drawn tongas rattled by too close. The open booths of the food sellers and the ironmongers were doing brisk trade in the cool of the evening.

The moon came up like a flare over the hotchpotch of baked bricks and splintered timbers on the flat roofs of the city. Age-old, tipsy-looking buildings leaned against each other for support. Glorious sacks of spices lay dumped together in the dusty doorways of the shops below.

Deans Hotel was the place to stay. It was an old colonial establishment full of foreign correspondents and genteel sightseers in creaking wicker chairs sipping gin and tonics on the veranda.

The spot Chris found for us had a spartan quality about it. He swung off the Khyber Road into Police Road and headed towards Jail Bridge. There, he pulled into a compound where an armed soldier stood guard over two men crouched behind bars on the earthen floor.

36

Keith caught a train to Delhi from the railway station at Peshawar. He had to be back in England by the end of the year and wanted to see the Taj Mahal before he left.

My mother wrote with news of Sebastian Snow. He had completed the southern half of his journey from the tip of Argentina. But when confronted with the big, bright highway hoardings and the rest of the paraphernalia connected with life in twentieth-century America, he had chosen to quit.

'He'd have been better off setting out from North America first,' said Lea.

'I suppose running through Europe was a bit like that. Busy roads certainly wear me out more than the running does,' I said.

'No way I'd ever dream of running across America!' Baz was adamant but we were unconvinced.

'Now the last time you made a statement like that …'

'I know, I know.' He grinned.

When we left Peshawar we ran along a pleasant tree-lined road that led to numerous military academies. Parrots flew from the branches of the trees on the outskirts. Green flags fluttered above the guarded perimeters of the artillery schools. From the top of the pass the plain had looked verdant and flat. Beyond Nowshera it became more rugged.

In 326 BC, at a place called Attock, Alexander's army spanned the Indus with a bridge of boats. Genghis Khan won a great battle there too, only to turn back after a division of his men arrived from Delhi muttering that 'the heat of the place slays men and the water is neither fresh nor clear.'

We crossed the high ravine over a double-decker bridge that resembled a long cattle wagon. A railway was laid above it. On the other side of the river was a barren sandstone area where simple dwellings had been dug into the rock walls.

On the way to Taxila we became aware of the inspection bungalows and rest houses situated close to the Grand Trunk Road. These were used by travelling officials in the days of the British

Empire. Sometimes we were even allowed inside to use the bathrooms, but mostly it was enough just to park up in the privacy of the walled compounds.

Already, after only a few days, the sheer number of people taking an interest in us had begun to feel daunting. Whenever Chris and Lea stopped the van to wait beside the road for us, more eyes than midges followed their every move.

The streets of Taxila were swarming with people, as were the streets of every other town we entered. Passing through them on foot was like being catapulted into a fairground whose operators had been overthrown by the rides.

Someone stood waiting around every corner to thrust a trolley or handcart directly into our path. We weaved between the iron-rimmed wheels of bullock carts and pony tongas. Cyclists would turn to stare after us and ride into someone else doing the same. Cows suddenly changed direction, just when we were overtaking, bundling us into doorways, or blocking our way entirely.

The real traffic never let up either. The buses, trucks and cars swinging this way and that added to the heat with fumes that stung our eyes and made the air wobble.

'Why are you marching?'

'What is your name?'

'Where are you going?'

'What is your country?'

'Baksheesh!'

'Baksheesh!'

We broke off running on 25 December. For the first time in centuries the Muslim festival of Eid fell on the same day as Christmas. Most of the merchants had already shut up shop. But the road was not as empty as we had been led to believe. An earthquake had occurred in the Karakoram ranges overnight, less than 200 miles away. Over five thousand people were reported to have lost their lives and scores of army trucks and ambulances were setting off for the mountains.

We spent Christmas Eve on a deserted campsite just outside Islamabad. Lea and I stayed up late wrapping presents that we had hidden from Zhenka for weeks, before slipping them into a pillowcase that hung above his sleeping bag. Jackals were scavenging for food at a nearby tip. I lay awake listening to their high-pitched howls and wondered how anyone could sleep through it. Outside, the air was still. A cloud fastened onto the tin pail moon and wedged itself between the brim like a long loaf of bread.

Next morning I was up early. It was the sort of crisp morning that was bound to get better and better as the day progressed and I wanted to make the most of it. No one was about at the campsite. I walked out through the open gates and turned along the lane that led into town.

A leggy man in shorts stood hunched up over big bunches of flowers, deftly weaving the different coloured petals together to make garlands. He had screwed up his eyes against the sunlight countless times. Now, even though still a young man, the skin above his cheekbones looked like cracked mud.

I made for a large, open expanse of grass where a few richly patterned marquees had been erected. Thousands of people dressed in colourful tunics and saris were knelt in prayer. The grass smelt as if it had been freshly mown. In the blue sky above the stretched canvas of the big tents I could see snow far away on the mountaintops of Kashmir.

When the crowds finished praying they rushed to the cake shops and I tagged along behind. The cakes were oozing sticky sugar and were dyed in Day-Glo limes and fluorescent tangerines. No one wanted the one I chose, but it looked more like a proper Christmas cake than the rest.

By the time I got back to the van, the bulging pillowcase was already half empty. Zhenka was knee-deep in a pile of wrapping paper.

'He's been! I told you he would find us. He always does!'

'I didn't think he would this time,' said Lea. 'He must have had a good map.'

'Where have the others got to?' I asked.

'The gas for the stove ran out when I was cooking breakfast and as it's a public holiday we can't get it refilled. So Baz and Chris are hunting for firewood.'

'That sounds exciting Zhen! Sparklers tonight!'

Throughout the afternoon, several Pakistanis arrived at the campsite with gifts of meat and sweets. Later, we lit the fire and Lea cooked our Christmas dinner while Zhenka played with a clockwork train set by the light of the flames.

The meal was delicious. For the main course we had beef with potatoes roasted in their jackets and a selection of vegetables. Added to this, as a special treat, were a few Yorkshire puddings prepared over the hot embers.

By the time we turned in, everyone was pleased that Eid and Christmas had been celebrated on the same day.

37

The Grand Trunk Road sounded impressive, but when Jeff first suggested we take that route across Pakistan and India I knew very little about it. He had pinned a large map onto the wall of his bedsit so that I could see for myself what an important road it was.

'It's here look: GTR!' he said, and pointed to a red line that was not as squiggly as the rest. There was a narrow desk below the map, on which a book lay open. Jeff pushed his spectacles a fraction higher on the bridge of his nose and looked down.

'"It runs straight, bearing without crowding India's traffic for fifteen hundred miles – such a river of life as nowhere else exists in the world",' he read. '*Kim*! It's an old favourite of mine. Rudyard Kipling's *Kim*. Did you know he was named after the Lake?'

Rudyard Lake lies between Stoke and the market town of Leek in Staffordshire. Lea and I had often gone walking there and we knew someone who lived in a wooden summerhouse on the shore.

'It must have held a special significance for his parents.'

Jeff closed the book but insisted that I read *Kim* and I took it home with me that same night.

Now, two years later, Baz and I were striding along the GTR on our way to Lahore. If the line denoting the road looked wide on our map, and the name itself sounded grand, the actual highway was a bit of a let-down.

Out in the country, the road often dwindled into a narrow lane, barely wide enough for two vehicles to pass without one of them scattering stones from the dust shoulder. Whenever the tarmac widened there were ample feet to fill the space – and if not feet, then a variety of hoofs and wheels.

On the far side of Rawalpindi, traversed after a long and tiring stint in the heat, we found ourselves in a region that appeared to have suffered great devastation. High embankments had been built along the Potohar Plateau to safeguard the route from floods. Weathered columns of tan-coloured earth rose from the abyss below the level of the road like shattered tree trunks.

'Paul Nash painted something just like this when he was a war artist at the front,' I told Baz.

'The whole area looks as though it's been hit by an earthquake.'

'Legend has it that Alexander's horse Bucephalus died here.'

'I'm not surprised.'

Like many legends, there were different versions as to how the horse met its end. One story suggested that a blow from a sword at the Battle of Jhelum, in 326 BC, was responsible. But the animal was thirty years old anyway, and most likely died of old age. Not so the 23,000 Indians who lost their lives fighting Alexander's 11,000 troops.

The Grand Trunk Road twisted between dull red boulders. Nothing but the tough acacia bushes seemed able to survive. Vultures sat amongst the buff rocks with their heads bent, waiting for more animals to come to grief on the road.

There were many small settlements anchored to the highway. Baz and I splashed through stagnant pools of water and shuffled warily over the debris of litter in the larger towns we came to.

'Somehow Baz, I thought it would be a lot easier once we were through the Khyber Pass. But dodging all those people and the traffic! I'm not sure I can handle it.'

Baz felt the same. 'It's the noise Kel. It feels like I stuck my head in a big fucking bucket that's being hammered on all sides!'

Soldiers in full pack went thumping across a long bridge spanning the River Jhelum. On the other side of the river stretched the open plains of the Punjab.

We ran on grass paths that wound through the trees under a blue sky. The sky looked bigger than the endless plains stretching into the distance and every so often a grey and white barred cloud would drift across like a roadside kilometre post.

The trees had enormous branches and had been planted beside the road for centuries. Palm squirrels with striped tails frenetically darted in and out of the shade at the foot of their wide trunks. Baz spoke of buying a birdspotters' book and pointed up excitedly whenever he saw something new.

Someone threw a stone at us on the edge of a crabby town called

Gujrat. It hit the ground in front of me, then flew up and whacked Baz sharply on the knee. The stone drew blood and Baz cursed. He was still cursing when we reached the industrial core of the province, a place called Gujranwala. Here, the air was already thick and heavily polluted by a large soapworks and the factories producing rubber and plastic.

A blind man with a pink face was playing the bagpipes on a toll bridge over the River Ravi. Both he and his son had a shock of white hair and there was a forlorn-looking bear beside them, standing on its hind legs and swaying to the music.

Canemakers and nut vendors sat on the pavements in Lahore. We stepped out of the road and up onto the kerb, took a few short strides through the bundles of goods tied up with blankets, then veered back into the road.

'Pavement or no pavement, it's all the same,' I said.

'Well, there are more horses on the road but only just.'

Many of the horses were pulling two-wheeled covered wagons called tongas. The wheels were wooden. They reached shoulder height and had bright yellow spokes that spun over the tarmac like sunflowers.

Kites were flying from a park over the road, dipping silently above the backstreet din. But if we stared at them for too long we were sure to come a cropper. Ahead was a busy intersection crossing the main thoroughfare – the Mall.

From here on I was looking for one thing only and thinking how excited Jeff would have been to see it. Zam-Zammah – Kim's gun – stood on a raised plinth in the middle of the Mall. Baz and I stopped jogging and nipped between the congested traffic for a better look.

There were no bare feet scrambling along the polished bronze barrel of the cannon as they had in Kipling's day; just the tiniest of birds pecking around the brick base beneath the shadows of the great iron wheels.

38

Chris parked the van in the grounds of the new National Athletics Coaching Centre. As luck would have it, an important meeting of the 1978 Asian Games Committee was in progress. Pakistan was due to host the next games in Islamabad and the country's leading athletes and coaches had assembled to discuss plans for the event.

The athletes were intrigued to find marathon runners already on the doorstep, and quickly sought permission for us to make use of the running water and to camp inside the gates.

The committee members wore smart blazers which all bore the same badge and they looked on with some amusement as we prepared for our overnight stay. Off came the lid of the trailer and out came our squeaky foldaway table and the four threadbare canvas stools. Whilst Chris filled the kettle and clamped the stove's rubber pipe onto the head of the gas cylinder, Lea clambered up to the roof rack and hauled down Zhenka's blue plastic tractor.

Everything we did was second nature by now: a tried and tested routine that we stuck to as the miles rolled by. When Baz and I went off to fill the water butts, Lea began to peel potatoes for a vegetable stew. Tonight however, the man responsible for catering at the complex intervened.

'Massala Machli is being cooked for everyone, Mrs Bowers. Only gentle for the little one on the tractor I am thinking. No chilli, no chilli.'

The spiced fish was delicious and we ate so much naan bread that we could barely move. Afterwards, a group of the athletes wandered over with a few crates and a wooden pallet. These were stacked high over thin sticks of kindling. Soon we were all sitting around a big fire.

Several of the athletes had represented Pakistan in the Commonwealth Games at Cardiff and Edinburgh, and most of them had competed at the White City.

One coach had been a long-jumper. He had won an AAA title and a bronze medal in the 1958 Empire Games.

'Herb Elliott was there,' he told me. 'And the man with the silver hair who looked after him.'

'Percy Cerutty,' I said.

'Oh, such a lovely man! Percy the pensioner who was always charming our ladies.' The long-jumper gave a shrill giggle and warmed his backside on the fire. 'Also Kelvin, I am on one occasion sharing a room with a Mr Arthur Lydiard. He was a nice man also, but more serious around the outer edges.'

Baz and I were facing each other on either side of the flames. We both looked up at the same time. Another hero. The big-chested man from Auckland who had written a book called *Run to the Top*, which became every runner's bible in the sixties.

'I read his book and trained like a Kiwi when I was nineteen,' I told the long-jumper. 'A hundred miles a week for ten weeks – a thousand miles. Then I finished third in the Midlands mile in my best time ever!'

'He knew what he was talking about alright,' agreed the long-jumper. 'Endurance training even for short distance events. But this is a big, big distance you are doing. It is exploration of a very different kind I am thinking.'

'I knew a poet once,' I told him. 'We were in Australia on a beach at St Kilda, just outside Melbourne. He had written a poem about a man rowing across the Atlantic.'

'Ridgway?' volunteered the long-jumper.

'Yes, it probably was John Ridgway. Anyhow, the poet would read out what he'd written and I would listen. I didn't understand much of it but I loved the words, the sound they made and how they fitted together. I can't remember the lines of the poem any more, but it had something to do with the soul-destroying rigours of a nine to five job – how that could lead some people to veer off and attempt something else or go nuts. It struck a cord even then. I think that's why I'm here doing this big distance.'

'I think most of us would settle for nine to five,' said the long-jumper. 'What about you Chris, why are you here?'

'It's not much of a story. I had a girlfriend whose father was the sports editor of the newspaper following Kel's journey. He suggested I fly out and take over the driving.'

Baz burst out laughing. 'I never knew that. Didn't it ever occur to you that he was just putting some distance between you and his daughter?'

39

'This morning I am reading in *The Pakistan Times*, stories of crisis concerning lack of food in India.' The British Leyland dealer dabbed the corner of a white napkin around the edge of his mouth to remove a blob of strawberry jam.

We were taking afternoon tea with him at the Lahore Golf Club whilst the van was being given a free service.

'Also, I am reading that they are having most unpleasant experiences from severe drought. It is causing villagers to riot, Mr Bowers. Even to storm the railway engine for the very water in its tank.'

The young boys employed to look for lost golf balls were showing Zhenka how to putt whilst we relaxed under the shade of the palm trees outside the clubhouse. Later, Chris and Lea went shopping. They returned with 45 packets of porridge oats, four dozen bananas and four dozen eggs.

Next morning we were all awake early.

'We are going to a new land today. There are lots and lots of big temples there, all made out of gold,' Lea told Zhenka.

'Do they fly kites there? If they don't I'm not going!' He stamped his foot on a blister I had been thinking of bursting.

After we had swept out the van and made our living quarters more presentable for the next customs inspection, Chris drove off in search of India.

Baz and I walked along the banks of a dried-up canal bed. Then we pushed through crowds following a wedding procession. Outside the walls of the Shalimar Gardens stood a horse-drawn cart. On the cart sat a young boy dressed in white and wearing a yellow turban. The boy yanked the handle of an old gramophone for all he was worth. Music crackled out of a big brass horn.

The bridegroom was blindfolded and sat astride a white horse. He wore a silvery grey tunic of silk that was all but hidden beneath the garlands of flowers hanging from his neck.

We dodged between his family and friends who were blocking the road, only to meet more groups of people massed together on their way to the markets and bazaars in the heart of the city. When we rejoined the Grand Trunk Road it was much quieter and we were able to begin running again.

We passed through a small village before we reached the border. Scores of vultures circled a graveyard there.

'India will be the most total experience,' Ted Smith had told me, months ago now, on the shores of the Caspian.

After the village the road became a lane. Soon we were hemmed in by high walls of thorn bushes, and we wondered if this was what the jungle was like.

At the Attari Road Land Customs Station a team of Pakistani labourers formed a chain, passing bales from one head to another until they reached the turbans of a group of blue-shirted Sikhs, who transferred the goods to a big truck that reminded me of pink fudge and tinsel. Chris and Lea were waiting for us.

'This is India!' piped up Zhenka.

'Yes,' I said, 'and the Golden Temple of Amritsar is only a few miles down the road.'

'I saw a bird with greeny-blue wings, Baz, and I wanted to paint its picture, but my paintbox doesn't have that colour.'

Chris had bought two maps from a tourist bureau to help us find our way through the city.

'It will be safer if we split up tomorrow,' he said. 'Some backpackers just told us that Amritsar makes Lahore look like a ghost town.'

'This seems to be the best spot to make for.' Lea pointed to a dot on the map that she had ringed with a red biro. 'It's the Punjab Government Tourist Hotel, on the main road to Delhi. They might let us park up in the grounds.'

During the night, heavy drops of rain began drumming the van's roof. It was such an unfamiliar sound that we found it hard to sleep. At my side Baz turned over, fidgeting and rustling inside his sleeping bag.

'Fuckin' bucketing down out there,' he grumbled as quietly as he could.

'Yeah, not at all what I expected on our first night in India.'

The rain was still falling steadily when we set off in the morning. A flock of vultures shook their dripping wings like black brollies as we ran by. Dogs tunnelled through the rotting flesh of a dead horse. The rain softened the stony ground at the roadside and people left the road in search of shelter.

For a short time we had the GTR all to ourselves and were able to leave the slippery path and run along the pot-holed tarmac instead.

Where the city spilled over into the countryside the muddy snouts of black hogs sniffed around a maze of corrugated tin shacks. Beyond the shacks were long winding rows of flimsy cowshed homes.

'Where are the bicycles? Where are the bicycles?' Baz mimicked the cries that usually accompanied us. 'Wat-append? Wat-append?' he shouted. 'By walk? By walk?'

Rain dripped from the end of his nose. We were both soaked, and to keep warm we jogged as far into the city as we could before the streets began to multiply. Then we stopped and ducked our heads inside the doorway of an empty shop. Out came our map. I had wrapped it in a plastic cover and rolled it up to carry in my hand like a baton.

The shopkeeper's round face was framed with a long shiny beard that he had tucked into his tartan turban. He took off a pair of steel-rimmed spectacles and held the map close. Baz guided him to the red biro ring and he raised his bushy eyebrows. Then he handed back the map and pointed down the street. As we turned to leave the shop, he stooped and held the flat of his hand a few inches from the floor.

'What do you think he means?' asked Baz.

'It's probably just a short distance,' I said. 'Not very far.'

Of course, I spoke too soon. We traipsed through the noisy back streets of Amritsar all afternoon.

At first we did not mind. Everything seemed of interest and was exciting to watch. We walked under the huge painted posters of cinema billboards showing chubby-lipped film stars whose paper faces were slowly peeling away in the storm. Tall Sikhs spat out red betel leaf juice that coloured the puddles of rainwater so that it looked as if a bloodbath had just taken place.

Massacres and real life bloodbaths were nothing new to Amritsar. In 1919, the British gunned down thousands of unarmed civilians in a park close to the Golden Temple. More atrocities followed less than thirty years later during the Partition of India.

Parks and temples came and went. We strode between painted cowhorns and a million feet – pedalling pushbikes, back-pedalling pushbikes, and pushing pushbikes. All with the same unpredictable nonchalance that would have seen us hospitalised within seconds had we tried to cross the city in a similar way.

We walked and walked. Our map was sodden and out of scale. All we arrived at was the conclusion that we had come too far.

'Let's double-back,' said Baz, 'but not on foot!'

I carried a few rupees in a back pocket sewn inside my shorts. We counted the money. It didn't amount to much.

'Not enough for a horse and carriage,' I said.

'What about a cycle rickshaw?' asked Baz.

'Yeah, we can just about run to that,' I laughed.

We waved down a rickshaw straight away. It was not difficult; they were everywhere. We climbed up and huddled together under the plastic canopy while the man studied our half-shredded map. Then he set off, pedalling slowly back the way we had come. Baz and I grew cold sitting in the rickshaw. We hoped it was not far and would not take long to get there. The man's thin matchstick legs struggled to top a rise, then pumped hard and fast along a flatish stretch.

He took us to a building site, applied a brake, and dragged both his feet along the road until the rickshaw slithered to a standstill. When I unrolled the map and pointed to the name 'Punjab Government Tourist Hotel', the cyclist nodded his head emphatically.

'You are standing on the foundations of the hotel you are asking me to take you to. There have been disputations but I am hearing that it will be ready very soon for you.'

Chris had parked the van in a side street close by. He had been run over by a cyclist when he went to ask for directions.

40

Outside Amritsar, villagers were harvesting wheat and other crops from fields protected by fences of cacti. The ditches were filled with marijuana plants. The land was green and flat and the main route through it could be traced by the customary line of trees.

A railway track paralleled the road but was not often visible from it. Every now and then a steam engine thundered between the palm trees on top of the embankments. Zhenka pressed his hands over his ears and yelled with excitement.

The GTR bypassed the larger cities such as Jullundur and Ludhiana. But the Hero Bicycle workshops were based in the latter and everyone on the outskirts seemed to own at least two wheels. Even so, we made good progress.

When we stopped at the milk bar of the Punjab Dairy Centre the manager treated us to ice-cold, pineapple-flavoured milkshakes. He sent one of his workers to a nearby village to buy eggs for us, and arranged for buckets of hot water to be brought for us to soak our feet.

'I am telling you without any question that this is a damn fine achievement you are doing.' The Sikh was tall and wide from drinking too many milkshakes. His forefinger and thumb twirled the tips of an impressive moustache about his cheeks so that they looked like two question marks.

'Even if we are doing only a little, then by small amounts and gradual you are going a long, long way.'

Later, much further down the road, Chris followed a sign that read 'PWD Rest House' (Punjab Works Department). After negotiating with the caretaker for a free overnight stopover in the grounds, he walked back to wait for us at the roadside. It had been a long day and we were both hot and dusty.

By the time Chris led us back to the rest house, Zhenka had made friends with a police inspector who was a guest there.

'Here's Baz,' Zhenka pointed. 'And that's my dad. They've been running.'

The policeman was sitting at a table under a large sunshade in the garden behind the rest house. He got up and dragged a couple of cane chairs across the lawn to the table.

'Your son Zhenki tells me you are running to Australia?'

'That's right,' I said.

'Will you have something to drink?'

We settled for orange juice and sat down beside him.

'So, how far have you come?'

'Just over six thousand miles.'

'How long did that take?'

'Nine months.'

The policeman made a quick calculation in pencil on the corner of his newspaper. 'That's about a hundred and fifty miles per week.' We nodded.

'The most I managed in any one week was two hundred and forty-three miles – right at the beginning, in England. But there are times when we get injured or become ill. When we set out I estimated that it would take fourteen months to reach Sydney.'

The man's smart khaki uniform was crisply starched. He tapped his pencil on a table leg as he talked, and the queries came out quickly because he was so used to questioning people.

'I know,' he laughed, as if he had read my mind, 'once a policeman, always a policeman.'

'Is that a saying in your country too?'

'Not exactly. I was educated in England.'

The policeman motioned for us to wait for him, then he disappeared into the brick bungalow. When he came out he was holding a large map of India. The paper map was glued to a sheet of faded red muslin decorated with a woodblock pattern of darker red dots. Together we unfolded it out onto the grass. He pointed to the spot we had arrived at and ran his finger along the GTR as far as Delhi. Then he hesitated and asked for directions.

'We had planned to use the main road from Delhi to Bombay,' I told him, 'and from Bombay to Madras. But this road south through the centre looks much shorter and is probably less busy.'

'You'd save two hundred miles easily,' agreed the policeman. 'Less truck traffic too, but ...' There was a brief pause whilst he searched for the right phrase. 'You see this stretch here, where the road crosses the Chambal River?'

We leaned down over the map. 'The road between Agra and Gwalior?' asked Baz.

'This is where the dacoits operate. Bandit country on both sides of the river. It's difficult terrain because the monsoons erode the land each year and leave behind vast areas riddled with ravines. The gangs set up roadblocks to rob unsuspecting travellers and then use the ravines to make their escape.'

The inspector glanced up from the map and wobbled his head a little. 'They seldom attack in broad daylight though, so if you find somewhere safe to camp each night you should be safe. One of the gang leaders used to be an athlete like yourselves. Pan Singh Tomar. He won a gold medal in the 3,000-metre steeplechase at the Asian Games in 1958. He was in the army at that time. But later, when he retired, there were arguments in his village over the ownership of a piece of land. Pan Singh and his brother murdered their enemy and made for the ravines. You'll see his photograph on the wanted posters once you reach that region. The police from three states have been after him for years – so far without success.'

'Tell me,' I said, 'are we likely to experience any trouble from the police in India?'

'Not while you are in my state,' the police inspector reassured me. 'Of course, I cannot vouch for the rest, but if they read about your journey in the newspapers that may prove helpful. Then again,' he added, 'the more publicity you have, the bigger carrot you become for a kidnapping. What about other countries, how were you treated by the police there?'

'Not so well in some places – even in England.' I walked over to the van and climbed inside. A small, brown leather suitcase contained a pile of correspondence accumulated along the way. At the bottom of the pile was a letter from the Metropolitan Police.

'Here we are,' I said, walking back to the inspector. 'Read this.'

The policeman cleared his throat, stood up and read it out aloud. '"Police are not in favour of events of this nature which would expose both the participants and other road users to potential dangers. You are therefore requested in the interests of safety to abandon this venture.'"

The inspector looked as shocked as we had been to receive the letter during our very first week on the road.

'At least we weren't arrested,' I laughed. 'That happened to me twice in Yugoslavia. I was scared stiff the first time, but when it occurred again only a week later I thought I was well prepared. I had taken the precautions of drawing a map of the world on a small sheet of paper with a matchstick figure running towards Australia.

'On a second piece of paper I had drawn a sketch of our van, complete with the fibreglass Michelin Man which had been screwed on top of the roof by one of our sponsors. The police superintendent stared at my two sketches. Then he asked me to produce my passport and I pointed to the little drawing of the van.

'I explained, as best I could, that while I travelled on foot, my wife, my son, and two friends drove ahead in the vehicle. Then I told him they would be looking for me now and wondering where I had vanished to.

'He seemed to understand but kept staring at my little sketch of the van and shaking his head. Eventually I persuaded him to send out a search party for the van.

'I found myself wedged between the superintendent and his assistant on the back seat of a police car. We went up and down the main road a few times without seeing the van anywhere. Each time this happened the superintendent and his assistant looked across at each other knowingly and muttered a few words. Then they both turned to me and muttered some more.

'Just when they were preparing to return to the police station, I caught a glimpse of the van! The car pulled across and flashed Jeff down. As soon as the superintendent saw Zhenka sitting on the passenger seat with Lea he picked him up and started laughing.

'Then he hoisted him up to the Michelin Man and I realised what he had been saying back in his office, when he'd shaken his head and stared at my sketch.

'He'd been asking why my son was sitting on top of the roof.'

41

There was a sharp rap on the rear doors of the van. Baz was already lying awake and he crawled out of his sleeping bag to investigate. Sampath Kumar stood outside, pointing to his wristwatch.

'It is six Barry, and I am following Ranjit's request and having you up and off by not later than six thirty.'

It was 21 January, 1975, and the Roadrunners Club of New Delhi had arranged an escort of runners to accompany us into the city. We were due to meet them at the Delhi border checkpoint, twelve miles down the road. That would leave us with a run of 25 miles to the national stadium itself where a big welcome had been organised.

We had met Sampath and Ranjit a couple of days earlier when they had ridden out on their moped in search of us. Ranjit had studied at Oxford and represented India in the 5,000 metres at the Rome Olympics. Now he was a professor of mathematics at St Stephens College, New Delhi. We warmed to him instantly.

Despite Sampath's insistence that we leave on time, we were still some fifteen minutes adrift when the van pulled off to head for the city boundary. The dawn air was cool and Sampath blew into his hands and kept his tracksuit on. Baz and I were full of running and immediately pared down to singlet and shorts.

Even though we were closing in on New Delhi, the road remained narrow. For the first few miles I counted less trucks and buses. By eight the GTR was more congested than I had ever seen it. The volume of traffic noise soon drowned out our conversation with Sampath. He was breathing hard anyway and knew how far it was to the stadium.

A large crowd had gathered at the city border checkpoint. I could just make out the bald head of our Michelin Man serenely sitting on top of the van like a rotund little buddha. Lea was cooking porridge on the trailer top and Sampath seemed surprised by the size of the portions spooned out to us. He declined all offers of a hearty breakfast but needed a few plasters for his blistered feet.

A television camera crew arrived. A man holding a microphone introduced himself.

'Ranjit Bhatia is saying that we are to be meeting with you here at no later than eleven precise.'

A grey Ambassador car (or as we know it, the Morris Oxford) cruised past a massive cow and pulled up alongside the television people. A photographer jumped out, opened the boot of the vehicle and climbed inside. Camera at the ready, he sat cross-legged and waited for us to set off.

Meanwhile, an olive-green army truck on loan from the Rajputana Rifle Regiment shuddered to a halt a few yards ahead of us. Out clambered ten of India's leading distance runners, including national marathon champion Ram Narain Singh.

Ram Narain wore a big grin and a Rupert Bear scarf wound tightly around his head. Babar, his coach, had a long white beard and was dressed in the traditional dhoti. The runners took off their tracksuits and gave them to a couple of soldiers who stood beside the truck.

Babar looked around for Ranjit. Sampath explained that he had not yet arrived. The coach rolled his head to and fro and tutted loudly. He was a stickler for time on the running track and just as punctual off it.

A few minutes later, there was an insistent peeping of a horn and the crowds surrounding us parted. Ranjit steered his moped between the onlookers and the athletes and asked if he could stow the machine in the back of our van. He had overslept and was sweating profusely.

'Quickly, quickly!' he reminded everyone, as he balanced on one leg to remove his tracksuit bottoms.

Once underway the pace was brisk. The army truck rumbled ahead on the opposite side of the road, while Babar clung to the tailboard and shouted instructions to his athletes. We could smell the diesel and already feel the heat from the rest of the traffic heading in and out of the city.

It felt strange to glance down at the road and see so many running shoes rhythmically pattering along beside our own, and it was hard not to run at any pace other than 'quickly, quickly'. The camaraderie and adrenaline saw to that.

Soon enough though, Ranjit's head developed an acute wobble. 'This is too fast!' he puffed. 'Marathon pace! I am telling you, we will be there too soon!'

We tried to contain our enthusiasm. We leaned back and looked around as we ran on.

The lower half of the tree trunks that lined the road were painted white. The dirt verge was wider than ever and we fanned out right across it. The marathon runners belonging to the rifle regiment were used to the chaotic Indian streets, and we were too by now. But when we came to the shanty overspill, hazards such as handcarts, bicycles and scooter cabs multiplied.

'This is where a marathon runner becomes a matador,' shouted Baz, as a white cow lurched in front of us.

'In India the cow is sacred,' explained Sampath. 'Before, when you are causing fatalities to the cows it is sentence of death. Now there is leniency, but you are still going to prison.' He pointed out a river that was also sacred, but he hadn't enough breath to name it.

The GTR widened as it flowed into the Mahatma Gandhi Road and on towards the city ring road and we moved into the lane reserved for slow-moving traffic.

Ranjit was hanging on, attempting to hide the discomfort our fast pace was causing him and yet unable to prevent his head from wobbling. To make matters worse, his spectacles kept steaming up and he could not see properly.

A Union Jack was waved from the window of a passing Dormobile near the Red Fort. Sampath's feet had begun to blister again and he discarded his shoes: throwing them up into the back of the army truck.

At our side, the Raj-Rif runners indicated some of the impressive landmarks. 'This is Kashmir Gate,' said Ram Narain, who was the least breathless. 'Over there, in the gardens, is a most splendid column and the ruins of a palace. The column is made of sandstone and was brought here by raft down the River Yamuna many ages ago.'

The river turned out to be the same one Sampath had tried to name earlier. It looked brown and uninviting but was sacred nonetheless.

A battery of cameras had been set up outside the entrance to the national stadium. Zhenka shielded his eyes against the popping flashbulbs as the van drove by. A lap of the track followed and we all crossed the line together. The run from the city checkpoint had taken over two and a half hours, but it had seemed much shorter in the company of the athletes.

When Ranjit recovered he introduced us to Mr Anand, the Director of the National Institute of Sports based at Patiala in a former maharaja's palace. Afterwards we were led to a conference room in the stadium for tea and biscuits. There, we met a tall, dapper looking gentleman from the British Embassy.

Mr Dowdall-Brown had white hair and a tidily clipped moustache that was more grey than white. He wore a red carnation in the buttonhole of his pinstriped jacket and walked with a slight limp. Earlier in the day, on his way back to New Delhi after a weekend break in the hills, he had been unfortunate to catch a train that crashed.

'They have complaints books,' he told us. 'Thousands of ledgers chained to little wooden shacks at every railway crossing in the country. You should read them. All India's past, present and future documented for everyone to see in those vast tomes. Remarkable.' Dowdall-Brown pressed his foot down onto the raffia matting and winced. 'For one nasty moment when the trains collided I thought I was going to miss you chaps. Wouldn't have wanted that. Nice little outing this. Went like clockwork too, didn't it? All down to that fellow Bhatia, the whole show, everything. Oxford man of course. Excellent, excellent! Must get everyone along for drinks at the club tonight – the Roadrunners and the Raj-Rif people. Thought we'd throw a bit of a party for you. This is just what we need Kelvin, just the ticket. Excellent!'

Dowdall-Brown had emphasised the word 'informal' when he invited everyone to the party. Nevertheless, it threw us into a panic.

This was the first function we had been called upon to attend – what on earth were we going to wear?

We rushed back to the van and helped Ranjit untangle the moped he had jammed between the two bunks. Then we set about choosing suitable evening attire from the tin chests on the roof. Most of our clothes had more creases than a concertina.

Chris was first down the catwalk. He sported a black leather bomber jacket over a brown woollen cardigan patterned with diamonds. The rigours of his part in our journey had rendered the backside of his blue jeans threadbare, but the underpants he was wearing were the same colour and so the holes were more or less concealed.

Next came Baz, resolutely sticking to his Mickey Mouse singlet to show off his suntanned arms and shoulders. The heavy carbohydrate diet we had both been enjoying made it impossible for him to fasten the top button of his trousers, so a safety pin had to be found.

Lea was the fortunate one. Ranjit's wife Ranee took her to the bazaar and she returned with two cotton skirts and a pair of leather thonged sandals.

Zhenka proved to be the most fashion-conscious among us. He rejected everything Lea found for him with the one word he had overheard all afternoon: 'Unsuitable, no ... unsuitable.' Finally it came down to: 'Wear this jumpsuit or stay behind in the van!' That did the trick.

I managed to find a shirt that did not look too bad. But my trousers were baggy and needed ironing. The big problem was what to put on my feet. Every pair of trainers stank to high heaven. Chris came up with the only solution.

'Go barefoot and tell everyone it helps to keep your feet in shape.'

I did, and later a journalist who was present used it in an article about the preparations of a long-distance runner.

There was a good turn-out at the club in the British Embassy compound. The Indian contingent quietly stood together in a corner drinking orange juice. They wore dark blazers with grey flannels and it looked as if they were not often invited to such gatherings. Dowdall-Brown saw to it that we had plenty to nibble and a great deal to drink. As the evening progressed I could hear Baz's voice booming out across the room in his broad Potteries dialect: 'There I am in the bushes, throwing up and having diarrhoea all at the same time, when some nutter taps me on the shoulder and asks the way to Pakistan!' A lot of hearty laughter followed and a few drinks were spilt.

Ranee Bhatia asked Lea how the journey was affecting our sex life.

'Well, it has to take a back seat, if you see what I mean. We go for walks away from the others and share showers whenever they're available.'

Ranee giggled. More outbursts of laughter came from a group of ex-pats at the drinks table. Baz was in the middle of another story.

'One morning I crouched under a bridge and was horrified to see what I'd deposited. Then, when Kel and I set off, we ran past several heaps of the stuff – same reddish colour and same shape. Like replicas of Australia steaming in the sun. Next bend we come to, there's this enormous elephant with an exploding backside. Elephant dung! And it was exactly the same as mine!'

42

Captain Dogra of the Indian National Institute of Sports was responsible for the day-to-day running of New Delhi's National Stadium. He had arranged accommodation for us in the changing rooms of a swimming pool behind the running track. The pool was closed to the public for the winter and a caretaker had been posted at its entrance to look after our van.

'I think you will be most satisfied Leona,' Ranee winked, 'even if there is no hot water in the showers you are taking.'

We spent one week in the capital and crammed in as much as we could. Zhenka and Lea went to the zoo with Ranee and her children. When they came back, Zhenka told me that he had already seen most of the animals roaming the streets.

One morning, Mark Tully strolled past the caretaker and approached the van carrying a reel to reel tape recorder in a black leather satchel. Zhenka babbled away non-stop until a microphone was held in front of him.

'So that's how we keep him quiet,' laughed Baz.

The interview, for the World Service, seemed to go well. One look inside our van had convinced Mark Tully that this was no ordinary overland journey.

Dowdall-Brown had a consignment of milk powder and orange juice sent over from the catering department of the Embassy. The message on the cartons read 'For Zhenka – happy travels.' A crate of ale also arrived mysteriously. Best of all came news that the British Embassy restaurant had been put at our disposal. Baz and I tucked into buffalo steaks and chips on a daily basis – sometimes even for breakfast.

Between the meals out we resolved to keep in shape with late afternoon training runs at the stadium. Most days we ran with Sampath, Ranjit and the rest of the Roadrunners. Afterwards, we would all file through the grubby alleyways to a little coffee bar close by and eat omelettes and toast whilst watching a half-naked madman twirl a bamboo staff about in the dusty square outside.

One day I was called upon to give a talk in the packed auditorium of a local college. Next, I was asked to present the medals at a three-day Inland Revenue Olympics. This event culminated in a grand social evening beneath the canvas of a colourful marquee. I sat cross-legged on the grass listening to a comedian tell jokes in Hindi that were not translated quickly enough for me to laugh in time.

Midway through our stay, a freelance photographer called Baldev befriended us. His keen eye quickly told him that the route to our hearts lay in our stomachs. Whilst his wife ordered their servants to prepare mouthwatering delicacies for us, he acted as our guide around the old city, clicking his camera when we jogged through Chadni Chowk or stood beneath the walls of the Red Fort.

Zhenka's favourite spot was in the centre of Connaught Place, where he saw skinny men shin up ropes that led nowhere, and flute players charm snakes out of their baskets. One man was a contortionist.

'Like Chrissy when he goes to sleep around the steering wheel!' said Zhenka, full of a new-found admiration for our driver.

Whilst in Delhi, we discovered that the Australian Government had decided to clamp down on immigration in an effort to reduce unemployment. This meant that we would need tourist visas to enter Australia. Normally such visas were not granted unless return tickets could be produced, or at least sufficient funds to purchase them. We had neither.

However, the interest in our journey had never been greater and the media coverage of our arrival in Delhi was about to pay dividends. Baz and I were shown into the office of a keen sportsman at the Australian Embassy. He was a big man with shearer's hands that strayed about the desk top as if they were searching for a fleece to yank hold of.

'We heard you'd be payin' a visit,' he grinned. 'Dowdall Brown's been on the blower half the bloody morning. Wants us to give you these.' He shuffled four visas towards us across the table and leaned back in his chair.

'Rafferty's running them ragged across the Nullarbor – doing the journey in record time so they say. I've given you five months instead of three. Reckon you'll need all of that after crossing India. Get yourselves an agent when you step off that boat. The dollars will come rolling in, you see if they don't.'

The man extended one of his big hands for us to shake.

'Bazza, I'm Barry. What say youz all come round for beers tonight?'

There were boomerangs on the walls of the Australian High Commission Club. Zhenka wanted to throw one of them across the room but the Indian waiter said he mustn't.

'Wait until you get to Australia,' Lea told him, 'and then you can go hunting kangaroos with a boomerang.'

'I don't want to hunt them, I want to climb inside their pouches and ride them.'

I dragged Zhenka away from the boomerangs and lifted him up to look at a picture on the opposite wall. It was a reproduction of the Sidney Nolan painting, *Burke and Wills*: two explorers setting out to cross Australia.

'Look,' I said, 'never mind kangaroos, what's that?'

'A camel! But I thought they lived in Afghanistan?'

'Well, supposing a few of the Afghans took their camels on a boat to Australia and went exploring with them?'

Zhenka looked hard at the two men on the camel and frowned. 'They don't look very comfortable,' he sighed.

'No, it wasn't a very happy journey for them. But guess what Zhen, the man who painted the picture came from Melbourne – the place we're going to – and his dad used to work the trams there, just like I did.'

'Dad ... do boomerangs always come back? Always?'

43

A thick fog had descended on the city whilst we were at the club. Chris peered intently through the windscreen as he drove back to the swimming pool.

'It's a real pea-souper,' said Lea.

Zhenka rubbed his eyes sleepily. 'Can you eat it?'

The caretaker came running to unlock the gates when Chris beeped the horn. He had been trying to get to sleep on a wooden pallet outside and wore a blanket wrapped around his shoulders.

In the morning, when I woke and looked out through the rear windows of the van, the fog had lifted. The sun hung in the air like a bronze gong.

A hockey team was practising on one of the pitches near the stadium. I watched them going through their warm-up routine as I doused my hands and face under a cold water tap outside the changing rooms. The men sprinted for a few yards, then slowed, and then sprinted some more: short bursts that quickened their breathing and drew mist from their mouths like puffs of smoke. Whenever the hockey sticks clashed, drops of dew flew up from the trimmed grass and the sound carried across the river.

'How's your head?'

I turned around. Baz had just taken a cold shower and was drying his hair on a grubby towel.

'Not so bad. Must be getting used to it.'

'Yeah, I think we must. I never felt better.'

It was our last morning in New Delhi and the Roadrunners would soon be turning up to run out of the city with us. Dowdall-Brown arrived bright and early. He had a telegram for us from England tucked into his breast pocket below the obligatory red carnation.

'"Passage secured on *MV Chidambaram*. Sailing from Madras 2 April."'

'So it's agreed then. We go through central India rather than taking the main road to Bombay and Bangalore.'

Baz nodded. 'Yeah, Ranjit seemed concerned about us taking

the back roads but he's contacted a few people along the way and arranged for us to stay with them.'

'We don't have time to run that extra two hundred miles anyway, if we're to be in Madras before the second of April,' I added.

By 10 a.m. we were ready to leave. Captain Dogra presented each of us with medals. Sampath and Ranjit handed out traditional gifts of silken scarves. Tarlok Singh, the Sikh coach, gave Zhenka a wind-up elephant named Babar.

This time we set off at a slower pace. The ring road was lined with domed tombs and rubbish tips and it followed the course of the river on our left. The river looked sluggish. I felt that way too. I glanced over my shoulder at Ranjit. His wobble was still there, but less pronounced.

Sampath had arranged a surprise for us six miles down the road. Tables and chairs had been set up outside a teahouse where a group of villagers were waiting to welcome us. Sampath's boss from the GPO placed garlands of orange flowers around our necks and made a short speech. Then, after a few glasses of spiced tea, we set off once more.

When we reached a town called Faridabad, Ranjit led us along a side street to Bhogal's Sports Shoe Factory. Here, amidst tubs of glue and cross-legged cobblers, the owner of the company fitted us out with new running shoes.

We finally parted company with Ranjit and the Roadrunners and left them waiting for an army truck that would return them to New Delhi.

The road to Agra and the Taj Mahal first passed through Krishna's birthplace on the banks of the River Yamuna. Pilgrims stared out of buses which showed the destination, Mathura, painted in big white letters across the top of the dusty windscreens. Large groups of them came pedalling past us on hired bicycles too.

One afternoon, on a lonely stretch of road between two such villages, Baz pointed up to the sky ahead. 'Vultures … see them?'

The dark gliding shapes looked like black coat hooks with wings as they whirled in tight circles far above a tree by a sharp bend in the road. When we rounded this bend we came face to face with a pack of wild dogs.

There were seven animals in all and five of them were tearing the flesh from the carcasses of three dead cows. The two dogs whose jawbones were temporarily unoccupied made straight for us. Instinctively, I dropped to my knees, frantically scrabbling in the dust to find a stone to throw.

'There are no fucking stones Baz!' I screamed.

Baz did not hear me. He was charging at the dogs like a madman, leaping in the air and waving his arms. Roaring and foaming at the mouth, he ran towards them like a Staffordshire bulldog with rabies. Bhogal's brand new, white leather shoes flashed in the sunlight as Baz lashed out at the dogs with his feet.

I closed my eyes. I did not want to look. When I opened them again, the dogs were back among the pack and pretending not to be interested any more. Baz was unscathed but shaking. I led him away from the dogs. He looked back over his shoulder a couple of times and his lip curled disdainfully.

'They didn't put up much of a fight, did they?' he muttered.

Later, from the safety of the driver's seat, Chris expounded on his theory of how such wild dogs should be handled in the future.

'Punch them on the nose,' he said confidently, 'that's their weakest spot.'

Baz stared at him with the same look he had given the dogs. For a split-second I thought they were going to come to blows. Instead he laughed incredulously.

'Baxter, you idiot! A dog's nose is too close to its fucking teeth! When did you ever pull a stunt like that?'

44

It was hard to imagine Krishna spending an idyllic childhood growing up in Mathura. The city was big, bustling and dusty. Anything faster than walking pace was out of the question. Baz attempted to distance himself from the barrage of noisy children by bursting into a hymn.

'To be a pilgrim!' he sang out devoutly. But that only attracted more attention and the crowd following us grew.

South of the city lay a large military cantonment known as the Civil Lines. Here, two neighbours – a captain and his colonel – both tried to outdo each other with offers of hospitality.

We sat on the veranda of the captain's bungalow and drank army-issue rum in the dark. Then we all trudged over to the colonel's place for more of the same. Some people were celebrating a wedding in the cantonment area. Lamplight marched the shadow of a trombonist across a red brick wall near the parade ground. Bugles sounded and a big drum beat in the distance.

'It's so romantic to marry at night-time,' said Lea to the colonel.

'Well, yes,' he agreed. 'Also it is not so hot and they are reducing the number of flies crawling over the sweet cakes.'

As we looked we saw what we thought might be the beginnings of a procession. Shrill voices and sudden peals of laughter set the dogs yapping. The stars were crammed into the sky overhead and the meagre light from the lamps in the city below had no effect on their brilliance.

'Nothing drowns out the sound of the crickets,' said Lea. 'It reminds me of the old Somerset Maugham plays I used to watch on the television when I was twelve. Thursday nights at about nine o'clock they'd be on. The typical British colonial type with his white trousers and his open-necked shirt, sitting on the veranda in his cane chair and all the tropical plants around him … and the sound of the crickets.'

The colonel eased a cigar from his mouth, blew a smoke ring across the moon, and changed the subject.

'How do you manage to cook for these hungry athletes, Mrs Bowers?'

'It's not easy. Sometimes I think they run on their stomachs instead of their feet. We try to vary a basic diet. At the moment that's dhal and rice. It depends whereabouts we are. Barry jots down almost everything we eat.'

The colonel turned to Baz and pushed a hurricane lamp towards his side of the low table. Baz selected a couple of entries at random from his diary and began to read them out to us.

'"Lea did a massive tea. After tomato soup we had rice with curried veg. Then pineapple cubes fried in batter and a rice pudding. Bloody great!"' He flicked back through the pages and paused. 'This is last November, when it was cold. "What makes evenings so delightful in Afghanistan are the glorious red sunset skies. The blue deepens to a dark turquoise in yet another impressive Milky Way sky. Lea cooked us an incredible meal. Fried mashed spuds and onions, tinned cheese, three bean salad, carrots, fried eggs. Followed by rice pudding with raisins. Two helpings. Unfortunately old pig face overdid it again and got stomach ache. Went to sleep serenaded by Beethoven's Fifth."'

The colonel's cigar waved around in his mouth as he laughed.

'That reminds me of when Kel was ill,' said Chris. 'Baz decided to give breakfast a miss. Since I wasn't eating porridge – nor Lea – Kel had a heyday, gluttoning himself on three bowls of oats, a dozen oranges and as many bananas, before setting off to run thirty miles.'

'How are you cooking such banquets, Mrs Bowers; do you light campfires?'

'We have a small gas cooker. Once though, we couldn't find gas anywhere and so we bought a kerosene stove. That's what I'm using now. It's slow and laborious – sometimes meals take two and a half hours to prepare and half the village gathers round to watch. It feels like I'm giving cookery lessons!'

The colonel looked amazed as he poured out more glasses of rum.

'Shopping can be difficult too,' Lea continued. 'Once, there were so many people following me and helping to barter for the vegetables that the crowd brought down the wickerwork awning over the shop. Of course, I got the blame for it. The local schoolteacher told me that few Europeans ever stopped at the village, hence the interest in me. He told me I was quite a specimen.'

The colonel laughed again. He had finished his cigar and would soon be turning in. 'Shall you visit the Taj Mahal?' he asked.

'We'll probably take a day off to see it.'

'Good. You will enjoy it. The last time I was there I met a young couple on holiday from another country. I forget which. They were blind. They carried white sticks and a camera, and they asked if I would take their photograph. Everywhere they went they asked someone to take their picture. The young man explained that when they returned home and showed their photographs, everyone said how happy they looked, and this they loved to hear. It was true: I have not witnessed a happier couple anywhere.

'These two people, being always blind, had never seen a photograph. The very word "likeness" meant nothing to them. Yet when I followed them into the marble dome of the Taj, they craned their heads back and stared up as though they really could see. Later, they told me that they had never heard anything so beautiful as the Taj Mahal. So, when you make your visit, you must remember to listen.'

'My grandfather always looked happy,' I said. 'He was blind from birth too. When he was a youngster he fell through the trapdoors of a pub whilst they were unloading the barrels of beer into the cellar. The landlord gave him a few coppers and told him to look where he was going in future. After that, whenever the brewery were making deliveries, he would do a round of the pubs and tumble into as many cellars as he could.'

'A profitable pastime, eh?'

'A businessman with bruises was the way he put it.'

45

When we arrived at Agra we stayed with the principal of St John's College. Ranjit Bhatia had sent word ahead and accommodation had already been arranged for us.

The room we were shown to was reached by climbing two flights of steep stone steps. It was light and airy and led out onto a flat rooftop that overlooked the grounds of the college. Baz carried an easy chair outside onto the roof and sat in the sun with a book. Lea pegged out washing.

'He's always reading, isn't he?' said Chris. 'The other night I caught him with a book in one hand and his toothbrush in the other.'

'That's nothing,' I said. 'I've seen him crouching under bridges with a toilet roll in one hand and a book in the other.'

We both looked at him through the open doorway and grinned.

'I wish we could stay here longer,' I said, testing out one of the beds with a bounce or two. 'My sleeping bag feels like cardboard, and have you felt the foam we lie on recently?'

'The foam *you* lie on,' Chris reminded me. 'All I've got are the van seats.'

The sound of footsteps clattered up the stone steps. Someone tapped lightly on the door.

David Reid-Thomas, the college curate, stood on the landing outside.

'Hope I'm not disturbing anyone. The principal told me you were here. Can I invite you all to supper, if it's not too short notice?'

After ten months on the road, our eating habits had strayed far beyond the boundaries of any table. The merest glimpse of a pristine tablecloth was apt to send us spiralling into a massive inferiority complex. Added to this, any polished cutlery laid in the correct formation had become as confusing as Urdu.

A broken blade on a fan that would not work hung from the ceiling of the dining room like the folded wing of a dead moth. As the curate sat down to say grace, Zhenka let loose a little belch and giggled. David winked at him.

'He slurps his soup,' whispered Chris when we were halfway through our first course. 'Always a good sign, that.'

David and his wife Helen came from Scotland. They had three young children and had been living in India for six years.

'I wasn't at all sure about David accepting this post. The children were tots – two of them anyway. Younger than Zhenka. My mother played merry hell with him for taking her grandchildren so far away from her.'

'I came out here first,' said David. 'I knew that Helen would love it.' He looked at her and winked. 'I know my wife. When she arrived I was at the railway station waiting with three trishaw wallahs. I sat the children with me in one trishaw, Helen's luggage occupied another, and Helen herself climbed into the third.'

'I wasn't at all impressed,' interrupted Helen. 'It was the middle of summer; I was shooing flies from the moment the plane touched down.'

'Anyway, off we went. The children thought it great fun – watching the trishaw wallah's matchstick legs pedalling us through impossible-looking gaps. They shrieked and clapped whenever the brakes were applied to avoid the cows. Unfortunately, Helen's ride was even more exciting!' David paused and looked across the table at his wife.

'My trishaw man was having a bad day. He couldn't keep up and didn't know where he was supposed to be taking me. Because of this he must have let his attention slip. Next thing I know, there's a big truck bearing down on us halfway across a narrow stone bridge. The trishaw swerved into a parapet and I went sailing over the wall.'

'Luckily, the river hadn't dried up completely. It usually does at the height of summer,' said David.

'Oh yes, I was so fortunate wasn't I – to land head-first in a quagmire of sewage!' Helen pretended to be annoyed. 'I spent my first fortnight in India confined to bed and full of antibiotics. Every now and then David would pop his head round the door and try to reassure me, saying "You'll love it Helen, just you wait and see!" I felt like killing him!'

'But not any more,' laughed Chris.

'No, not any more. India's a wonderful country. I wear saris, cook a mean curry, and my mother thinks her grandchildren are enjoying a marvellous experience.'

David grinned, waggled his head like an Indian, and looked down at his plate. The curate was a messy eater. The white tablecloth in front of him was spattered with saffron.

'You mentioned the railway station.' Baz steered the conversation to another mode of transport.

David nodded. 'Agra has six of them. Did you know Barry, that there are six thousand steam engines still operating in this country?'

'I've seen some real old workhorses on the narrow gauge lines,' said Baz, 'and bullet-nosed jobs too on the wider tracks. Back in England they'd be in museums: here they're thundering between palm trees, larger than life.'

'It sounds like you're something of a railway enthusiast, Barry,' said Helen.

'I used to be.'

'A gricer!' added David. 'That's what they're called. We had one stay with us last Easter. Remember the chap from Rotheram, Helen?'

'How can I forget; our visitors' book is virtually full of the locomotives he logged.'

'Yes,' agreed David, 'he was very serious about it all. His favourite stretch of line was on the east coast, the Parlakimedi Light Railway. There were these little engines there that had been built in Stoke-on-Trent in 1910.'

'I love railways,' said Helen, 'but not in that sort of obsessive way – more as a means of exploring India. People live on the platforms here you know: vast communities, thousands and thousands of them.'

'When we left Afghanistan and entered Pakistan there were so many people swarming around we thought it would be impossible to carry on travelling the way we were,' said Lea. 'Then when we reached Amritsar it was even worse. But between the towns the countryside is beautiful and less hectic.'

Helen nodded. 'When you've seen the Taj Mahal you must visit Fatehpur Sikri. How far away is it David?'

'Oh, no more than twenty-five miles.'

'It's a city that was built in the sixteenth century and then abandoned after only fourteen years. Nobody knows why.'

'A sandstone version of the *Marie Celeste*,' said Chris.

'Exactly,' said Helen. 'And if it's peace and quiet you're after, I know of no better place.'

46

The streets leading to the Taj Mahal were full of craft shops selling alabaster models of it that reminded me of white blancmanges. None of us felt comfortable taking a day off to indulge ourselves, but as we had already ignored the Golden Temple of Amritsar, we went anyway. Perhaps our reluctance to view one of the Seven Wonders of the World had something to do with the transient nature of the nomads, and how much we had begun to identify with them since we had been on the move. I thought back to Afghanistan and how thrilled we'd been to explore the dune-covered walls of the caravanserais, built of mud, not marble. But they had been created as safe havens for traders and travelling people like us. Also, there was a strong sense of impermanence as the ruins were left to crumble and the desert engulf them.

The Mughal monument at Agra was quite different. It had taken 20,000 men over twenty years to build. We paid our two rupees and followed a Punjabi family though a high-arched gateway carved out of red sandstone. It was a clever device, intended to enhance the brilliance of the vast marble dome once you emerged out of the shadows and stepped down into the enclosed garden.

I picked up Zhenka and crossed the smooth paving stones lining a narrow strip of water. Ahead of us, a little girl in a yellow sari trimmed with crimson dipped her hand into the pool and watched the big reflection tremble.

The memorial to Mumtaz Mahal – the lady of the Taj – is undeniably beautiful. I agreed with Lea that Emperor Shah Jahan had at least achieved some feeling of transience in that the central dome above the tomb appeared light enough to float away.

Inside the high chamber, moved by the echoes of soft-voiced Urdu prayers, I whispered to Lea, 'What an incredible statement he's making, creating a building like this in memory of the woman he loved.'

Lea was less certain about his motive. 'He's buried here too, you know. And anyway, she died giving birth to their fourteenth child. I think she deserved it.'

In the afternoon Chris drove us out to the empty city called Fatehpur Sikri. For three hours we wandered in and out of palaces, mosques and deserted law courts.

'If only every city were this easy to walk through,' said Lea in a soft voice. The silence made us all speak in whispers.

'It feels like the past is eavesdropping on the present,' remarked Baz, lowering his voice without realising.

By the time we returned to St John's, the hubbub outside the fort at Agra felt strangely comforting.

'It was altogether too eerie, too unnerving ... such quiet seems unnatural for this land,' Chris said to the curate.

'I don't think the holy men would go along with that, Chris.'

'No, I suppose not. But it's early days yet, David. We've got the whole of India to cross. Perhaps one of us will find peace of mind before we're through – if that's what you're getting at.'

'I wasn't, but you're right. Now, Barry tells me that your particular calling is confined to the chessboard. How about a game this evening? I may be a little rusty but the Lord moves in mysterious ways.' He laughed loudly and wagged a finger.

The journey from Agra to Gwalior is 74 miles long. It was the one stretch of road that our friend Ranjit had been perturbed about us taking because of the same dangers we had been alerted to weeks ago by the police inspector.

Mike Artus's itinerary notes more or less confirmed what we already knew, but I read it to the others just the same.

'*A narrow road ... tarmac to one car width, with hard shoulders ... Dusty in dry weather, and muddy in rains. Night driving between Agra and Gwalior is not advisable as dacoits still sometimes descend on the traveller.*'

If my own thoughts were directed to sudden attacks, then so too were those of Lea, who returned from the bazaar before we left with an armful of toilet rolls.

Saris and glistening limbs swayed above the paddyfields as we ran. And the drumbeat of diesel generators pumped sound through the still trees. Water cascaded from wheels turned by lumbering buffalo goaded into day-long circles of the same dusty path. And on the edges of the logging camps the elephants curled their painted trunks around the fallen timber.

For a short distance we ran through the state of Rajasthan before entering Madhya Pradesh.

We jogged between avenues of palm trees and eroded Mughal ruins. Baz listed the birds that perched above us on the telegraph wires and those which hopped along the wooden sleepers of the narrow gauge railway track – grey-hued pigeons, blue jays, bee-eaters and black Indian robins.

It occurred to me that if Baz was both birdspotter and trainspotter there should be some special name for his rare breed. It would have to be a combination of twitcher and gricer. 'Twicer' was all I could come up with, but thinking about it got me over a few more miles on a hot day in the jungle.

Beyond the town of Dholpur, the central arches of a red sandstone bridge had been swept away by the River Chambal. Covered ox carts were queuing to cross a narrow pontoon bridge, whilst the heavier motor wagons were ferried from one bank to the other.

This was the very heart of the central Indian badlands. When the serious day-long rains came, the wide river would burst its banks and lop off great chunks of land all along the Chambal Valley. Each monsoon season the swollen waters swept in unpredictable torrents to carve out fresh ravines. When the rains ceased and the height of the river dropped, all that remained was a maze of thorny canyons. Such land was useless for cultivation and, like the grand palaces at Fatehpur Sikri, whole villages were abandoned overnight.

Since the twelfth century this constantly changing landscape has bred generations of outlaws. So many kidnappings, rapes and revenge killings had taken place that the Chambal was known locally as the River of Revenge.

Camels were wading in the shallow water on the far shore as we jogged across the rattling sheets of metal that were laid over the pontoon bridge. The camels were likely to have come out of the deserts of Rajasthan, taking one of the old trade routes to Uttar Pradesh. Perhaps the bundles they carried were what the bandits came looking for.

Once across the bridge the road climbed steeply out of the valley and we ran past a well-cultivated field that had escaped the ravages of the river. Clusters of scarecrows leaned over the crops and looked to be in the throes of animated conversation as the wind tugged at the rags attached to their wooden limbs.

There were flowers beside the road. Hundreds of paths meandered away through the scrub and vanished into the jungle beyond it. Between long stints of running I swallowed salt tablets and stretched out on top of the trailer which Chris carefully parked in whatever shade there was.

Once, I fell asleep and woke to find a woodcutter standing over me with a long-handled axe resting upon his shoulder. I rubbed my eyes as the man cradled the end of the wooden shaft in his big knobbly hands with fingers that resembled the roots of a banyan tree. He fixed his large brown eyes on me and I waited for him to smile or at least tilt his head. But he did neither.

'Easy to see how the dacoits operate,' said Chris, fuelling my worries. 'This bloke appeared from nowhere.'

I stared from the axe-head to the spiky bushes in the ditch that dropped away from the road and imagined Pan Singh Tomar on his way to rob us – hurdling the felled branches deep inside the woods.

'He could easily have been a dacoit!' I told Baz later.

But Baz thought I was being paranoid. 'Or a woodcutter?' he suggested, pissing me off.

'It's alright for you, Baz,' I shouted. 'You only have yourself to think about.'

'That's unfair, Kel. You know very well that we all look out for each other.'

'Do we now?'

'Yes we fucking well do!'

'As long as your needs are catered for first, Baz.'

'My needs? You're joking. You're fucking joking, aren't you? Who's the one who gets up first every morning. Who gets this bloody circus on the road? I do that for everyone's sake, not just mine.'

'You just don't seem as concerned as I am about the others whenever the van doesn't show up or isn't where we thought it would be, that's all.'

'Bullshit! Fucking bullshit! If you're feeling worried and paranoid 'cos you've brought Lea and Zhenka with you, don't go blaming me!' With that he began to accelerate away: it was invariably what happened whenever we spoke our minds.

Baz was used to living on his own. He was good at sticking to a routine. He had demonstrated that often enough by now and it had paid dividends all the way. But young children can play havoc with routines and I don't think I fully appreciated how difficult it must have been for Baz to accept this.

For my part though, perhaps things went deeper. I felt that the pressures to make a success of the journey were all on me. Baz had joined in to help, and if he chose to quit, no one would point a finger or consider him to have failed. I think I envied him in this respect and every so often my feelings surfaced and grew into full-scale resentment.

We ran on through the jungle and argued along the way. Not that the arguments resolved anything. They didn't. They just drained us at a time when we could have done without it. Baz even began to think that I had never really wanted him to join us; that he had misread my letter. Later, I wondered if the jungle didn't have something to do with our stubbornness. Falling out in the middle of a desert left us feeling that it was no big deal. We were small fry and our rantings infinitesimal. The jungle just didn't offer that perspective.

47

On arrival at Gwalior, we handed over a letter from Ranjit addressed to the principal of the Lakshmibai National College of Physical Education. Accommodation was found for us at the top of the racecourse grandstand of a former maharaja.

Our rooms were cool and carpeted, each with its own bathroom. A cook was on standby for the duration of our stay. He insisted on bringing us 'tea bed' if we failed to turn up on time in our private dining room just along the veranda.

The principal also saw to it that his students met us. Three hundred athletes and staff turned up to hear an impromptu talk about our run.

'No gang of fucking dacoits could be more scary than this!' whispered Baz as we were led up onto the stage in the assembly room.

Later, we were invited to attend a gymnastics display, hastily arranged in honour of our visit by the local cotton mill workers. The lads met weekly in the old part of town and a beat-up jeep was sent to collect us. We sat on gunny sacks in the back and tried not to fall out when the gears crunched and the jeep jolted over the ruts.

Our young driver told us that he was older than his grinning companion. But neither of them looked old enough to have a driving licence. In the tight grip of such small, thin hands the steering wheel reminded me of an old-fashioned bicycle wheel. The feeble beam from the headlamps bounced up and down through the unlit back streets.

'It is dark now, too dark,' the lads explained. 'If it wasn't you would be seeing the clouds of cotton dust we are breathing in. So we must unclog our lungs daily by exercise.' The youngest of the two coughed on the fluff that hung in the air outside the textile mills. A small pig squealed from an adjacent alleyway that had proved too narrow for our jeep. And yapping dogs chased amongst the ribbons of discarded rags and rubbish.

The shadows of the inhabitants who passed along the streets mingled with the shadows of those who had paused to talk, or to yawn, or simply to catch their breath. And the noisiest shadows of all were the ones bent double, who spat out what had been sucked in at the looms.

'Life, my father is telling me, well, we are full up with it. So I am thinking there is no room for any more!' The youngster thumped his chest. 'We are congested inside ... and on the outside it's no different.' He stood on the brake pedal and flung everyone forward one last time.

The lads from the cotton mill cheered when we clambered out of the jeep and a couple of them ran forward with bright garlands of marigolds. They led us to a mud-walled square lit by a single hurricane lamp which hung from the branch of a tree. Chairs had been arranged for us at the foot of the tree and a table had been placed there too, with five plastic beakers and a bottle of orange juice.

When we were seated someone introduced us in Hindi and the lads all clapped.

To start the programme one of the older boys began to spin around like a hammer-thrower, twirling ball-shaped wire baskets of red-hot coals in glowing circles overhead, creating rings above the clapping hands. Then, a skinny thirteen-year-old performed rapid acrobatics inches from our feet, with his arms and legs hooked together, flattening his face on the hard ground with each somersault, whilst two friends preceded his orbit on their knees and swept away the sharper stones.

The young cotton mill workers pretended to fight each other with wooden staves and flashing knives. And they took part in rural-style wrestling matches waged in a dirt pit ring. This was the Chambal, the badlands of central India, and they were showing what they could do. How it was for them to grow up here. Practising useful skills taught by men from the villages. Skills that might help them to survive.

On the morning we left Gwalior, the principal telephoned the commander-general of a border security force academy, 22 miles away on the road to Nagpur, to ask if they would put us up for the night. Then we were handed singlets bearing the college crest and half a dozen PE students turned up to accompany us for the first hour's running.

One student was Tibetan, another Ethiopian, a third came from Fiji, and yet another from Assam, one of the far-off Indian states bordering China and Bhutan. The lad from Fiji looked to be the better runner if an effortless style was anything to go by, but I ran beside the Ethiopian.

His body was so thin and his shoulders were so narrow that his head looked out of proportion; almost like a baby's. He had dark hair clipped into short tight curls that brought to mind my grandmother's knitted tea cosy. Looking at his legs as he ran at my side, made me think of another Ethiopian who became the first great runner to emerge from Africa.

I used to subscribe to a magazine called *World Sports* and in one issue there was an article devoted to this man, with a wonderful photograph of him training in the hills above Addis Ababa.

I can see the picture now – a whole page of it. Abebe Bikila was his name. A tall Abyssinian clad in a dark sweat-stained singlet and blood-coloured shorts. He won the Olympic marathon in 1960 and again in 1964, before an automobile accident led to his early death in 1973. The times I stared at that photograph and dreamed of pounding across the same red earth on some distant quest.

It helped to have the PE students running alongside us through the city. They chose the easiest route out to the open road beyond and it felt good to be running fast again. The Tibetan strode ahead with Baz. Earlier he had come to our room in the grandstand to give me a picture of the Potala Palace in Lhasa. I had asked if he knew anything about the art of *lung-gom* or 'trance walking' as described by Alexandra David-Neal in her book *Magic and Mystery in Tibet*. But he had only been a small boy when his family fled from the Chinese invasion and his recollections of life there were hazy.

After seven miles the students turned back to face the fort on the mile-long plateau at Gwalior, and Baz and I were on our own again. The road was narrow – dangerously narrow – and we ran on the red shoulder as it wound through bush-covered hills and sugar cane plantations.

Lea and Chris had stayed behind to shop.

'The tin cans of sugar were black with flies,' they told us when they caught up. 'Zhenka's asleep in the back with the mosquito net around him – they're everywhere.'

The military academy lay along the banks of a lake full of crocodiles. A mounted officer ordered a platoon of soldiers to line the road as we approached.

'So as to be inspired by your example!' the commander-general later told us.

A guest room reserved for VIPs had been made ready for our overnight stay. The glass doors of the room folded back in hinged segments that opened onto a patio of dull pink marble overlooking the lake. A major and his wife and daughters stopped by for sherry and rum. They took the same walk each evening.

'The sun is simply splendid at this time of the day and from the patio here the views are magnificent. Agreed?' said the major.

'But we have no swimming,' spoke out the youngest daughter.

'Of course there is no swimming. The lake is for the sun alone to bathe in, and for fishing. Tomorrow I could be fishing with you, agreed?'

Baz shook his head.

'We have a long way to run and a ship we mustn't miss,' I said.

'There is always something we are having to miss. Isn't that the way?' The major looked from daughter to daughter and then scanned the wide green water and made as if to cast his line. When the sun dipped into the lake I watched for ripples and saw instead the water turn from green to dark pink, like the cool marble underfoot.

Next morning, a servant wearing a spotless white tunic eased open the door of our room and quietly strode inside carrying a large silver tray. After 'tea bed' we said a leisurely farewell to our hosts at the academy and made our way along the road and over a bridge spanning the River Sind.

The area we ran through was hilly and it was hot. The sun

shone on the hills and had all but burnt up the bushy vegetation. The colour of the land was a light brown. Outcrops of a lighter coloured rock were wedged into it. Each was crowned with a white Jain temple.

In the narrow-laned capital of the former state of Datia, the thatched roofs of the mud houses had been replaced by dark red conical tiles. High above them, on a scrubby hill, rose a seven-storey palace which Edward Lutyens considered to be the finest building in all of India. The building dominated the landscape for many miles around. When Baz halted on the fringes of the old town to look up at it, two farmers from a neighbouring village approached him.

'The Gobinda Palace once belonged to the Maharaja of Datia,' said one farmer.

'You should be visiting him before you go on your way. He is practising every kindness and his new palace is on level ground.'

The second farmer's fingers strayed into his greying beard so that when his head gave the inevitable nod it looked as if he were tugging it from side to side.

It was a short detour to the maharaja's new home and we were all too intrigued to let slip such an opportunity. The heavy iron gates snagged on the long weeds choking the entrance. Chunks of paint fell in copper-coloured flakes as we pushed against the rusting bars.

Once through the gateway, we ambled down an overgrown drive towards what we presumed to be the new palace. The building looked at least as ancient as the older version, if less majestic.

The maharaja himself stood before us in front of two pillars, casting an insignificant shadow across the chipped flagstones and fallen masonry. Over his right shoulder, high on a hill in the far distance, the deserted palace was festering with shiny cupolas above an architecture that appeared to be both complicated and extravagant. Its former resident looked neither of these things.

The maharaja was a little chap. Down at heel but not dismayed. He was wearing the frayed jacket of an old brown suit with crocodile skin patches stitched unevenly onto each elbow, over a long white tunic and baggy pantaloons.

He immediately introduced us to three of his children.

'There are eight of them in all,' he told us, 'all females, every one.'

The three daughters we met were plump and jolly, and they made a bee-line for Zhenka, each tugging him this way and that as they showed him around their palace.

The hall we entered was full of heavily varnished oil paintings; family portraits of bejewelled ancestors wearing wonderful turbans that looked as if they could topple off their heads and out of the ornate frames at any time.

The first room we were shown into was filled with carved tables, statues and Victorian vases. The next contained hanging daggers and shotguns. The maharaja drew our attention to the sepia photographs on the walls of this room. Hundreds of pictures of roaring tigers were frozen in time by bullets and the shutters of cameras. Tigers and leopards were arranged in neat rows – stripes and spots cascading down the steps of the old palace.

There were two stuffed tigers in the lounge: one with a cobweb looped about the claws of its raised paw, and the other with a child's marble replacing its left eye. Zhenka fed them with biscuits whilst everyone drank milky tea beside a palm-fringed lake infested with crocodiles.

'My daughter bagged the tiger with the glossy coat not far from here six years ago. One rarely sees a tiger nowadays and hunting is forbidden anyway – but there are still many panthers in the jungle.' The maharaja beckoned me aside and lowered his voice.

'There is poaching still. The tiger is a valuable commodity. Listen, if you are ever experiencing a difficulty with the sexual act, then I am telling you to smear liberally your penis with the kidney fat of a tiger! I can vouch for it. Also, when a birth is expected they are saying that a tiger's nose will tip the scales in favour of a boy – though this I cannot vouch for.'

48

A long convoy of armoured vehicles rumbled towards Jhansi. The dust thrown up by the wheels stuck fast to the sweat on our arms and legs.

In 1853, when the last raja passed away without having produced a male heir, the British pensioned off his wife and took full control of this region. Four years later, at the time of the Indian Mutiny, the Rani led a rebellion at Jhansi where the British contingent were all massacred. When reprisals were called for, she escaped to the fort at Gwalior. There, disguised as a man, she charged out on horseback to meet the British and was killed. Since her death, the rani of Jhansi has become central India's Joan of Arc.

At first, we ran through wooded hills, and then between shoulder-high wheatfields. Eventually we reached an arid plain. The road across the plain led to the town of Babina where a busy market was being held on the banks of a lake. Uneven rows of baskets full of fruit and cosmetics flickered in and out of sight behind silver-bangled ankles and the colourful saris of the women who had walked for many miles from the surrounding villages.

Some way beyond the town we crossed a long bridge over the Betwa River. On the other side of the river the road wound through scrubland until it skirted the shoreline of a large artificial pool at Talbahat. Men were fishing from narrow punts in the middle of the murky water. Wading birds and ruined shrines were reflected at its edges where the reeds had been cut back.

Close by, Chris discovered a dak bungalow and was able to park the van out of sight in a far corner of the compound. This achieved without attracting too much attention, he and Baz set about assembling their camp beds outside under the first faint smudges of starlight. The temperature was not dropping as much as it had done only a few weeks ago at the onset of dusk. Consequently, nights inside the van had become unbearably stuffy.

Chris tucked a flouncy bundle of mosquito netting under an arm and dragged his sagging camp bed onto the open concrete veranda of the bungalow. That afternoon, whilst waiting for us to catch up, he had occupied his time by reading the wildlife section of a travel book I had picked up in New Delhi.

'Guess how many people die from snake bites in India every year,' he asked Baz.

Baz was fumbling in the half-light behind the trailer, cursing the two bent metal rods that held his bed together.

'No idea,' he shouted.

'Ten thousand it said – ten thousand! And then, in the very next line, they try to reassure you not to cancel your trip by adding that on the whole it's quite rare for snakes and humans ever to come into contact.'

Baz stopped trying to fix his bed and looked with longing towards the back of the van. 'Makes it sound like those ten thousand poor fuckers who got bitten went looking for snakes,' he grimaced. 'Just think: suicide by snake bite!'

It was dark when Lea began preparing our meal. Clouds of gnats circled the oil lamp on top of the trailer. Some fell into the vegetable stew.

'The Jains wear masks over their mouths so they don't accidentally swallow anything living,' volunteered Chris from behind the pyramid of mesh that he had hung above his camp bed.

'There'll be nothing left to swallow by the time Kel and I have reached Madras!' grumbled Baz, as he spat something out into the darkness. Then he spluttered and stood up. Blood trickled from his nose. 'Fucking nosebleed now.' He swore and tilted his head back to stem the flow of blood.

The night was still. Our clothes felt sticky and uncomfortable. A pack of jackals were howling in the jungle. Zhenka fidgeted on his bunk inside the back of the van. I sat next to him entering a few comments into our logbook. Beads of sweat dripped onto the pages as I wrote and made the ink run into illegible blotches.

We were up early. There were to be no more late starts. Not if we were to avoid running during the hotter parts of the day. Dawn was the best time of all.

We re-entered the state of Madhya Pradesh between the villages of Gona and Malthon. The area was densely forested and the jungletops cast welcome but deceptive shadows that would intermittently vanish to reveal scattered wheatfields or black boulder-strewn slopes. The road dipped and climbed, dipped and climbed, sometimes towards blinding sunlight, never once towards a cloud.

More truckloads of soldiers overtook us one day and we in turn strode past foot patrols of armed policemen carrying full packs near a bridge over the River Dhasan.

'Word has it that dacoits have been seen nearby,' explained a major between neat shots of whisky from a silver hip flask concealed under his cap.

Many of the villages we came to comprised just a handful of huts that were little more than withered leaf lean-tos. Most of these were unmarked and unnamed on our map.

We continued to stay overnight in the grounds of the various inspection bungalows, rest houses, circuit houses or dak bungalows whenever we could. For two rupees the caretaker, or chowkidar, would usually allow us the use of the bathroom and a small amount of cold water – though acquiring the latter was more time-consuming than simply turning on a tap.

Once, Baz and Chris were led off in the dark to collect water from a well situated near the walls of a small fort. The chowkidar showed them how to use a pulley system that scooped up the water in a loop of bobbing clay pots.

'Trouble was, Kel, after we'd filled them, the fucking buckets went flying when the fruit bats came at us!' Baz looked serious when he told me this. 'You should have seen them. Bloody big wings flapping over the turret walls in the moonlight. I tell you, we were off, water or no water!'

We sat in the dust with our backs resting against the hub-caps of the van's wheels, and shook with laughter.

Drums were beating. We could hear small bells and many voices drifting out of a clearing where a temple must have stood, hidden by the dark.

'While you were away at the well I had my palm read by a woman in the dak bungalow,' I said. 'She told me she could see water; that

I would one day live close to water. Curiously enough, it ties in with an I Ching reading on our wedding night five years ago. Kris Hemensley was there too, you know, the poet who lives in Australia. Friends had come from London. They told us that a throw of the coins had changed the course of their lives forever.'

49

Narsimhapur was what I imagined a Himalayan town to look like. The houses were all two storeys high. Many of them boasted wooden balconies decorated with an intricate fretwork to which several layers of chalky gesso had been applied. The balconies overhung the road. Our stop-start passage beneath them took us through the same unhurried floodtide of lurching cows, smoky two-stroke scooter cabs and ever-questioning pedestrians.

The town stretched for three miles and the district had an abundance of impressive temples. Sandwiched between such places of worship was that mossy residue of the British Empire – the church spire. Close to the outskirts, the jungle had been pruned back to provide space for animals to graze. Thin white cows with enormous eyes nosed aside a tangle of felled branches and nibbled on the yellow grass.

Beyond Narsimhapur the land was less populated and the dense jungle stretched for many miles. One day, shortly after breakfast, Baz tugged at my singlet to indicate something he'd seen on a small patch of ground at the roadside. A crudely hacked slab of stone stood balanced on a wider base littered with offerings from passers-by. We both stopped running and walked over for a closer look.

There was the broken head of a stone god that appeared to have been removed from a temple, a brush without bristles, two horseshoes, a few coins, coconut shells and a crescent-shaped metal charm. Nothing Baz and I had on us seemed remotely fitting to leave behind. Half a toilet roll, however significant to the traveller, could never be considered suitable talismantic material.

When we next slowed to a halt it was to read a simple notice nailed to a tree. For the benefit of any foreigners who could not read the language, two pictures had been painted upon a weather-warped sheet of plywood. The first showed yellow flames licking the trunks of palm tress. The second was an animal bearing the unmistakable markings of a tiger.

There was a violent thunderstorm that night and the extent of the damage caused by the downpour made us realise how impractical it would have been to try to cross India on foot during the monsoon season. Many homes in the villages had been washed away, whilst the wattle and daub walls and woven twig rooftops of those still standing looked in a sorry state.

'The monkeys threw mud at Chrissy when he tried to take their photo,' laughed Zhenka as he wriggled under the van with a spanner in his hand.

The last day of my twenty-eighth year was cool enough for us to cover 44.4 miles – the most I had managed so far. Distant thunder was still rolling on the morning of my birthday. We celebrated with pancakes tossed into a grey overcast sky, and then set off for the town of Lakhnadon. Light gusts of wind lifted the damp foliage overhead as we ran. The breeze grew stronger as the day unfolded until it blew the narrow boat-shaped leaves down into the wet grass beside the road, and slowly cleared the sky of clouds.

By noon, Lea and Chris were sunbathing. They had driven on ahead some two miles and parked within sight of a narrow bridge. Chris was lying on top of the trailer. Lea had climbed onto the roof rack to sprawl across two foam cushions.

The men who silently rolled the boulders into the road ahead went unnoticed. Their intentions, most probably, were to force Chris and Lea out of the vehicle to remove the barrier. At that point they would attack – assuming there were no more than two people touring with a small child.

The plan backfired when Baz and I strode around the bend, so the dacoits chose more devious tactics. At first they pretended to be roadmenders and told us the bridge was unsafe. Then they actually helped us to remove the stones. But when we looked up we realised that a second barricade blocked our exit on the other side. We were trapped!

'This is serious,' I said, stating the obvious as I turned to the spot where I had last seen Baz.

But Baz had gone. He was already halfway across the bridge, running as if his feet were on fire.

I flung myself after him and heard the van crunch into gear

behind me. I leaned forward and concentrated on not letting my head tilt back – 'That way you don't tense up,' H had instructed years back. And I wondered now, in hysterical flashback, if my old coach had ever been chased down the road by a gang of bandits armed with axes.

'Don't look back either – the chasing group will think you're afraid of them,' was another choice understatement of his.

I didn't look back, though I doubt if this fooled them into thinking they'd all get a real pasting if they came any closer.

Baz had succeeded in rolling one stone aside before I caught up with him. Together we hauled and pushed a further two out of the path of the van, leaving just enough room for Chris to drive through.

Baz took one quick look back.

'They're coming after us!' he screamed.

Out of the corner of my eye I could see other men running along dirt paths between the tree trunks on our side of the river.

We sprinted for as long as we could, neck and neck along the narrow road. When the pain forced us to slow down we only eased up gradually and even then we still ran strongly.

Baz unclenched his fists. His fingers were bleeding from where he had yanked the rocks out of the way.

'Were any of them carrying guns?' I gasped. 'Perhaps we shouldn't be running side by side.'

'I don't think so,' panted Baz. 'I didn't see any. Besides, they wouldn't shoot us, we're tourists.'

That statement shocked me. Baz loathed tourists. I never thought I would hear him admit to being one. He was obviously too shaken up to think properly and was clutching at straws now.

'They did have knives though,' I told him, 'and axes too!'

'They weren't knives, Kel, they were fucking great machetes! We could easily have been hacked to pieces back there.'

50

We entered Seoni in twilight, at walking pace. We were tired out. Flashes of lightning lit up the narrow streets. Elephants shook their dusty ears like dark cloaks with each clap of thunder. And the fruit bats flew closer and closer, causing us to duck our heads and race for cover.

On the way into town the rain had flooded the roads and washed away the banks of the lakes and rivers, making the nets of the fishermen heavy with mud as they hauled their catches ashore.

Earlier still, when the sun had momentarily broken through the clouds and the grass was steaming, a cyclist had approached us, pedalling from the jungle with a small sack dangling from the handlebars of his maroon bicycle.

The man stopped pedalling when he saw our van and freewheeled to a halt alongside the trailer. Quickly, he fished a red-lined notebook out of his sack and thumbed back the wavy pages until he found what he was looking for. Then he handed over a letter protected by a plastic cover and printed out in several different languages:

'Shri Mahadeo Maruti Thakar is a mill hand, working in Narsinggiraji Mills at Sholapur in Maharashtra. He has a hobby of cycling. He is in the habit of making journey on bicycle for long distances, to visit holy places and take Darhsana. He recently makes a journey of 4,600 miles in 40 days, from Sholapur to Sorati Samnath. He now desires to visit Nepal soon.'

One by one, we all signed our names in his notebook and told him about our journey as best we could. When Chris asked if he would pose beside his bicycle for a photograph he first entertained us with a little dance – swivelling across the muddy road in a pair of down-at-heel trainers.

We changed states, leaving Madhya Pradesh for Maharashtra, and the weather stayed mixed all the way to Nagpur.

Once, we waited inside the musty porch of a boarded-up church as a frightening storm broke overhead. At the height of the downpour a wizened old man came slowly walking along the road, dragging a wooden stool through the puddles. He set down the stool at the foot of the church tower, then balanced on it to grab a red and white bell rope, giving a mighty tug as though he were trying to haul himself to heaven. Rainwater tumbled over the rusted guttering and muffled the sound of the clanking bell, but the noise still sent the birds flying from their damp nests under the eaves and out in a circle over the jungle.

At Kamptee the sun came out. Children were playing chasing games on dirt piles beneath dripping lengths of bright blue and green dyed cotton, hastily strung up to dry. Cardboard cots were swinging in the doorways of huts and the yells of babies waiting to be fed rose above the clatter of power looms on each side of the street.

A truck overturned as we ran into Nagpur. There were piercing screams, a terrific crash and thick clouds of dust. Two women who had been perched on top lay in a crumpled heap. Later, we read in the newspaper that the driver had swerved to avoid a madman who was happily squatting in the middle of the road. Three people had been killed in the accident.

We spent three nights in Nagpur: two of them in the noisy car park of the city's public rest house, and the third at the bungalow of an English mining engineer.

Howard Dudley came from the West Country.

'I go home for good next year,' he mused. 'I'm retiring. Can't go on forever, but the thought of it scares me to death.'

He pushed a photograph at me. A blurred snapshot taken by a cabin mate to commemorate their first overseas posting. Howard had a big, generous face that had been pink when his ship docked in Bombay thirty-nine years earlier. The picture showed him stepping ashore wearing starched khaki shorts and carrying a selection of brass-hinged measuring apparatus across his shoulders.

I could recognise him still. The tousled hair had gone and he was plumper now, but there was no mistaking him.

'Back home,' he paused, 'they use handsome to describe almost anything.'

Howard had been brought up in a close-knit tin mining community and did not relish the thought of going back. Whenever he referred to his birthplace it was as if he were trying to describe some mythical place that had never really existed. A land of half-crowns and halfpennies to which there was no return.

'I'm not fool enough to think it won't be a struggle – without servants I mean. But at least I don't have to do any cooking. I'm married, you see, so that's all attended to. My wife lives in Cornwall still. The company I work for allows me generous leave, but whenever I'm over there I can't wait to get back here. The wife thinks I'm mad. She hates it. Hates it she does. Prefers to do her own cleaning and would do next-door's too rather than live in India.'

Howard signalled for tea to be brought out. We were sitting at a table on his lawn with a splendid neem tree for shade.

Before we left he spread the skin of a panther across the grass and Zhenka squeezed his toes inside the animal's mouth and waved a toy rifle.

'My friend shot this panther while it was lying asleep under a tree. But Carlo had no hunting permit so I ended up with him.' Howard looked down into the viewfinder of his old box camera. 'Just think son, when you grow up you can come back and go hunting for real!'

Zhenka shook his head and pulled his foot out of the dead panther's mouth. He wanted to be off.

51

The squat trees along the road out of Nagpur were full of red blossom and birdsong. But the temperature had shot up and the air was badly polluted by cheap petrol and fumes from the twin smokestacks belonging to the Kanwan ferro-magnese plant. Breathing in was like chewing rust.

'I'm trying not to swallow too much,' gulped Baz, wiping his cracked lips with the back of his hand. 'When I do, the roof of my mouth feels as tacky as a fly-strip. And it tastes fuckin' awful!'

'Howard reckoned it would top a hundred before the week was out,' I said.

Because it was so hot we did more walking than running. I put on my bush hat with the cotton flap that covered the back of my neck. Baz wore his butcher's cap. We dipped our hats into the rivers or the water tanks whenever we came across them. Then we scrunched them up over our heads and let the water trickle down our faces as we walked.

All we seemed to talk about were milkshakes and beer. I told Baz about my favourite deli in the Melbourne suburb of South Yarra, where I moved to when I left Percy Cerutty's camp at Portsea. It was run by a Greek family and I would stop by each morning on my way to work and buy a pint of chocolate-flavoured milk to swig as I walked between the sprinklers across the grass flanking the tan horse riding-track outside the botanical gardens.

'I never tasted any milkshake to match those we had a few days ago at the Sheri Punjab Restaurant.' Baz swallowed hard, even though he meant not to.

A good-natured mob of youngsters had surrounded the van one evening on our way from the rest house to Howard's bungalow. Someone had a message for us but had been hard pressed to deliver it.

'There are two letters for Mr Kelvin Bowers awaiting collection at the Sheri Punjab Restaurant. Please to follow me.' The voice had bellowed out above the usual hubbub, and somehow Baz had spotted the messenger.

When he knew we had seen him, the cyclist had pedalled off down the unlit back streets that led to the old part of the city. Chris had driven after him, doing well to keep up along the narrow cobbled lanes. When the road became too narrow we had followed on foot until we found the bicycle propped up outside a restaurant that looked more like a milk bar.

The restaurant turned out to be the headquarters of the Sheri Punjab Cross-Country Club. Its owner, a seven-foot-tall Sikh, turned out to be club president. He had appeared in the doorway like some apparition in the desert, balancing a tray of ice-cold milkshakes on one hand.

'Lea didn't fancy hers and thought it safer if Zhen left his too,' chuckled Baz, 'so I scoffed the lot. Wonderful they were. Best fuckin' milkshakes I've ever had in my life!'

'It was all down to Ranjit,' I laughed. 'He'd been in touch as usual. Though it beats me how they found us.'

We ran on. And it grew hotter.

'Blowtorch weather this,' said Baz. 'Think of something cold!'

And so I thought of ice exploding into cracks beneath the feet of Eskimos. But Baz interrupted my thoughts.

'I remember wanting a piss during a school cross-country run one winter,' he told me. 'I was crying from the cold when I fished out my dick. It was shrivelled to buggery and the piss squirted all over my shorts. When I got inside the changing rooms after the run, my fingers were too numb to button my fly. The PE teacher, the smug bastard, was prancing about in his fleecy lined tracksuit. "What's the matter Bowler?" he says. "Jack Frost bitten yer willy?"'

We were both in an argumentative mood when we reached the van.

'Why on earth didn't he park in the shade?' I asked Baz. 'There's a bloody big tree not ten yards away.'

Chris was slumped in a bunk.

'What's the matter with him?' I asked Lea.

'He's feeling rough. A headache came on yesterday.'

'Well, lying in this bloody oven's not going to help much, is it?'

52

One week's running separated us from Hyderabad: our next mail pick-up point. The expectation of news from home, snippets of gossip sealed inside folded blue aerogrammes delivered to tumbledown post offices all over the globe – this was the carrot dangled before us under an Indian sun.

I had put seven thousand miles behind me by now. But our journey was about to be jeopardised from an entirely unexpected quarter.

Chris's day-long headaches did not go away. In fact, they grew worse. At first he attributed them to the increased glare of the sun through the windscreen and spent more and more of his time lying in the back of the van.

After one long stint on the road, we arrived to find Lea looking worried. There was a copy of the *Traveller's Health Guide* on the seat beside her. And a thermometer.

'His temperature's a hundred and two,' she said. 'It could be any one of a number of things, but Chris has taken the same precautions as the rest of us. He's had all the vaccinations. I can't understand it.'

It was March. Hot days followed one after the other with no let-up. Chris's headaches grew less persistent, however, and we all heaved a sigh of relief.

One afternoon, Baz and I walked into a town called Pandharkawada, and went looking for drinks. The only shopkeeper in sight was fumbling with a brass padlock at the doorway to his shop.

'Kabaddi! Kabaddi!' he offered in a rush by way of an apology while he shooed us away.

Kabaddi is a popular Indian sport and the local championships were entering their final phase that very afternoon. Consequently, most of the small town had gathered to watch at a court across the road from the rest house where Chris had parked.

For once Lea had no crowds to contend with. No questions to answer, no helping hands that mostly got in the way during mealtime preparations. By the time we had eaten, the floodlights had been switched on to illuminate the court, and the loudspeaker announcements sounded loud and hysterical. Intrigued, we sidled over to watch and were given front row seats beside the mayor.

Kabaddi used to be called Hu-Tu-Tu, a name which Zhenka found instantly preferable and one which he delighted in reciting for the remainder of the night. The rules seemed complicated. Sensing our bewilderment, one of the organisers gave a rapid explanation while we watched.

'You have two teams. Each team made up of seven players who attack and defend within the marked area. You are following?'

I nodded.

'The server of one team must cross into the opponent's half, where, as in the game of tag, he must touch one of the opposing players without being trapped and lifted from the ground by the rest of them. You are following?'

I nodded again and hid my blank look behind a pair of sunglasses.

'Which team do you support?' I asked politely.

The man indicated a marked preference for the team wearing dark shorts. Whenever he leapt to his feet and cheered, or hung his head in exasperation, so did I. When the final whistle blew I threw my arms in the air and congratulated my fellow supporter with a hearty slap on the back. Minutes later, I watched horrified as the wrong team climbed a little rostrum to receive the cup.

'We are losing it,' the man next to me explained. 'Badly! Didn't you know?' Then he moved away furtively and sat somewhere else.

Following the fast-moving Kabaddi championships, Zhenka felt bored with his life in the van. Bored that is, until he discovered the old steam traction engines which stood parked or abandoned outside most of the rest houses in the area. The first two models he found had been built in Yorkshire in the 1920s and they were still in good working order.

Soon, the search for the great rusting giants became a regular treat which Zhenka eagerly looked forward to each afternoon. Once the van was sorted, Chris would help him scramble up into the shaded open cabs, where he'd turn wheels and pull levers amongst the cobwebs and weeds. If the enormous wheels were not too hot, Chris would perch on them himself and pay his driver pebbles to make trips back to England or on to Australia.

Zhenka made pretend engine noises or puffed out his chest and shouted 'Tu-Hu-Hu!' Sometimes I heard him as we approached.

We entered a new state, crossing into Andhra Pradesh over the Penganga River. The road cut through fields of hacked sugar cane stumps whose dried leaves were stacked about the flat landscape like grim funeral pyres.

Many drums were beating on the road to Adilabad, filling the blank spaces on our map with unnamed villages that we rarely caught sight of and never once passed through. Old men at the roadside sheltered beneath large dusty brollies and stretched out their wrinkled necks, like tortoises, to stare up as we ran past. Farmers covered their oxen with blankets and sensibly drew our attention to the sun.

Once or twice, whilst we were reduced to walking pace, several ox carts wobbled by along the pitted road. Small bells jingled from leather collars attached to the yokes across their necks. We looked up from the books we were reading. Baz bent back a corner of *Seven Years in Tibet* and folded the covers shut. I kept my page with my finger. The book was a slim paperback by Malcom Lowry, *Ultramarine*. Most of the carts carried bales of cotton piled high and swaying. Some rumbled by loaded with families. The people on the carts stared down at us and then they began to remonstrate with their drivers for not stopping in the shadows of the trees when they had the chance to.

We saw more monkeys in the Satmala Ranges. If we left the road to relieve ourselves we would send them into a leaf-scattering stampede amongst the trees.

In the hills it was cooler. But the hilly region did not last for long. On the plain below, there were paddyfields and groves of palm trees. In the far, far distance, waterwheels that looked no bigger than delicate stick insects somersaulted out of view in the turquoise haze.

Gigantic grey boulders and sharp pointed rocks dwarfed the town of Nirmal. Small forts, half ruined, crowned the heights. A cockfight was taking place in the middle of a narrow street. Feathers flew in the dust scuffed up by the crowds of people who were watching. Our arrival reduced the number of spectators by at least half as they chased after us instead.

The lake at Nirmal smelled of oceans. When Baz drew up a bucket from a well in the grounds of an inspection bungalow there, the water from its brim tasted as salty as the sea.

Borne by the hot breeze, masses of dragonflies floated across our path over the black sticky tarmac for two days or more. We watched the dragonflies drift across the River Godavari, one of the holiest rivers on the high Deccan Plateau, then crossed it ourselves over a long bridge constructed from big blocks of masonry.

Upstream from the bridge, an important earth dam formed part of a vast drought relief programme. The land badly needed something to revive it. Even the black boulders and weird-shaped hills looked as if they had been left in the oven too long.

Beyond the dark humps of the big boulders we came to large stretches of red sandstone and found ourselves crossing a desert dotted with hundreds of palm trees. After a time, acres of Day-Glo rice shoots spilled lime green onto the red plain where the road swung into Kamareddi. Here, we met a blond boy doing wheelies on a bright red bike.

'Come and meet my dad,' he said.

Tom Garrett was dressed in frayed denim shorts that had been jeans before his sharp knees started to poke through. There was a make-do-and-mend feel about the man that was refreshing and it extended to his whole family. The Garretts numbered nine in all. The youngest was a little girl of six, and the eldest a boy of seventeen.

'Tom,' he muttered, chewing on a yellow pencil in the corner of his mouth while he extended his one free hand for me to shake.

'Your son insisted we pay you a visit,' I explained, 'but we've obviously chosen a bad time.' I motioned towards the group of men behind him who were busy clamping together several long steel poles.

'Naw.' He waved a sheaf of drawings at the men and told them to come back after lunch. 'Busy or not, always find time for folk passin' through. Wife'd slay me if I didn't. Besides, it's good for the kids. They just love meeting new people. Get it from their mom, I guess. Most sociable sort in the whole of Michigan!'

Tom led us along a dirt lane to the house they were renting, whilst his son rode ahead demonstrating bike tricks for Zhenka.

The Garretts had come to India for three months to build a windmill in a village situated eleven miles away.

'It all started when I met an Indian missionary who was over in the States looking into the construction of homemade windmills,' he said. 'Now I'm no big fan of religion, but this guy was going for it some, and his belief in how much better life would be for a whole village with just a minimum investment sort of took a hold of me. So, I bought me a *Whole Earth Catalogue* and *The Handbook of Homemade Power*. Next thing you know, Marlene tugs open the blinds one morning and there's a twenty-foot-high windmill in the backyard.

'Neighbours had a dicky-fit mind you. Threatened all sorts, but in the end they raised enough dollars to pay for the whole shebang. Flights included. The lot. Well, that's Detroit for you!

'Marlene took less convincing than I did. She cancelled the milk and loaded a suitcase full of Kool Aid before she'd even looked at the map. Boy did she get a shock though when the plane touched down at Bombay. Mary, that's the little one – well, she went missing straight off.

''Course, we ran screaming to the police. God almighty, did we kick some butts. Found her though, curled up a-snorin' behind a hold-all in the middle of all our baggage. Baggage! That's some understatement. Only reason we left the kitchen sink behind was because it wasn't big enough.' Tom's eyes sparkled. He could hardly believe it himself. He was just telling it the way it was.

Mrs Garrett hugged everyone and begged us to stay put with

them 'just one day'. To lend weight to her argument she pointed a podgy finger at Chris.

'That lad looks drained now. You boys can go running out and back a little ways, but I think a day's rest in a cool room would do him a power of good. Don't you Tom?'

Tom handed us beers from a crotchety fridge and searched for a bottle-opener amongst the debris on the kitchen table. The beers were cold. We gulped them down fast, and all our resolve to notch up more miles despite the heat disappeared along with the liquid.

The next morning, while Baz and I set off running, Chris stayed behind in bed. Mrs Garrett said she would help us to stock up with vegetables. She and Lea went shopping in the village. Zhenka stayed behind to play in the garden with Mary.

In the evening, because the air felt clammy, everyone decided to go swimming. We trooped back into the village and out across the other side along winding paths between the boulders and the bushes. The reservoir looked muddy but that didn't deter the Garretts.

'Everyone bathes on this side,' Mary told us, 'and the far end is for washing your clothes.'

The children ran laughing and splashing into the muddy pool and Lea and Mrs Garrett waded in after them.

Clouds were rolling with a distant sound of thunder and a hot wind plucked the dark water into waves. Zhenka stood beside me on the bank and patted the mud pies he'd made with a spade as we watched the lightning flash for a long time across a line of faraway hills.

The path back skirted paddyfields and we squelched home barefoot in the dark, while the frogs croaked and the thunder rumbled closer. No one had taken towels with them but everyone had dried off in the heat by the time we reached the house.

Mrs Garrett cooked tuna fritters – Tom's favourite. When Tom returned late from working on the windmill he told us that the villagers had just killed a cobra.

'They rooted it out with sticks,' he told Mary, who squirmed around in her chair while Zhenka wrinkled up his nose. 'Just you watch out. There'll be more of them now that it's getting warmer. Fine time for the legs of your campbed to snap, eh Bazza?'

Tom pushed back his thick black hair and picked up the bottle-opener. 'Now where did I put that darn refrigerator?'

54

The storm returned on the day we said goodbye to the Garretts. Slabs of stone, flat as tabletops, glistened in the fields on each side of the road. The falling rain felt warm on our shoulders. It quickly flooded the uncambered road, and for a short spell we enjoyed splashing through the puddles. Soon though, the fields were under water and so we sheltered inside the van.

When the storm was over and the dry scrubland had sucked up most of the surface water until only steam remained, we began to run again. We ran through paddyfields and an unexpected forest of trees with narrow grey trunks that looked as fragile as wisps of smoke.

'Did you see the steam train back there?' cried Baz, soon after we had rejoined the others. 'It was green and black with windshields.'

Zhenka looked glum and handed him a sketchpad. 'I didn't see it Barry. Can you draw one for me?'

'And the plovers too. Did you hear them? They were going mad.'

Zhenka shook his head. He had also missed the plovers.

'I saw the blossoms though,' he said. 'Pink, orange and white. Lots and lots and lots. Your elbows are lumpy Barry, where the mozzies have sucked your blood.'

'Last night Zhen, I counted twenty bites after eight months without a single one.'

Zhenka looked alarmed. It was hard to imagine there still being any blood left inside Baz.

'Mum says this trip is falling apart,' he confided. 'The 'mometer in Chris's mouth is boiling!'

We ate coconut, melons, bananas and mandarins. Then we went back out onto the road and ran again in the heat until we were both dizzy with hunger.

It was early in the morning when we came to Hyderabad. Sugar cane was being harvested in the fields on the outskirts while the sun was low and not yet fierce. The neat stacks of lopped cane were covered with yellow straw and their long soft shadows crept over the stubble to pinpoint the passing season like a sundial.

Mist hung in white snatches above the Hussain Sagar Lake, but the ragged clouds were lifting and we could see the vapour trails of two jets reflected in the blue water as we ran towards the city.

There was no one to meet us at the state capital's athletics stadium and all the envelopes bearing our names had either been opened or sent back to England. Anxious to find a doctor or a hospital where Chris could receive attention, I asked to see the President of the Sports' Council.

He emerged from behind a closed door, wrapped in a towel and playing a violin. 'Because there is so much that must be attended to, I am having the massage and the music lesson both at the same time. Now I am told that I should be welcoming you also. These are impossibilities that you are asking.'

The greasy man in the towel wobbled his head. The rolls of flesh around his waist wobbled too. He suggested we try the fever hospital first. It did not sound very reassuring.

The busy streets in Hyderabad were full of Morris 8s and Standard 10s. When Chris parked the van outside a bookshop and asked directions to the hospital, the owners of the property, who lived next door, offered to let us camp in their adjoining backyard.

At the Hospital for Infectious Diseases, Chris was examined by a doctor who took a blood sample. In a different part of the building, Lea, Zhenka and myself updated our cholera vaccinations.

I sat down next to a small boy from New Zealand as the needle was plopped into a vat of boiling water.

The lad looked at us incredulously.

'Don't say you didn't bring your own syringe?' he asked. 'My dad wouldn't go anywhere without our own syringes. He says you're asking for trouble if you don't bring them along with you. I mean to say, just look at this place. This is Filth City with a capital F!'

'New Zealand must be spotless,' I ventured.

'Oh it is. My dad says it's about the cleanest place there is. That's why they brought me into the world there!'

'I hope they didn't get dirty doing it,' Lea whispered in my ear as she struggled to keep a straight face.

I looked towards Zhenka. His lip had taken a downward turn and was quivering.

In the meantime, there was a muffled thud, and I swung around in my seat. The pristine little Kiwi had keeled over. Fainted with a capital F, and now the nurse was stooping over him on the grubby floor.

55

The bookshop was in a busy district known as the Gun Foundry, halfway down a hill on the main road to the city centre. The shop shared a dusty yard with the adjoining building and both were enclosed within a high red brick wall. Next door was the Ashoka Talkies Picture Palace.

Chris parked our van close to the wall in a quiet corner of the yard. Then he went out to find an auto-rickshaw – 'rockets' we called them – to take him back to the hospital for the results of his blood test.

When he returned he was beaming.

'Malaria, they reckon it was. But there are no traces now. I just feel weak still, from the after-effects I suppose. Anyway, that's a relief, isn't it?'

In the evening we decided to eat out at a place we had seen around the corner, the Blue Diamond Chinese Restaurant. At the last minute Chris said he had better stay behind and catch up on some overdue letters.

'I want to let my mother know I'm back on my feet again,' he told us.

Two hours later, when we pulled back the big wooden gates to the yard, the Ashoka Talkies had just started up and a neon sign dangling from a side wall of the cinema bathed the van in a harsh blue light.

Baz shielded his eyes from the glare and rushed across the yard.

'What does he think he's up to?' he shouted. 'He's left all the bloody doors open!'

The van was empty.

Overhead, the frenetic soundtrack of a Bollywood film thundered from a shaky speaker bolted to a corner of the Picture Palace.

'Where the fuck is he?' mimed Baz.

Across the yard, a door opened and a beam of light fell on the stone columns and the wide stone steps leading up to the house. The woman who had told us we could stay hurried outside.

'Christopher is collapsing,' she said. 'He is inside, and we are sending for a doctor.'

We followed the woman back up the steps into a hallway and along a corridor. She placed a hand on an ivory doorknob, then hesitated.

'Inside, you will meet my mother-in-law, Mrs Mistry.'

Behind us, a high-pitched nasal voice began a long drawn-out wail to emphasise some dramatic development in the Ashoka Talkies film showing next door. The sound filtered down the corridor even after the front door was slammed shut.

We braced ourselves and shuffled into the room one by one. Chris was wearing a pair of blue and white striped pyjamas that I couldn't remember having seen before. He was stretched out on top of a vast double bed under a soft canopy of white mosquito netting that hung in folds all around him.

The Picture Palace badly drained the power supply in the immediate vicinity, dimming the room's single low watt electric lightbulb until it was scarcely brighter than a candle flame.

I stared at the fine cotton mesh draped over the bed. It reminded me of the cobwebs covering Miss Havisham's wedding cake.

In the darkest corner of the room sat a robust-looking Indian lady, whose long grey hair had been brushed back so frequently as to leave her severe eyebrows permanently raised. The pained expression on Mrs Mistry's face had nothing to do with Chris's predicament. Photographs, hanging askew in the half-lit room, indicated she had looked as sour since birth.

Mrs Mistry pointed to Chris. 'Your friend is unwell but I have sent someone out for a doctor.'

She glanced up at the ceiling where the blades belonging to a motionless fan hovered over us like the propeller of a grounded bomber.

'As soon as the film is finishing, the fan can be turning. He is very hot, your friend. But we must be patient.' Mrs Mistry wobbled her head to herself in agreement, and continued. 'He can remain here. It is the coolest room in my house. And the rest of you can stay in the yard outside.'

Chris wearily flung an arm across the coverlet, opened his eyes, and blinked at us through the mosquito net. 'I remember feeling dizzy,' he muttered. 'Then I rolled off the bunk and hit my head on the medical chest.'

The doctor looked like Rabindranath Tagore and had a long white beard that hid his stethoscope. After examining Chris, he stressed how high his temperature was and left a pile of cardboard pill boxes on a table beside the bed. Mrs Mistry was given instructions on what should be taken and when. On no account were we to leave until he was feeling much better.

'And he must be eating more too, before you go,' added Mrs Mistry, when she told us what the doctor had said.

The next morning, when I popped my head around the door, the fan was whirring effectively and the room felt cool. Chris was sound asleep. On a tray beside him – under the mosquito net – was a glass of untouched milk and a biscuit from which he had taken one small bite.

The rest of us joined the family for breakfast in a front room overlooking the yard. Vikram, Mrs Mistry's teenage grandson, supervised the servants in her absence and sat beside his father at the head of the table.

'He has Parkinson's disease,' Vikram explained as he tucked a bib under his father's chin and raised a spoon to his mouth.

We ate eggs and chappatis while the daughter-in-law talked to us about the great misfortune of their family.

'My husband, Arnand, had a good job with the bank. He is the manager before this happened to him. Then we used our savings for treatment in America. One day he is to go back there for more treatment.'

After breakfast, Vikram's mother jammed a bundle of rent books into a large leather bag and ran to meet a taxi that drew up outside the gates.

Vikram followed us outside. It was sweltering in the stony yard. Now that we were unable to run, we couldn't decide what else to do. Finally, Baz made up his mind to visit the Salar Jang Museum, a short ride away.

'When we stayed at Howard's, he told me it compared favourably with the Victoria and Albert, in London,' Baz said, before climbing into a 'rocket' at the entrance to the yard.

Lea and I spent the rest of the morning cleaning out the van. In the afternoon I sat with Chris, glad to avoid the heat. He was still not eating and asked me in a whisper to smuggle out what he had left.

'Can't face these,' he said, furtively producing three sticky buns from under the netting. 'But I could murder a Pepsi, Kel.' He glanced at the door. 'Don't let Ma Mistry see you bring it in though. It's on the banned list, along with my bloody ciggies!'

In the evening, soon after Baz returned from the museum, Vikram invited us into the house for a mutton curry followed by slices of melon. Baz had only just finished demolishing three tubs of ice cream and several small bananas, but couldn't bring himself to miss out on any meal. Instead, he undid the top two buttons of his trousers and trooped inside behind us.

Mrs Mistry never deigned to join the rest of her family around the dining table. Perhaps the sight of her trembling son being spoon-fed caused too much pain. Her room was at the far end of the dark corridor which divided the house. Sometimes, if the door was ajar, I would catch a glimpse of her – sitting cross-legged on a wicker stool with her back to me – praying for all she was worth.

She prayed mostly for her son, of course, and now there was Chris to pray for too. But it was during a time when rice was being rationed and she also prayed for an end to that.

A few days later, Chris felt recovered enough to sneak out from under the mosquito net and join me in a grubby back street café close by. The café was next to a corrugated shed where the cycle-rickshaw wallahs took their bikes to be mended. Several young employees sat on the pavement pumping up flat tyres and joking with the boot-polishers across the street.

Inside the café we chose a table well away from the window and unfolded our map of India. Chris rolled a cold bottle of Pepsi slowly back and forth across his forehead, and sighed.

'You've no idea how good that feels.'

We'd come to the café to fix a date for moving on – out of earshot of Mrs Mistry – and it felt as if we were part of an escape committee hatching plans to tunnel free from Colditz.

'I know my temperature's not as high,' said Chris, 'but I'm suffering serious post-chappati-hoarding stress and if I see one more sticky jam bun I'm liable to throw myself under a double-decker!'

'There's just over a fortnight before our ship sails from Madras,' I told him.

'How far is it?'

'Four hundred and thirty-seven miles.'

'Shit, that's cutting it fine.'

I nodded. 'Even if you were up to it – which you're not – and we left tomorrow, it would still be touch and go in this heat.'

I looked down at the map. 'Baz has ringed a place on the coast called Bandar Fort, near Masulipatam. He says it's only two hundred and twenty-one miles away and once we've reached the Bay of Bengal, then we'll have crossed India on foot. So we can drive the rest of the way along the coast road to Madras.'

We ordered two more Pepsis, then set off back.

A formidable shape in a crimson sari sat with her knees apart on the steps inside the yard. The old woman was waiting for us and she was spitting dust. It had been a black day at Gun Foundry and she was lucky to still be alive.

Vikram had been aiming his air pistol at the lizards on the brick wall outside. Growing tired of this, he and Zhenka had then taken the pistol indoors. Somehow the gun went off in the corridor and a pellet had narrowly missed the grandmother as she bent down to pray.

56

It was four in the morning when Chris slid back the bolts on the front door. He had taken off his flip-flops because they made a slapping noise on the tiled floor of the corridor. Barefoot now, and still wearing the blue and white striped pyjamas Mrs Mistry had found for him, he eased open the door and crept outside.

Lea and Zhenka were still asleep in the back of the van. Baz and I had already swung open the big gates to the yard. As soon as Chris put on a pair of shoes and climbed into the driver's seat, we jogged out into the deserted main road and ran down the hill.

It was still dark. The streets looked wide and unfamiliar because they were empty. A group of bicycle-rickshaw wallahs were sleeping in a row under an iron railway bridge at the foot of the hill. Each lay across the padded back seat of their bikes with their skinny legs draped over the handlebars.

'This reminds me of the last time we set out so early,' said Baz. 'Remember, in Istanbul? After I'd flown out to join you.'

'Yeah, we tried to beat the crowds of people rushing to work, down at the waterfront, and those soldiers thought we were nuts racing past them on that big bridge over the Bosphorus.'

'It seems a long time ago now,' Baz reflected. 'Who'd have thought that we'd end up running away from some well-meaning granny in the depths of India.'

'Did you see Chris's face?' I asked.

'He looked so desperate, Kel,' chuckled Baz. 'Like Steve McQueen in *The Great Escape*!'

'I hope we're doing the right thing by pushing on. But if we stay we'll miss the boat. It's as simple as that. We just have to put our faith in Ma Mistry's prayers!'

The twin beams from the van's headlamps rose and fell as the vehicle bounced over a pot-holed section of the road. Ahead, the sky was growing pink. A few youngsters were trundling heavy carts towards us or operating the steel levers of a complicated mechanism used to extract juice from the sugar cane.

We stopped for breakfast beside a vineyard owned by a man named

Krishna. A line of grape pickers were slowly moving between the rows of vines, rattling tin cans full of stones to scare away the birds. Lea found an empty can for Zhenka and he piled it full of pebbles he had collected along the way, and then joined in to make as much noise as he could.

Afterwards Krishna brought out cold beers and orange juice and had it not been for us worrying about missing our sailing date, we would have accepted his invitation to stay. Instead, we pushed on.

A grassy path helped to loosen our stiff legs after the enforced lay-off in Hyderabad. But there was virtually no breeze to cool us, and the wide leaves of the palm trees hung limp under a hot sun. The greater the distance we put between Ma Mistry and ourselves, the wilder the landscape got. When the grass path became overgrown with thorn bushes and cactus plants we swung back onto the hard surface of the road.

The route to the coast cleaved through a stunning valley of palm trees and boulders. Toddy collectors wearing loincloths shinned up the tall trunks as fast as monkeys to retrieve the small clay bowls of sap.

Halfway through the valley we met a tall man who told us that he taught PE at a village school over the next rise. He waved to one of the men climbing a tree. Then he pulled out a bottle from the saddlebag of his bicycle and said that it was coconut toddy and that we should try it.

'This is doing you the good of ten elephants,' he boasted as he removed the cork with his teeth. 'But you had better be finishing it – half each, in one go. Otherwise I am thinking this bottle will explode!'

Baz wiped the neck of the bottle with his vest and stared at the cloudy liquid inside. A few of the toddy collectors slid down the trunks they were climbing and crossed the road to watch.

'You first,' I said, when Baz offered me the bottle.

He shut his eyes and gulped greedily once or twice, before taking a longer swig. Then he opened one eye to see how much was left and pushed the bottle into my hand.

I drank the toddy slowly, keeping the bottle up to my mouth

until it was empty, and I spat out the sediment that had gathered at the bottom. It did not taste as fiery as I had expected it to. Nor did it taste of coconut.

The men looked at us admiringly. The PE teacher gently slapped us both on the back. If we could down coconut toddy in one go, then we were true athletes.

There remained only one question now. Could we continue running in a straight line?

Straight or not we made it through the valley, and across a scrub-covered plain dwarfed by granite ridges. When we came to the next village we stopped at a water pump to refresh ourselves. Baz pushed the long wooden handle up and down vigorously, whilst I sat underneath a spray of warm water. Then we changed places.

By the end of the day Baz was feeling unwell. His nose started to bleed on the last stretch and when he tilted back his head to stem the flow of blood, he tripped over a stone and gashed his knee.

Come nightfall Baz was also suffering from a prickly heat rash between his legs. The nights felt sticky and uncomfortable now. Even outside on a camp bed under the stars there was no guarantee of a decent night's sleep. Baz tossed and turned. And when at last he did drop off to sleep, it was only to be abruptly shaken awake by Chris, who had seen rats running in and out of the van.

Baz rolled over and buried his head under a pillow.

'Ants, cockroaches, spiders, flies, mosquitoes, crickets and wasps,' he moaned. 'Now rats! Better send for Roy Fowler!'

Chris looked at the moon and lit a cigarette. He slid open the van door at the front and reached inside to switch on the radio. A few short bars of the familiar World Service signature tune woke the rest of us. Then someone with a plummy voice announced that London was covered in snow.

57

Men, women and children from the villages were widening the narrow road between Nakrekal and Suriapet. The sound of pickaxes breaking up boulders rang out across the paddyfields, where a red sun was rising.

We jogged between thatched huts, past a woman grinding spices in a chipped white bowl. Patches of mist strayed about the palm leaves in the treetops like a strange grey fruit, and men descended from them clutching clay pots of sap.

The road was busy. An accident had already happened. Dead cows were being dragged away and splinters of pale blue wood were all that remained of a cart. Close by was a truck, with a caved-in radiator, and the word 'rocket' scrawled across the top of a shattered windscreen.

There was a café on one side of the main street through Suriapet, and a stall selling fruit on the other. Chris and Zhenka went inside the café and waited for us, knowing we were sure to stop. Lea crossed the road and began to haggle over the price of melons with a thin-faced woman at the stall. She was in a bad mood by the time she squeezed past the tables to rejoin the others.

'They think it's their God-given right to rip you off,' she stormed.

Chris looked drained and said nothing. Zhenka made bubbles in his Pepsi by blowing through a soggy straw.

A band of Banjara gypsies reached the café before we did. They danced and sang in the doorway, barricading all exits with their swirling red skirts and ivory-bangled arms and ankles. Tiny mirrors and silver trinkets had been sewn onto their tight-fitting tops and they sparkled in the sunlight like the chandeliers from a doll's house.

When their hands snaked out for payment, Lea jumped to her feet and began to sing to them instead. The gypsies looked astonished. They had come for rupees, not a musical recital. But they smiled anyway, before moving on. Zhenka clapped, and even Chris found sufficient energy to wobble his head in a bemused way before stumbling back to the van.

Every day was hot now, and we lost our tempers more in the heat, both with one another and with those who crowded round us whenever a halt was called.

'Rest house, that's a joke!' shouted Lea one night as she flung a bowl of potato peelings into a circle of staring eyes.

Baz and I spent as much time as we could on the road. We preferred running to the goldfish bowl alternative back at the van. But there was a limit as to how far we could run each day with the temperatures up in the hundreds.

When we had to stop – to eat and sleep – the curiosity of the villagers made us feel uncomfortable. All we craved was a decent wash, but this drew more onlookers than ever – particularly when the rest house bathrooms were locked. Then we had to find a well and heave up buckets of water to empty over our heads.

The village lads opted for less troublesome solutions: racing barefoot over the slippery backs of their half-submerged water buffalo to dive into the muddy pools in which they wallowed. This of course, attracted less attention than we did.

It was harvest time. Oxen, pulling overloaded carts of sugar cane, lurched along the highway night and day in slow-moving convoys. One afternoon, Chris announced that he had packed in smoking. The very next day we came to a plain full of tobacco plantations.

More bands of gypsies were on the move too, making for an annual fair held on the banks of the River Krishna. It was growing dark when we reached the spot. Bolts of silk billowed from the bamboo poles of the stalls as the moon crept up behind. We listened to fortune-tellers, and stood laughing at each other in front of funny mirrors. We saw a wall of death and a blind lion in a flimsy wooden cage who was poked with a pointed stick to make him roar.

A day later, a wagon carrying empty ribcages overtook us at Vijayawada. It swung into a bone yard on the edge of the local cemetery. A wild girl with thick matted hair ran out through the gates of the cemetery to hurl a wooden spear at us. The spear fell short and clattered onto the road, and the girl ran back shrieking, and disappeared amongst the graves.

At Kankipadu, the children jeered as we jogged through their village and Baz got hit by a stone on his ankle.

We were running on empty. And the Indian Ocean? Where on earth was that?

58

'The water tastes saltier than a sumo wrestler's jockstrap, if that's anything to go by.' Baz ditched his drink and slammed the enamel mug back where it belonged.

'We must be close by now,' I said. 'Anyway, I've gone and done a stupid thing, Baz. I've told Zhenka we're off to the seaside today.'

'That's it then. We have to get there. Otherwise there'll be bloody hell to pay.' Baz looked down at Chris. He was lying half out of his sleeping bag on a camp bed that matched our sagging spirits.

'C'mon mate.' He gave him a gentle nudge with his knee. 'Not much further.'

The two of us strolled away from the grounds of the rest house and turned down an empty street that led to the coastal road. It was that magic time of the day when most people are still rubbing the sleep from their eyes and haven't yet picked up anything to throw.

We broke into a hobble that almost became a jog. After a few hundred yards we were jogging. Slowly the tight muscles in our calves began to loosen and our ankle joints grew less stiff. Soon we were very nearly trotting – a comfortable prelude to full out striding. And the road was still empty.

Flocks of egrets were taking off from the paddyfields adjoining the road and water dripped from their big white wings as they flew overhead.

Some of the fields of crops were protected by prickly hedges of cacti, others by scarecrows kitted out in striped pyjamas. A mobile dairyman was making for the village we had just left – pedalling his bicycle erratically and causing the milk to slop out over the tops of the two shiny metal churns fixed to its yellow frame.

The route to the coast took us along the banks of a canal fed by the River Krishna. Mango groves lined the canal and there were flimsy huts that required rebuilding after each monsoon. The women who lived in the huts were standing waist-deep in the water, beating their washing against smooth slabs of stone. A few of them ran for cover in their long underskirts and hid behind the reeds until we had passed.

We came to a sugar factory in a town called Vuyyuru. Carts pulled by oxen were queuing to be unloaded in the shade beside the giant tanks of molasses.

There had been a dispute that morning on the other side of town. Word was spreading fast. Two local policemen had beaten up one of the drivers transporting sugar cane to the factory. Now, his workmates were retaliating and planned to block the road ahead. A bonfire of old truck tyres was already blazing. Heavy cartwheels were being rolled from the blacksmith's and manhandled into position across the tarmac.

Baz and I pressed on. We hoped that Chris was not far behind and that he would manage to drive the van through whatever barrier was in place by the time he arrived.

It was two in the afternoon when he caught up with us at Masulipatam. Puzzling symbols were chalked on the mud doorsteps of the houses as if to ward off evil intruders, and rice paste had been used to daub the shopfronts with strange signs.

Baz and I sat perched on a couple of plastic crates outside a café where men were gossiping about the flare up at the sugar factory. When we asked for drinks, a youngster wielding a machete scalped two coconuts for us and rammed a straw inside each. Chris drove up but left the engine running and stayed behind the wheel.

'Ask them which road leads to the sea,' he shouted across to us.

I finished drinking from my coconut and went back inside the café to look for the lad with the machete. When I found him I placed my palms together and then dipped them forward in front of me in imitation of a dive.

The boy looked blank. But he was good at his job, and he pointed to the machete and patted the top of a coconut.

I shook my head and tried again, this time pawing the air in what I hoped was a passable doggy paddle. Being a non-swimmer, even on dry land, can be a bit of a drawback. But he seemed to understand what I was getting at.

We walked out of the café together and he looked long and hard at the van and its occupants. Then he waved down a boy on a bicycle and asked me to repeat my mime show.

The young cyclist's grin was as wide as a lopped coconut, and his hair was the same colour. When he slid down from the saddle of his bike he was scarcely tall enough to reach the handlebars.

I did the doggy paddle all over again, after first diving in with my palms pressed together. You could almost hear the splash.

The boy looked me up and down. He was no fool and was not going on any mission with a madman. Finally, with a sweeping self-assurance, he tilted his head from side to side.

I studied the wobble. I had crossed India on foot and had seen heads rolling this way and that on every street corner. Now there could be no mistake.

This wobble was affirmative. He knew what we wanted, where it was, and he was willing to take us there for the price of a few coconuts.

The lad on the bicycle led us out of town at a fast lick. Baz reckoned that seven miles would see us at the Bay of Bengal. He said he was going in, 'no messing'. I wished I could take the plunge too, and doggy paddle out until I was as far from the shore as the man on my grandfather's matchbox would have been.

The lane was winding and narrow, and there was no traffic on it. Every half mile or so our coconut-haired escort swivelled his head around and smiled at us. Once, I thought I heard the sound of the sea and I glanced across at Baz. But it was just the side of the van brushing against the tropical bushes that hemmed us in all the way to the coast.

The bushes were too high to see over and too dense to wander in to. The only gap through them lay trapped in the sun like a furnace.

'Any other day we'd be easing up in this heat,' cried Baz.

'We couldn't slow down now, even if we tried,' I told him. 'The mere thought of the Indian Ocean is pulling us along like a magnet.' I thought of Mahatma Gandhi, marching to the sea to break the salt law. It was an afternoon of high emotion and the adrenaline surged inside us like a tidal wave.

Just then, there was a sudden squeal of brakes in front of me, and our tiny guide made an abrupt about-turn.

'No route! No route!' he explained with a shrug before pedalling back down the lane and out of sight.

We stopped running, looked at each other, and then stared down to the spot where the hard surface vanished in a forlorn-looking dribble of melted tar. Where the road came to a full stop, so too did the high barrier of tropical vegetation.

What was left was a view. The first we had seen since leaving Masulipatam. There was a greeny-blue horizon flecked with crashing white lines that wriggled in the heat. It was the Bay of Bengal.

To reach it we had first to cross a vast expanse of slimy brown mudflats.

Baz took a minute or two to make up his mind, then began to untie his shoelaces. I did the same. He stepped out of his trainers, peeled off his socks, and strode to the very edge of the tarmac strip and prodded some big leafy plant with his bare toes.

When there was no squelching noise or rising bubbles in the mud, he turned and gave me a thumbs-up.

'This plant's holding firm,' he said. 'Besides, the sun would dry out the estuary in no time.'

What he said made sense. And the way he said it too – so positive. It reminded me of how we got to know each other in the first place.

Each Sunday, a small group of athletes met up to run from my home in the woods. The run took two hours, sometimes longer. It was the endurance portion of our weekly training and we loved it. One Sunday morning, someone invited Baz along. I had heard his name mentioned by the local athletes but I knew nothing more about him at that time.

It was a hilly course and a hot day. We were bunched together in a group at the halfway mark where there was a wide ford to cross. Everyone else slowed to file across a plank bridge, but Baz ran straight through the water splashing and yahooing. That was how we became friends.

Now I strode past him, just as determined – heading for the Indian Ocean.

The mud came up to my knees. For one terrifying moment I

thought I was going to carry on sinking into it. When I didn't, I should have stayed where I was, but instinct dictated otherwise and as I struggled to lift my foot clear I lost my balance and toppled forward face down.

Baz yanked me out and looked me in the eyes. Or at least where he imagined my eyes might be.

'Fuckin' hell, Kel!' he said, picking up his trainers. 'What the fuck are we doing here?'

59

The drive south along the coastal road to Madras took two days. Baz and I lay on our bunks in the back of the van as it bounced along the pot-holed highway. We were not good passengers. Having moved so slowly for such a long time, even a moderate speed seemed too fast. We buried our heads under the pillows and left it to Chris to get us all to the state capital in one piece.

On arrival in Madras, he drove straight to the British Embassy. Ranjit Bhatia had been in touch. Members of the local running clubs were keen to meet up with us. The secretary of one such club, Tony de Souza, rushed straight over to the embassy as soon as he heard we were in town.

'Call me AJ,' he said. 'Everyone in Tamil Nadu is calling me AJ – look, even on the briefcase.'

AJ asked to use the telephone. He dialled a few different numbers and left the same message each time.

'Ranjit is telling me you are running across the world. So we are welcoming you with our arms opening wide. First stop I am taking you to the Dominic Savio School. The younger pupils are having their holidays and an empty classroom is accommodating you.'

The Catholic school lay just off the South Beach Road, right behind the cathedral of San Thome where the remains of Doubting Thomas are thought to lie. Inside the classroom, the small wooden desks had been stacked together in a corner next to a blackboard on which someone had stuck a page from a newspaper called *The Hindu*.

The newspaper carried a full page spread about marathon running together with a photograph of Baz and myself that had been taken in New Delhi several weeks before. The article focused on the history of the event and the inherent dangers associated with various feats of endurance. It took the form of a discussion between Dr K. Venkateswarlu, a leading research scholar in physical education, and a Dr G. S. Sundarajan who was an authority on sports medicine. There were also photographs of the double Olympic marathon winner Abebe Bikila, and a graphic picture sequence of Jim Peters staggering towards the finishing line in the 1954 Empire Games race at Vancouver.

'I can see you've been busy AJ,' I said, tapping the blackboard.

'Ranjit wrote something for *Athletics Weekly*. I am a subscriber. Here ...' AJ bent down to rest the briefcase on his knee and released the two metal clasps with his thumbs. He dipped his hand inside and handed me a copy of *Athletics Weekly* dated 22 February, 1975. The magazine contained a feature by the sports journalist Cliff Temple headed 'England to Australia – Running!'

Ranjit had written: 'No event in athletics has attracted as much attention in Indian sports circles in recent years as Kelvin Bowers arrival in Delhi after nine and a half months of gruelling running.'

'There is much interest here too, in Madras. We are even staging two special races in your honour over the next few days.'

His hand dipped back inside the briefcase and he pulled out two certificates to show me.

'We are asking for both your signatures on these. They will be awarded to the fifty finishing soonest. Also, Kelvin, I am extending my invitations for Barry and yourself to take part physically – yes.'

'We look forward to it, AJ,' I told him.

AJ moved closer to the blackboard and pointed out the wobbly knees of Jim Peters in the news cutting he'd stuck up. 'This man I am having for my hero since a young boy.' He sighed.

'I wrote to him once,' I said, 'and he wrote back telling me what it had been like training for that marathon in 1954. He said he quit after Vancouver because he was too scared to pack up his job and send his wife Frieda out to work so that he could train full time. They had a mortgage and two kids, and anyway it just wasn't done in those days. On my way to India, I met a Canadian couple who were there in the stadium on that day when he collapsed. They couldn't remember who won the race but they never forgot Jim Peters.'

Later, AJ took us to meet Arnold Satur, whose four daughters were the young starlets of the Don Bosco Athletic Club. Arnold also owned a factory that produced ice.

'You must see the ice house during your stay,' he insisted. 'It has been built on the shore a hundred and fifty years before I am making my factory. Giant blocks of ice were stored there after a journey by sailboat from the lakes of North America.'

'In the days of the Raj it was unthinkable to serve drinks without ice,' added AJ. 'Now we have prohibition there is plenty of ice and no liquor!'

'Well,' Arnold winked, 'perhaps a little can be found, for our visitors.'

The Kelvin Bowers and Barry Bowler 5-Kilometre Beach Race took place on a Saturday morning, at six a.m. to avoid the heat. There were 350 competitors in all and their ages ranged from eight to forty.

Baz and I lined up too.

When the gun went off, there was a mad scramble over the loose sand as everyone made for the edge of the shoreline where the wet surface was firmer. The leading group were too fast for us – skimming over the soft sand in their bare feet before striding out close to the incoming waves.

The marina beach is the second-longest beach in the world. Fishermen were hauling their boats ashore to unload the morning's catch. Once or twice the ropes and nets crossed our path, and when we hurdled them clumsily we lost a few more places.

At the statue of Mahatma Gandhi, each competitor was handed a ticket before turning around to run back. On the return stretch we both made up some ground and Baz eventually stole a lead on me when we hit the deep sand in the finishing straight.

When the race was over, we signed the certificates and presented them to the first ten finishers in each age group. Then AJ handed us a microphone and asked us to describe our journey to India.

On the last day of March, the National Track Club held the Kelvin Bowers and Barry Bowler 5-Kilometre Road Race. This time the early start was at the request of the local police who were anxious to minimise any traffic congestion along the route.

Once again, a monument to a prominent Indian politician played a key role in the race: to signify the starting point on this occasion. It was a flat course from the statue to the sports stadium and the chosen roads were free of traffic. The chief of police had been invited to start the race. He stood on a platform of creaking wooden pallets commandeered from Arnold's ice factory and raised the starting pistol high above his head.

'He looks like some South American revolutionary,' whispered Baz, leaning forward.

When the gun jammed without going off and the fidgeting runners remained where they were, the policeman mopped his brow, then pulled a shiny whistle from the breast pocket of his jacket, and blew as hard as he could.

The shrill whistle sent the faster runners surging down the road. Baz and I were among them, but only just and we were struggling to keep up. At the halfway mark AJ rode alongside on his 350cc Enfield Bullet. The leading group had broken away, but according to him we were catching them fast.

Baz took up the chase first and towed me past three runners wearing the red shorts and yellow singlets of the Don Bosco club. Then, I held back and waited until we turned a corner and I could see the big concrete stands of the stadium rising above the rooftops in the leafy street.

'C'mon Baz,' I panted as I swept past – hoping the sudden change of pace would catch him out.

The race finished with a lap of the cinder track, and the winner was already crossing the line when I ran into the stadium. There were two more runners ahead of me, but not enough distance left in which to catch them. I finished in fourth place and Baz was sixth.

Arnold threw a party after the road race and AJ found enough alcohol to give everyone a sore head the next morning.

It was April Fool's Day, and so no one paid much attention when Chris said we must somehow stow the trailer into the back of the van. But while we'd been at the road race, Chris had been to see the shipping agents.

'It will cost almost twice as much unless we can find a way round it.'

'Will it fit inside?'

'If we take the wheels off it might.'

We spent the rest of the morning rearranging what was already inside the van and taking everything out of the trailer so that we could lift it once the wheels were removed. By lunchtime, we were ready. Taking the wheels off had made a big difference but it was still going to be a tight squeeze.

We waited for AJ to arrive and then, on the count of three, heaved the iron chassis of the trailer up level with the top of the bunks and slid it along inside.

There was half an inch to spare. Chris looked exhausted, but he was jubilant. 'Australia, here we come!' he shouted.

60

The stevedores on the dockside wrapped heavy sacking around the steel chains secured to the underside of the van. Then, a man in charge signalled to the crane operator and the vehicle was gently hoisted out of the shadows and up towards the deck of the *Chidambaram*.

Chris gazed up as the van swung overhead. He felt no better than he had done almost three weeks ago in Hyderabad. But he was looking forward to the sea voyage and the prospect of a decent rest in an air-conditioned cabin. The Satur family had turned up to wave us off and AJ too, with a man who exported hockey sticks riding pillion on his Enfield Bullet.

Zhenka stood in front of the funnel on the top deck with Lea. He was wearing his Don Bosco running kit and holding on to a red and yellow balloon. Suddenly, a loud blast from the ship's hooter made everyone jump. Zhenka's balloon sailed into the air and the *Chidambaram* eased away from the docks.

The Indian women leaning over the ship's rail were tearful. The beginnings of a sea breeze snatched at the hems of their saris as they waved to their relatives. Chris took one last look at India and then went below deck to find the cabin he was to share with Baz.

Two days passed before we next saw him. Baz said that Chris wasn't eating: he'd had nothing at all since the party in Madras, and only a mouthful then. After some persuasion, Chris agreed to see the ship's doctor. He waited for some forty minutes behind a group of Indians who were coughing and sneezing, only to be shown to a barber's chair. Further along the passage the queue for the doctor's surgery stretched halfway around the ship. At least half the *Chidambaram*'s passengers and crew seemed to have acquired ailments in need of urgent medical attention. When Chris finally got to see the doctor he was handed a small bottle of aspirin.

That night I dreamt we were sailing on a vessel carrying a diseased cargo that no port would ever grant us permission to unload.

The crossing to Penang took four and a half days. According to Captain Sujit Choudhuri, the Bay of Bengal had never been calmer.

Which was just as well, for the ship sank in heavy seas a few years later.

On the night the Captain extended an invitation for us to dine at his table, Chris decided to put in an appearance. The first-class dining room was strictly out of bounds for tourist class passengers and the migrant workers, who found themselves permanently segregated in the lower reaches of the ship. This left a select little group who dressed for dinner and met for drinks each evening in the half-empty saloon.

Everyone was seated. A tide of white-topped waiters had just swept in bearing the first course, when a sudden hush stilled the sound of the cutlery and the chatter.

Dressed in a faded green singlet and Ma Mistry's striped pyjamas, a forlorn, half-recognisable figure appeared at the far end of the dining room. Whether Chris had not yet found his sea legs, or the sheer effort in dragging himself up from the cabin had simply proved too exhausting, his entry through the swing doors transfixed the diners.

Adopting a walk not dissimilar to Alec Guinness in *Bridge on the River Kwai*, he threw out first one leg and then the other, and tried to keep up with each as best he could. Had the ship been rolling, perfect balance may still have been arrived at in this manner. But the ocean was as flat as a chappatti. Chris looked around at the staring faces until he spotted us sitting with the Captain. Then began the most unorthodox navigation of the ship's dining room the head waiter had ever witnessed.

Once seated, Chris took one sip of mulligatawny soup and grimaced, his mouth twisted like that of a gargoyle. Fiercely clutching his spoon in one hand and his stomach in the other, he rose to his feet and stumbled towards the nearest exit.

Soon after the ship reached Penang there was a knock on the cabin door. We had last seen Stan Erbrink pedalling his bicycle past the Desert of Death in Afghanistan. Now, the bronzed Dutchman strode inside our cabin and gave us each a warm hug.

'I was here two days before you, after cycling from Bangkok. I couldn't believe it this morning when I took my coffee and read in the newspaper that you were also due to arrive.'

Stan ruffled Zhenka's hair and picked him up. Then we all went ashore and walked through the streets of Georgetown.

'The day after we met,' Stan told us, 'the nomads tried to push me off my bike. They chased me and threw stones when I wouldn't stop. Afterwards, I thought about you guys and wondered what would happen when they saw you approaching on foot.'

'They chased after us too,' I told him. 'Probably the same bunch if they were camped close to the road.'

'I caught one of those terrifying buses from Kandahar to Kabul,' said Stan, 'crouched on the roof with the bike so it wouldn't get stolen. Midway there, in the hills, it started snowing. A regular blizzard it was, and I wished I'd cycled. That was the worst stretch of the whole journey.'

'God, it was cold for a couple of weeks,' Baz remembered. 'We took a room once in a hotel outside Ghazni and they had these big metal stoves like old boilers.'

Stan came back to the ship after we had seen a little of the town. He ate a meal with us on board and then Baz took him to see Chris.

'I think you'll be surprised to see how much weight he's lost. Whenever he goes to a doctor they fob him off with a different diagnosis. Now we can't wait to disembark at Singapore.'

Stan agreed. 'There will certainly be a good hospital there. In the meantime he should try and eat a few biscuits at least. And take plenty of drinks too, otherwise he'll dehydrate.'

Chris seemed pleased to see Stan again. If the rest of us felt jaded after crossing India, it was quite obvious that the young Dutchman had lost none of his zest for the great outdoors. His exuberance was infectious too. In next to no time a sizeable map of Australia covered the cabin floor and Chris was out of his bunk and down on his hands and knees beside the others, pointing out the unsealed stretch of highway linking the western coast with the east, and joking about the roo bars Baz would have to fit to his legs.

When Stan went ashore we promised to meet up again in Sydney. The *Chidambaram* sailed from Penang the next morning. Four days later, on 10 April, Zhenka burst into our cabin and tugged my arm excitedly.

'Skyscrapers, Dad,' he screamed. 'I've seen them, come and look!'

We raced to the topmost deck, where the funnel was, and joined a crowd of people who were pointing to the blue horizon over the bow of the ship. Zhenka pulled my arm again. 'See them?' he shouted.

Way, way off still, but clear as crystal, the wafer-thin blocks of concrete and glass poked up out of the water like fresh shoots of rice.

I looked down at Zhenka. A middle-aged lady from Japan, dressed in a nun's habit, was kneeling on the deck holding out a pair of glitzy purple opera glasses for him to look through.

'It's taken a year for us to get here,' I told Zhenka.

'I know,' he said. 'I'll be four soon, won't I?'

61

Two people came aboard to meet us when the *Chidambaram* docked in Singapore. Born in Stoke, Peter Taylor now had a log cabin home in the Rockies, but was temporarily based in Asia to teach geophysical research to an American oil company. The sprightly 74-year-old who accompanied him up the gangway was a Mr J. S. de Souza – no relation to AJ, but a lifelong devotee of athletics just the same.

After the introductions, Jocelyn de Souza gave me a typewritten schedule detailing our movements for the next twenty-four hours:

11.00: To be met on board by J. S. de Souza and Peter Taylor.

12.00: To be brought to Sloane Court Hotel.

13.00: Lunch.

14.00: To be met by Lau Teng Chuan, Singapore AAA President.

15.00: To be met by press.

And so on …

That night, when the last of the engagements were over, Peter Taylor took us out for drinks at the Marco Polo Hotel. Earlier, down at the docks, he had watched our van being winched from the deck. Now he was intrigued to hear how we had managed, cooped up together for so long.

'I financed an expedition of my own once, so I can appreciate the problems,' he told us. 'I was based in Australia, but I wanted to climb an unconquered peak in the Himalayas. I wrote a book about it afterwards called *From Cooper's Creek to Lang Tang II*.'

Baz wanted to know about the Nullarbor and how it compared with the emptiness we had already experienced in Afghanistan.

'Well Baz, don't expect to see any trees! There are no trees, no bloody water, food, people, birds, animals or anything else, either. It is in the same class as the Gobi Desert, the Chubut in Argentina, and the Tibetan Plateau, though a bit better than the central Sahara.'

Peter would lean forward in his chair when making a point and then settle back into a more relaxed position whilst observing how we reacted to what he had said. It reminded me of the way Chris played chess. Peter had thick greying hair and a tidy moustache that was a fraction darker. Lea thought he looked like Omar Sharif. He was in his early fifties and married to a much younger woman who had just given birth to their first child. On Thursday he was flying home to see his son for the very first time.

'I'll be chopping logs this weekend,' he sighed. 'It'll be the woodstove, the wife, and the little one – and the rest of the world can go to hell!'

Next morning, when Mr de Souza called at the hotel, we told him that poor Chris had been feeling listless for weeks and that he had not regained his appetite despite taking various medicines. Mr de Souza quickly reassured us that all would be well. His daughter was a nurse. He would telephone her straight away.

By midday Chris had been admitted to Middleton Hospital for tests. Later, when we visited him he looked alarmed.

'A nurse just took my temperature,' he said. 'It's a hundred and four degrees!'

Lea told him not to worry. 'They'll soon bring that down Chris. Then they'll isolate the virus and you'll be off to Australia to obtain a cure.'

'No,' he shook his head despondently, 'they reckon I'm very ill. This is a free-of-charge hospital for suspected typhoid cases. That's what they think I've got – typhoid!'

It was our turn to look worried.

'They won't let me leave the hospital for at least a month. I'll miss the ship. And who'll drive the van when you get there? I tell you Kel, it's a nightmare – a bloody nightmare!'

There were four days left before our ship sailed for the port of Fremantle. From what the doctor told us, it seemed highly unlikely that Chris would be on board. I took a taxi to the shipping agents and explained what had happened. The vehicle documents – including the all-important carnet – were registered in the driver's name and required amending before the van could leave the country. I rushed back to Middleton Hospital where Chris wrote out a shaky note, handing over responsibility to me.

Then the British High Commission came to our aid. Our journey had received good coverage in the local newspapers and they were delighted to lend a helping hand. It was decided that

Chris should stay with Mr and Mrs Thorpe to recuperate once he had been discharged from hospital. John Thorpe worked for the High Commission and had been responsible for the press release that first alerted the media of our arrival.

One afternoon he and his wife invited us to their home for lunch. The Thorpes were great fun, and good at pulling strings: before we left, Chris's ticket for the sea crossing had been swapped for an airline ticket at no extra cost.

On the eve of Peter Taylor's departure for Canada we accompanied him to the Raffles Hotel where Lea enjoyed her first Singapore Sling. Next stop was the rooftop garden of the Hilton for more of the same.

'Chris and I spent days inside the van,' Lea explained to Peter, 'sheltering from the heat, from the cold, from the rain, or simply trying to avoid the crowds of people outside. Some days, to help pass the time, or just to remain sane, we'd list the luxuries we planned to treat ourselves to when the journey came to an end. Now he's stuck in some hospital bed surrounded by people who speak a different language, while the rest of us are here, enjoying ourselves.'

The day Peter left, we were scheduled to appear on national TV. Jocelyn de Souza drove us to the studios and introduced us to the presenter of *Sports Parade*. The man looked uncomfortable the minute he saw us. Something was clearly wrong but he wouldn't tell us what it was. Eventually, the producer beckoned Mr de Souza to a corner of the room. After a few minutes he rejoined us.

'There is a big problem Barry,' he said in a low voice. 'The government maintains strict control over what is broadcast to the people, and the man responsible has just vetoed the length of your hair!'

'What? That's ridiculous!' I shouted.

Mr de Souza shuffled his feet and tried to calm me down. 'They say it is OK for the interview to go ahead with you Kelvin, because your beard hides most of your hair, but ...'

'Baz and I ran through the Khyber Pass together Jocelyn,' I said. 'They can stick their squeaky clean policies.'

He put his hand on Baz's shoulder. 'Not to worry Barry. The same thing happened when David Bedford was due to compete in a race here. He refused to trim his hair, so the customs officers prohibited his entry.'

Our last day ended on a brighter note. We first took afternoon tea with Peter Tripp, the British High Commissioner. Then the local Lion's Club presented us with a cheque to cover our hotel expenses. In the evening, Jocelyn treated everyone to a meal out with his family at Fattie's Restaurant. We climbed a dusty staircase in a hallway lined with signed photographs of all the famous people who had stopped off in Chinatown to eat there. Prince Charles was among the faces I recognised.

We waited on the landing while Jocelyn chose a spot next to the window and requested that two tables be sandwiched side by side so that we could all sit together. We looked out on the ragged army of cooks feeding the rest of Chinatown in the bustling street below.

After a waiter jotted down our order, Jocelyn told us a little more about himself. He had been a sprinter, winning the 220-yard Malayan title in 1925. Later he had represented Singapore as an official at the 1948 Olympics in London, and also the 1956 Olympics in Melbourne.

'My grandchildren from my first marriage live in Australia,' he said, beaming with pride. 'Guess what? They recently competed for New South Wales in their age group and won three bronze medals. Now isn't that something?'

When the first course arrived, Zhenka turned up his nose like a rabbit sensing danger.

'What's that?' he asked Lea.

'It's soup. You like soup. It's your favourite.'

'Dad said there was a shark in it. I heard him. I'm not eating sharks. They eat people.'

'Just try a sip. You'll like it.'

This conversation was going nowhere and Zhenka knew it. To lend extra weight to his views on the matter, he suddenly grabbed a set of chopsticks from the table and hurled them out of the window. I jumped up, only to see them bobbing in a large vat of simmering noodles on an outdoor stall directly beneath us.

62

When the *Centaur* sailed for Australia on 15 April, 1975, Chris was confined to his sick bed in a restricted wing of Middleton Hospital. Earlier in the morning I had stopped off to see him on my way to the docks. He already looked in much better shape. Ice-packs had succeeded in lowering his temperature and he was slowly beginning to eat again.

While I was there, the doctor walked in with the results of his tests. 'Sorry, it's thumbs down Chris. Typhoid I'm afraid. You're going to have to join your mates in a few weeks' time.'

'Don't worry,' I told him, 'we won't leave Perth without you. Besides, who'd be mad enough to take over the driving?'

Once aboard the ship I set about locating the others. They were shocked to hear about Chris, and we decided to keep it to ourselves for fear of causing any panic.

'If news leaks out that a few of the *Centaur*'s passengers have been in close contact with a typhoid case we're scuppered,' whispered Baz. 'They won't let anyone ashore!'

The Indian Ocean was as calm as the Bay of Bengal. We spent the best part of the smooth crossing dodging deck games and cocktail parties. Gradually, it began to dawn on us that the jungles of central India were less formidable than a saloon bar lined with fruit machines.

A large contingent of Australian pensioners was returning home from a package cruise to Singapore. A couple of them had seen our van.

'You the guys we read about? Must have been some trip, eh! Tell me about the campsites. Do they have hook-up facilities for campervans?'

'Most countries don't have campsites,' I tried to explain.

'No call for them I guess, with the hotels being dirt cheap.'

Later, when most of the passengers had retired to the main lounge to watch a cabaret show, Baz and I paced the near-empty deck. It was a clear night and I half hoped we would spot lights flashing along the coastline.

'All the stars,' said Baz, gazing up. 'I miss them since we stopped running. When I stood on the rooftop at the Hilton and looked down twenty-three floors, the city lights were a poor substitute.'

'Derek lives in the hills outside Perth,' I said, 'right on the edge of a National Park – you won't want for stars out there, or kangaroos!'

We were going to be staying with two friends of mine who had immigrated to Australia a few years after I did. 'Ten pound Poms who stayed put when they got there,' I grinned.

Derek and Rita Hoye once lived in the same street as my grandparents. He rode a motorbike with a big old-fashioned sidecar attached to it. They had two small children, still in nappies. Rita and the kids would squeeze into the sidecar and they would all set off on touring holidays to the Lakes or North Wales.

Derek was a runner. That was how I knew him. We both ran for the same club until it folded. Sometimes he would give me a lift to one of the races and I would sit in the sidecar and pretend to be a fighter pilot. In the days before the slag heaps were grassed over we used to run up and down the half-lit terraces to the council estates where the street lamps were brighter.

The ten pound assisted passage had provided the Hoyes with a great opportunity to ditch their industrial roots and look for something better.

'It will be good to see them again,' I told Baz.

'Yeah, Lea tells me Derek's still running.'

'He said he was, in his last letter. And he's looking forward to showing us the paths through the National Park.'

There was a faint speck of light on the horizon that could have been a boat. But we stopped walking anyway and leaned against the rail.

'Nine years ago now, I remember my friend Kris and I came up on deck to look for Australia. It was dark, just like this, but colder. Some of the other passengers had wrapped themselves in travel rugs and were listening to a boxing match on a short-wave radio.

Cassius Clay – as he was known then – defending his world title, against Joe Frasier, I think.

'After the long voyage we were both excited to be so close to land. It was the mid-sixties and everyone seemed fired up with optimism. Kris planned to write a novel and I wanted to run a four-minute mile.'

63

When the pilot boat brought the customs officers aboard they wanted to know where our return tickets were.

'We don't have any,' I admitted.

'Then you must show that you have sufficient funds to purchase them.'

'Well … we don't actually have any money yet, either.'

The man confronting me looked dismayed: this meant extra work for him, a special report. He dug into his black bag to find the relevant forms and ushered us to one side while the other passengers were checked out. Satisfied with everyone else, he then cleared a space on the table in front of him and deftly shuffled our passports together like a cardsharp.

'Mr Bowers.'

I stood up and went back over to the table.

'Take a seat,' he said.

I sat down and waited while the poker-faced figure in the dark blue uniform filled out his special report.

'The Australian Embassy in New Delhi granted us tourist visas for a stay of up to five months,' I told him.

'Visa or no visa, I can't let you into the country unless you can prove to me there'll be money to get you out!'

The *Centaur* reached the boat terminal at the port of Fremantle on 20 April. It was almost midnight, too late in the day for any of the passengers to disembark. We stood beside the funnel once more and scanned the faces peering up at us. It was drizzling and the iron tracks that carried the wheels of the giant cranes glittered like snail trails along the harbour front.

'There's Derek!' I shouted. 'See, with John and David.'

The two youngsters wore tracksuits and held aloft a big white cotton sheet with a message daubed upon it in capital letters: 'KEL AND BAZ! RUNNING FROM STOKE TO SYDNEY!! WELCOME TO AUSSIE!!!'

Zhenka climbed up onto my shoulders and began to wave both arms in the air. Everyone – on the ship and off it – seemed to be waving and grinning. We hurried to a lower deck so that we could make ourselves heard above the din. As we raced down the stairway, a muffled voice announced from the terminal office that disembarkation would commence at 8 a.m. When we were close enough to hear him, Derek shouted that Rita would collect us in the morning. After a short while the people on the dockside began to disperse, tooting their car horns as they drove off.

The first person up the gangplank the next morning was Michael Adams from the British Consulate. He had already contacted customs officials to explain about our journey, and now offered his personal assurance that our return to England would be arranged in due course by the people backing us. Within minutes he was leading us briskly past the queue of passengers filing ashore.

It had stopped raining and television camera crews were at the terminal. They filmed Baz and me jogging beside the liner on which we'd sailed. Soon afterwards, Rita drove up and we climbed into her car.

'The lads were so excited they didn't want to go to school this morning,' she told us.

Lea laughed. 'Zhenka was excited too,' she said. 'After we turned in last night he just wouldn't go to sleep.'

Rita glanced over her shoulder at Zhenka who was curled up asleep on his mother's lap. 'He looks really well, doesn't he? You all do.'

'We are,' nodded Lea. 'Totally unscathed and raring to go. Apart from Chris that is!'

'What's happening about your van?'

'The chap from the British Consulate has arranged for it to be towed to a lock-up until we're ready to collect it. Of course, that won't be until Chris arrives.'

Derek and Rita's home in Glen Forest was an eighteen-mile drive from Fremantle along the Great Eastern Highway. It lay at the end of a wide cul-de-sac ringed with single-storey houses built in the hills edging the Darling Range escarpment. The houses backed onto the John Forrest National Park. There were big lawns in front of them and tin letter boxes that reminded me of bird tables.

A few of the sprinklers were rotating, sending showers rainbowing over the grass.

'It's a lovely spot Rita,' said Lea as the car pulled off the road.

'Yeah, we're happy now we've moved up here. But it was a struggle when we first came out. They put us in some temporary hostel for immigrants just outside Perth. I wanted to go back to England but we stuck it out. Glad we did now, of course, but at the time it was awful and it stayed that way for a few years.'

Derek didn't get home from work until late afternoon. As soon as he walked through the door he wanted to take Baz and me for a run in the National Park. We followed him along a springy path that led through giant ferns, down to a creek where there were several deep rock pools. The forest was full of jarrah trees – massive eucalyptus that were too tough for the termites. Consequently, vast tracts of them had been logged in the past to provide millions of railway sleepers and the timber needed to prop up the mining shafts.

'We'll picnic here this weekend!' Derek shouted to us over his shoulder.

The light was fading in the forest by the time we turned around, and it was a steep climb to reach the road.

'Look!' whispered Derek. 'A kangaroo. See him?' The animal shot past, through the ferns in front of us.

'You'll see lots of them. I don't think I've ever been for a run at this time of day without seeing at least one.'

'Like the deer in Hanchurch Woods at dusk,' I said.

There was a meal waiting for us when we arrived back at the house. 'First things first,' said Derek, handing us a beer each and tapping the fridge door. 'This little sheila's full of tinnies. Fair dinkum or what?' He tried hard to sound like an Aussie, but his Potteries dialect was an instant giveaway.

The elder boy, John, glanced at his mother and winced. 'Dad's a drongo,' he muttered to her under his breath and they smiled at one another.

'Anyhow lads,' went on Derek, 'here's to the last lap!'

The three of us clinked our cans of beer together, then sat down at the table in the kitchen. John wanted to know how many people had crossed Australia on foot.

'I'm not sure John,' I said, 'but my guess is that you could count them on one hand.'

'You'd need both hands to list those who died trying to cross it,' his father told him, between swigs from the cold can. 'Dehydration: that's the most common killer in the outback.'

'I never really went near the outback the last time I was here,' I said. 'Unless you can call Percy Cerutty's camp at Portsea the outback. Most of the population are townies. Coastal dwellers too. They don't often venture into the interior.'

A week after we arrived, Derek drove the two of us back to Fremantle so that we could run from the port to Perth Council House where the Deputy Lord Mayor handed us a letter addressed to the Lord Mayor of Sydney.

Derek and Rita put us up at their home for the next month while we waited for Chris to rejoin us. During that time we ate butter, drank tap water, and Zhenka watched *Sesame Street* and played on the swings with the kids from next door. At weekends we went on picnics and Baz and Lea swam in the rock pools down by the creek. Sometimes Rita invited their friends over for a barbecue. And so we got to know the neighbours, and the postmistress and the grocer in the little row of shops just off the main road, that was in fact Glen Forest.

When the FA Cup Final was televised live from England we opened more tinnies whilst the boys played Monopoly in the room next door. It was winter down under and the nights were clear and cold in the hills.

Chris flew into Perth airport on 21 May. When he stepped from the plane he was faced with the same problems we had encountered on trying to enter the country without an onward ticket. Fortunately, we were there to meet him, together with Michael Adams from the British Consulate. He looked well and told us that he had enjoyed his stay at the Thorpes once he had been discharged from hospital. Now he was back with us we were able to collect the van from the port after it had been steam-cleaned and checked by the police. There were other details to attend to before we could leave.

British Leyland's head office in Sydney faxed their Perth-based dealer and instructed them to give the van a full service and new tyres. We filled our trailer with more plastic water carriers to take with us across the desert, and also purchased space blankets to help keep everyone warm when the temperature dropped drastically at night.

We were all set for off. Only one obstacle remained. The day after reaching Perth, Chris had gone into the city to renew his International Driving Licence – only to learn that he must first take a written test to obtain a Western Australian licence.

He quickly arranged to take the test, glanced at an Aussie version of the Highway Code for a few minutes, then promptly failed.

'You told me it was only a formality,' I said, when he got back.

'That's what I thought it would be. Don't worry, they're letting me resit the test tomorrow.'

'Thank goodness for that.'

64

The following morning, Chris re-sat the test to allow him back behind a steering wheel. This time he was better prepared.

'Right,' he said afterwards, waving the new licence in front of me. 'Let's go!'

Our journey had recently been featured on a top-rated television programme called *This Day Tonight* and a good-sized crowd came to St George's Terrace to wave us off.

We left from Perth Council House at 11 a.m. on 3 June, 1975. The Lord Mayor told me he had been swimming that morning. It helped him to focus on the day's various functions. He stepped in a puddle of water as we posed for photographs outside.

'No shots of my shoes,' he joked with the cameramen.

Zhenka grabbed hold of his blue plastic tractor and dragged it down from the van onto the wide pavement. Then he sat astride it and propelled himself pell-mell towards a group of well-wishers.

'What d'you say little 'un?' asked one man as he hopped aside.

'Well, if you sit on a chair too many times, it's so comfortable you don't want to move.'

That about summed it up. I for one had not kept in shape. After running in one direction for so long the idea of any out and back training session seemed less appealing than it once did. Baz reckoned I'd grown lazy. Either way I had lost some of the incentive whilst Chris was cooped up in Middleton Hospital. And when the days turned into weeks and there was still no sign of him, the stamina that I had built up slowly began to ebb away. Baz, in the meantime, had been out running with Derek most evenings. No question mark hung over *his* present condition.

Still, I told myself as I tugged on my tracksuit bottoms, I should easily be able to run myself back into shape during the next couple of weeks.

After the mayor had shaken our hands we headed east, along St George's Terrace and Adelaide Terrace, towards the Swan River, crossing over the causeway at the end of the street. It didn't take us long to reach the suburbs. Once we had left behind the shopping arcades and the high-rise buildings, it felt as if someone had lifted a lid off the landscape and that we were involved in it all again. The sky was blue.

A woman who had watched the TV feature waved us over to her garden fence.

'I came out here forty years ago,' she beamed. 'From Bolton. Can you tell? My son found me the other day – don't ask me how. We talked for an hour long-distance on the telephone and he sounded like he was in the next street. So clear. We've not spoken before – ever! He was a baby you see, when I last saw him.' She waved an envelope. 'I'm still in a state of shock. This arrived just now. It's a ticket home. He's paying for me to go and stay with his family – my family. I'm a grandmother!'

The woman pushed a plastic bag folded over with brown sticky tape into my hands. 'I didn't have wrapping paper. It's for your little boy. My friend made it. A koala. She makes lots.'

The smooth wide road climbed out of suburbia and stole into fields at the foot of the Darling Ranges. It felt wonderful to be on the open road again and we were both tempted to quicken our pace. Baz in particular seemed determined to press on at a fast lick. I dropped back and let him go. Perhaps he was trying to prove a point. I should have been more prepared for this last overland haul to the Pacific.

It had taken us two and a half months to cross India. Now, Western Australia alone looked almost the same size. And three thousand miles of our journey still remained. But we were not unduly worried about the Nullarbor, despite what Peter Taylor had told us, and the Shell map's recommendation that travel across the desert be avoided during June and July because rain was likely to render the road impassable.

There were no bandits in Australia. Nor any problems with the language. That had to count for something. We were no longer afraid to draw attention to ourselves at nightfall and planned to light campfires in the outback when it grew cold.

Our route over the Darling Ranges, by great good fortune, passed through Glen Forest. Rita had cooked a curry for our lunch. Derek took photographs in the garden, whilst Zhenka said goodbye to Patch the dog from next door.

We each grabbed the opportunity to take a shower and then stumbled back out into the bright sunlight. At the top of the street, where we turned right to rejoin the Great Eastern Highway, I took a last look back. Derek and Rita were in their garden – waving still – and the sprinklers were arching loops of water across the lawn.

The highway rose and fell in gentle undulations through the tall trees for most of the afternoon. Chris had been instructed to drive to a place on the map called The Lakes. But it was further than we'd estimated. Dusk came, and with it, a biting chill. The run that had begun so effortlessly under a blue sky ended in a starlit walk to a couple of petrol pumps and a roadside café – The Lakes.

Lea stood beside the trailer wearing a thick coat and warming her hands over the hurricane lamp. Meat stew was bubbling in a big pan on the cooker. Inside the van the space under the bunks was packed with food supplies. An Irish whisky cake had been included for Chris's twenty-first birthday – due to be celebrated in the middle of the Nullarbor.

Baz and I slouched over mugs of steaming tea. The foam cushions on the bunk lids and the curtains on each side of the back windows felt damp. After we had eaten, we waited for the lights from the café to go out and then wandered across the road to the bushes for a pee. The cold night air had stiffened our leg muscles and crouching was out of the question.

Sheep were bleating somewhere in the dark. Above us, the moon had humpty-dumptyed and come to rest upside down in a sky blazing with shooting stars. This was it alright. The final slog. I rinsed out my toothbrush in a tin mug of cold water and spat white toothpaste into the grass.

65

The second day out was worse than the first. Far worse. If ever there was a sure-fire nominee to join the ranks of whinging Poms, that morning it was me. I had slept badly on the thin foam sheeting and woke with a painful groin. After hobbling awkwardly along the side of the road for just a few miles it became difficult to pinpoint exactly where it hurt most. The pain seemed to have spread to the rest of my body. Each step was agony.

I had obviously underestimated the level of fitness required to cover such long distances each day. The stiffness would go away. I knew that. But it would take a few days of easier running. I looked up at the road ahead. Baz was just visible on the brow of a hill. He wouldn't be too impressed if I asked him to cut short our daily mileage.

By midday I was limping badly and feeling totally depressed when a car pulled up beside me. A lanky schoolteacher in knee-length shorts sprang out.

'G'day, I'm Bob.'

Bob Shorter taught at Bakers Hill Primary School and wanted to know if we could make a short detour to meet the schoolchildren there. A detour, in my present state of wellbeing, however short, sounded a ludicrous proposition. But I let him talk me into it.

'The kids watched you leave Perth on the TV yesterday and decided to do a project on your journey across Australia. We thought we'd try and link it all the way back to the first settlers and the explorers and prospectors who set out to pursue their dreams. The white man's dreamtime if you like.'

Bakers Hill was little more than a tidy cluster of bungalows set amidst neat, rolling countryside. The sort of small country town in which you would imagine there to be a great amount of dreaming and very little else.

By the time we reached the school gates there were about sixty pupils assembled outside on the grassy playground along with a few of their parents who had been rounded up to swell the numbers. As we drew closer, I tried to substitute my limp for a couple of light-hearted hops and gave a broad grin to indicate that I was in fine fettle for this little amble across the continent.

The children intended to collage a frieze around the walls of their classroom, showing the route we planned to take from the Indian Ocean to the Pacific. We told them about the places we had passed through on the way to Australia, and about the wild animals and the bandits.

One little boy had already drawn a camel for the frieze.

'It came all the way from Afgrannystan in search of gold!' he told me, looking up with big wide eyes. 'Mr Shorter calls camels "ships of the desert". Is that how you got here?'

We stayed talking in the playground for over an hour. But when we came to leave, the children wanted us to join them in the classroom to see their school play. Chris, Lea and Zhenka offered to stay behind instead, whilst Baz and I sneaked back to the highway.

Northam, the next town on the map, was much larger and less pretty. Farming communities from the eastern wheat belt depended on the place for their supplies, and both the railroad and the River Avon ran through it. Bob Shorter, the schoolteacher, had once lived in a mobile home at a caravan park there. He strongly recommended the piping hot showers. Unfortunately, a power-cut plunged the whole area into darkness soon after we arrived, and the hot shower turned into a cold trickle.

The hot water was back on again the next morning and we delayed setting out so that my sore leg muscles might feel the benefit. ABC Radio had contacted the local council who in turn passed on a message to the caretaker of the site. Could we look in on 'Legs' Dwyer before we left Northam?

John Dwyer ran the local radio station from his wheelchair in a cluttered studio on the way out of town. We spent half the morning chatting with him over the air, and chose a couple of records for the children at Bakers Hill.

When we did start running I was pleased to find that my groin felt less painful. But it still caused me to limp, and for a few irritating days Baz took to calling me 'Legs' Bowers. This wouldn't have been nearly so bad had Chris not overheard him – for he knew what my middle name was. From then on they both referred to me as 'Legs' Les, or the snappier version whenever drink was involved.

After the radio broadcast, motorists began to wave at us and toot their horns. Several people even stopped to wind down their car windows and hand over a few dollars.

'Good on ya, mate!' they would cry, before accelerating away.

Gradually, we were moving into a much bigger landscape with a widening sky above it, and fences that drifted further apart each day. Sometimes there were sheep grazing in the fields. Sometimes white cockatoos screeched from the trees.

The one constant object at our side was a giant water pipe that ran above ground for over 300 miles from the Mundaring Weir in the John Forest National Park all the way to the eastern goldfields. This pipeline was the ingenious brainchild of an Irishman named O'Connor: a brilliant engineer who had been called upon to provide water for the new settlements spawned in an arid region by the great gold finds of the 1880s.

Whilst bottled water changed hands under the counter for more money than champagne in the pubs at Coolgardie and Kalgoorlie, Charles Yelverton O'Connor found his project beset by criticism and lack of funding. In 1902 he finally cracked and his body was discovered on a beach in Fremantle. Less than a month later, the pumping stations he had designed were brought into operation and fresh water gushed out of the pipe at Mount Charlotte Reservoir on the eastern rim of Kalgoorlie.

There was no such water shortage the day after we first sighted an updated version of the long pipeline. Rain bucketed down on the road to Cunderdin. The storm felled a tree that missed our van by inches.

If gold fever created townships, it emptied them just as quickly. And the population dwindled in many other places too, making it difficult for us to recognise a genuine ghost town from one that had died a natural death or suffered some other calamity.

Meckering had been flattened by an earthquake in 1968, but the town's name still survived on a pristine sign that led nowhere. Just beyond the empty space, a wrecked car was hanging upside down from a tree, with 'Drive Safely' plastered on its side.

66

The wind rattled the chains of the children's swings in a deserted playground next to the council caravan park at Cunderdin.

We arrived there with drops of rain dripping from our noses, and our aching legs spattered in tangerine-coloured mud. After hot showers in the draughty concrete toilet block, we put on clean running kit, then zipped up our nylon rainsuits and hobbled outside to a nearby roadhouse.

Chris was inside the café, hunched over the flashing lights of a pinball machine in his black leather jacket. Zhenka had put some money in the jukebox and was dancing to David Bowie. We drank hot coffee from mean-sized mugs that needed refilling twice before we were ready to leave. And then we hit the road again.

It was still raining, so we moved off quickly and I felt the warm liquid slop about inside my empty stomach. Beyond Cunderdin, the landscape swelled, even though the rolling clouds pressed down upon it. There were big truck tyres abandoned beside the road, laid flat like frayed rubber nests full of empty cans of Swan lager.

Kellerberrin had the right-sounding name for the next place we came to. Like most of the shanty towns straddling the piped water supply, it consisted of one main thoroughfare. Midway down this wide street stood a solitary hotel with an imposing façade and a veranda decorated in wrought-iron lace work.

A group of children were playing in the dust on the pavement under the veranda. They were barefoot and were wearing their jeans rolled up at the bottom, like Huckleberry Finn. At the end of the street, just before the small town stopped dead, there was a caravan park with a noticeboard outside advertising electric blankets.

We had not gone far when a beat-up Holden with bald tyres and no suspension ground gamely to a stop a few yards ahead. The drunken Aussie who was driving sat behind the wheel and waited for us to draw level before he swung open the car door.

He nursed three cans of Swan lager under his left arm and used his free hand to prop himself up against the bonnet as he made his way round to the hard shoulder. We sprawled on the red clay by the side of the car – out of the glare of the sun – while he told us all about himself.

His name was Barney, and he grew up in a big drum, which accounted for his stooped shoulders, or so he said. Barney's grandfather had beat the drum on a street corner of Kalgoorlie during the surge for gold in the late 1880s.

'There was bands all over 'Goorlie in them days. Real money to be made, even for a musician, accordin' to my dad. But the story goes that the old feller popped one cork too many and got kicked out of his band. Anyhow – whatever – he put a knife through one side of a drumskin and then slit his own throat. When I came along, my granny stuck me inside the big drum to sleep. She couldn't be affording any cradle.'

Barney finished his drink and gazed at the black swan on the empty can. Then he held the can upside down and watched the sunlight catch the last dribbles.

'Where can I take you lads?' he asked.

We shook our heads. 'No thanks Barney, we don't need a lift anywhere.'

He got up, climbed inside his car on the passenger side and slammed the door shut.

'Only wankers and Abbos go walkabout!' he shouted through the open window.

We lit our first campfire a little way beyond the town of Doodlakine. Chris and Lea had already carried several fallen branches back to the clearing where the van was parked; enough wood to keep a good blaze going until we turned in. Zhenka had helped too, trailing behind them with armloads of kindling.

We boiled water on the fire, pouring it into plastic buckets afterwards to soak our feet. By this time Lea had got Zhenka ready for bed. He wore a warm woollen dressing gown over his pyjamas, and knelt on the ground to push his Dinky cars through the dust by firelight. Chris had several new music cassettes that he had brought over from Singapore. His taste in music had changed since meeting Baz, and that went for the rest of us too. He turned up the volume of the cassette player so that we could hear above the sound of the crackling logs.

'*I was lying in a burnt-out basement with a full moon in my eyes ...*'

Baz joined in, rocking back and forth on his haunches and warming his hands over the fire. Neil Young was his all-time favourite and 'After the Gold Rush' was an inspired choice given our current location.

We all looked up, through the sparks, and saw two shooting stars fly off at an angle and then disappear as if they'd just dropped, sizzling, into a black vat.

'Even the sky looks bigger,' said Lea, 'and unfamiliar too – like we'd not long been born or something.'

'This is as close as we ever get to the people who came here before us,' said Baz. 'The very first settlers I mean, who made fires just like this and watched stars fall through the sky.

'*Flying Mother Nature's silver seed to a new home in the sun. Flying Mother Nature's silver seed to a new home ...*'

The road became straight, but it was also hilly: long drawn-out climbs, where the crest of each rise never seemed to get any closer, followed by swift downhill stretches that were over far too quickly.

Halfway up one such hill – just past a small place called Carrabin – Chris used his foam shaving cream to spray out a message for us on the tarmac, adding an artistic squiggle to indicate where he had parked the van. Both of us missed the sign completely, but fortunately Baz spotted the roof of the van.

'What else should I have expected from a doctor's son!' he said to Chris when he took him back to look at the message. 'You can never read their bloody prescriptions can you? Fat chance we've got Baxter, heading for the desert with you carrying a spray can!'

We left the road. A wide path of compressed sand lay next to the pipeline, hidden from the highway behind the shoulder-high scrub. Maintenance crews in pick-up trucks used the track to gain access to the water pipe. It reminded us of the time we strayed from the main road in Iran to follow a flattened trail left behind by the construction gang who were laying an oil pipe between Tehran and Tabriz.

The route ran straight as an arrow, and there was a pleasant give in the surface of the ground. Underfoot a busy thread of bulldog ants marched over the sand, and when the sun dipped the saltbush looked blue, and the silver pipeline appeared to float across a vast inland sea.

It was relaxing not to have to consider any vehicles suddenly creeping up from behind, and to know that what traffic there was would remain out of sight for as long as we kept to the track. That way, it was also easier to imagine the impact such an endless repetition of horizons had on the pathfinders lost in this brittle scrub stubble. To do the vision justice, we had to blank out the pipeline and the telegraph poles too; not to mention the debris of smashed bottles and empty beer cans that littered the outback wherever four wheels could manoeuvre.

Tar was daubed around the foot of the telegraph poles to prevent them from being toppled by the termites. Green parakeets sunned themselves on the wires and sent their own messages screeching down the line.

Topping the longest uphill stretch – a climb that led into Southern Cross – was a notice fronting a deserted mine: 'You are entering the goldfields.'

67

Many of the settlements that had once been prominent stopovers on the cruel haul to the goldfields had main streets that were wider than those in the cities. They had been arranged that way so that the Afghan cameleers could turn their camel trains round without causing too much upset. Now, so spacious an entrance to the town of Southern Cross merely emphasised the acute lack of activity. A few cars had been left parked in the middle of the street, but apart from a lone flag fluttering above the post office, nothing was actually on the move.

As we walked by, a bell attached to the door of Mollie Taylor's Tea Rooms gave an optimistic jangle, and out came a couple wiping cake crumbs from their mouths. They both seemed delighted to have found someone else to talk to, and vied with each other to have their say.

'She's never shut up since we left Queensland!' the man complained.

'Hark at him,' said the woman. 'He should be finding a sheila who's taken a vow of silence besides fidelity.' She stressed the last word to indicate what a strain it had been to keep such a promise.

'Fi … what?' The man gave a belly laugh.

'Do youz two live here?' the woman asked, desperate to have a conversation with someone who belonged somewhere. 'Lol and I live out of suitcases. Always have done. Always will.' She looked at him and gave a frown. 'If we stay together that is. See the caravan – that white one?' There was only one caravan in the middle of the wide street. 'It belongs to my mother-in-law. We borrowed it for our job.'

Marlene and Lol were to look after a caravan site on the coast. The owner had not yet met them but Lol reckoned that Marlene could sweet-talk her way into any situation and that the vacancy was as good as theirs. 'That's how I got myself into this fix.' He grimaced.

'We just left my sister,' Marlene told us.

'Marlene's sister …' Lol blew through his teeth until his cheeks puffed out. 'She's a gold digger alright. Now when youz two get to 'Goorlie, be sure an' look her up. Hay Street – that's her patch. Red bulbs in the window-box and the same colour in the light socket!'

We parted company with them outside the tearooms, and strolled on.

'When I first left school I got a job as a complaints clerk at a glassblowing factory,' I muttered to Baz. 'There were three different baskets of correspondence on my desk. One of them was headed "Lost in Transit". I think that's what's happened to Marlene and Lol.'

Either the driving outside Southern Cross got sloppier, or there were more animals to knock over. Whichever it was, there seemed enough dead meat about to keep the state going on barbecues for the next few weeks. We ran past the remains of emus, kangaroos, foxes and dingoes. Burnt rubber zigzagged across the bitumen wherever sleepy drivers had jammed on their brakes. Sometimes there was broken glass too, mixed with the shiny peel-back rings from the lager cans, and the whole show twinkled like peculiar fireflies all along the highway.

Chris stopped at Joe's Roadhouse in Yellowdine to fill the petrol tank and the water containers. There was a gap in the map for the next 70 miles, and from this point on it would be wise to plan well ahead.

The desolation was sheer bliss. We stayed on the sandy trail and ran in silence most of the time. Kangaroo prints were everywhere and a wild turkey once shot out of the bushes and scared us. Every so often we would spot something other than a beer can that was man-made – like a metal windmill or a microwave tower. It brought us back to earth, or at least to the earth we were more familiar with.

One afternoon Lea baked scones and Zhenka played with the dough on the trailer lid, making canoe shapes and snakes. At bedtime, I had been reading stories to him by torchlight, all about the pioneers and the explorers.

'Look Dad,' he pointed. 'The explorers have to paddle their canoes through the snakes. We haven't seen any real snakes yet have we?'

Even Zhenka was enjoying these quiet times. While we were

running he played football with Chris as often as he could and went for long walks into the bush with Lea.

'The bandits have all gone, haven't they?' He looked disappointed, and so when I didn't say anything a faint ray of hope crept across his face.

'Mum says there aren't any bandits here, but I think it's a good place for them to be, don't you? As long as they don't take my tractor.'

We didn't see a single building between Joe's Roadhouse at Yellowdine and the Rock Hotel in Bulla Bulling. We reached the solitary truckstop late one afternoon. A strong wind had blown up and was bending back the three-foot high bushes nearest to the roadside. Bulldust swirled around a pile of rattling tin where a prefabricated wall stood tethered to the hinges of a splintered door.

'Last neighbours pulled out twelve months back,' came a voice from the shadows in the doorway of the hotel opposite.

'I signed yer book for yer mates. They was towing a little white trailer behind 'em. Said yer would be here soon. The *Kalgoorlie Miner*'s been on the phone asking if we'd seen yer.'

The voice belonged to a small dark-haired man who introduced himself as Leaning Mario of Bulla Bulling. His real name was Mario Mimosa and he was from Venice. He and his wife had been behind the bar of the Rock Hotel for the past eighteen years, and were now naturalised Australian citizens.

'Come on in. I'll shout yer a beer, and then we'll ring the radio people up. They're keen to speak to yer too.'

We followed him into a room where a young Aboriginal boy was playing pool. The pool table took up most of the space in the small room and we had to squeeze past to get by. At the bar, cans of antifreeze were stacked on top of a portable TV and Hungarian salami dangled from hooks above the rows of bottled spirits.

The Aborigine was called Benny. He had lost a bet on a horse in a race that had just been televised. Now his concentration lay solely on his pool game, and he quickly began to pot the few remaining balls left on the table, finally slamming the black into the pocket before handing the cue back to Mario. Benny looked at us and smiled.

'He sweeps up for me sometimes,' Mario told us. 'Never enough though, eh Benny?'

The young Aborigine smiled again. A big, wide grin shaped like a boomerang.

'Only thing in the bar that's not covered in dust is that damn smile of his!' said the Italian, slowly pulling on the handle of the pump.

There was a gondola tattooed upon Mario's upper arm. He hitched up the sleeve of his thick winter shirt so that we could see it better. Then he flexed his muscles to show how the boat floated over the ripples of skin.

'A gondola pulling a schooner, eh?' He laughed the kind of laugh you hear in vineyards when they're busy picking the grapes. Then he became thoughtful.

'At one time, forty trucks a day came by and the truckies all stopped here for their beer and meals. One Sunday I counted thirty-two trucks parked out there, and we wasn't supposed to be open. So, I built a big fire round the back and we barbecued steaks on shovels. Harry Evan's birthday it was. Now it's down to just a couple of trucks a day ... if we're lucky. The mines are closed of course, and the rest of the town up and left. That railroad out there took whole towns with it.

'I still keep my pigs and chooks. I tell you something for nothing – they talk about Mario's pork at every roadhouse in the state. I kill 'em, pack 'em in salt for forty days, and hang 'em high for two weeks more. You never tasted anything like it. I'll get a plateful. It's on the house. Then we'll phone the radio people. You can tell them you're eating Mario's pork.'

We drank another beer, this time with Benny, while Mario retreated into the kitchen. When he came back, his wife was with him.

'This is Maria,' he said. 'We are Mario and Maria Mimosa.' He spoke slowly, emphasising each name. 'Mmm ... mamma mia! It's the sound I made when she first caught my eye.'

Maria said hello, then busied herself behind the bar, rummaging about in a cardboard box full of beer mats and bills. She was much taller than her husband, with long black hair. And despite their eighteen years at Bulla Bulling, she was still beautiful.

'What did I tell you Mario? You never really look do you?' She waved a small photograph at him, and Mario snorted and snatched it from her hand.

'Here,' he said, 'look … you'll be interested in this.' He passed the snapshot across the bar. It was a picture of two young men with crew cuts, standing in front of a horse-drawn covered wagon outside the Rock Hotel.

'Americans they was. Walking round the world. See the one on the left? He joined in after his companion's brother got killed in Afghanistan … I forget their names.'

68

We stopped off at the graveyard on the run into Coolgardie. Ernest Giles was buried there. He was a West Country man: an explorer who had been involved in the race to reach the southern coastline of Australia, and, more notably perhaps, the first European to stumble onto the world's biggest monolith. Giles discovered Ayers Rock in the Red Centre in 1872.

Twenty years on, a man named Arthur Bayley pocketed his find at Fly Flat and rode into Southern Cross with 554 ounces of gold. Evidence of what happened next lay all around the cemetery. Entire families were wiped out by outbreaks of typhoid when thousands of prospectors set up camp in an area that was plagued by flies and was without running water.

The city of tents became Coolgardie. Hotels went up, and even a mosque for the Afghan merchants and cartage handlers, who planted date palms outside their doorways. The population spiralled to 15,000 before the century was out, but there were over a thousand burials in the five-year spell after that first strike.

'Christ,' said Baz. 'Typhoid! Chris was bloody lucky, wasn't he?'

A cold wind was blowing the topsoil over the graves, piling up the spent flower petals against the foot of the tombstones. An iron gate that we had left unlatched clanged against the fence whenever a strong gust of wind blew, and more than once we turned our heads around to see who was coming.

Overhead, clouds were piling up in the sky too. Big drops of rain fell from them and splashed onto the dusty earth, trickling into the jars that had been left behind with some of the flowers.

We moved on from the cemetery and made for the caravan site. Two families of Poms were waiting there for us, alerted to our imminent arrival by the *Kalgoorlie Miner*. Colin and Rita Olderson were employed by the local council as caretakers of the site. They lived there, with their five young children, in a converted single-decker bus. The caravan parked next to the bus was the home of their friends, Mick and Doris Ward. They had three children.

Colin Olderson led us to the shower block.

'Come and have a bite with us when you're ready,' he smiled.

After a long hot shower we sat in the bus and ate fish and chips with them, whilst Chris and Lea walked into town to catch the post office before it closed. The two families were anxious to let us in on their big dream. As soon as they had saved enough cash, they planned to buy a couple of double-decker buses in Sydney, and drive them overland to London.

Fifteen-year-old David Ward was the kingpin around which this wonderful idea revolved. The sandy-haired boy had a mania for maps. Where other boys his age listened to pop music and followed football teams, David wanted to follow in the footsteps of explorers.

He sat us down in the snug caravan bedroom he shared with his younger brother, and gestured to a narrow shelf tightly stuffed with old fold-out maps. The collection of miscellaneous pathways and tracks meandered from Timbuktu to the Trent and Mersey Canal, where his father had once taken him fishing.

'You'll be crossing the proper desert in a few weeks' time,' David told us. 'And the road across it is still only partly sealed. It's named after John Eyre. He set out from Adelaide in 1840, with a companion called Baxter and a few Aborigines.'

'Get away,' said Baz. 'Not another Baxter?'

''Fraid so,' laughed David. 'And guess what? Some way into the expedition the Aborigines murdered him!'

Baz didn't bat an eyelid. 'Never take a man named Baxter with you on any expedition; they're sure to get speared or go down with typhoid!' he said.

'Somehow – even though he was left without a horse and had no water – John Eyre survived, together with an Aborigine named Wylie. When they walked into Albany the two men had covered over fifteen hundred miles.'

'This double-decker adventure David,' said Baz, 'was that your idea?'

The boy gave a little snigger, 'S'pose it was.'

A museum had not long opened its doors on the far side of town. Doris Ward now knew exactly where to look whenever her son went missing.

'He spends more time there than he does here,' she said. 'I'm sure he's just itching to drag you off there right now. Isn't that so David?'

The museum was in an old court building on Bayley Street. David was our guide. He took us to see a quaintly shaped coloured bottle retrieved from the old camp, and a thonged leather purse that had once held gold. In the topmost room there were many photographs of the men who had flocked to the goldfields. Thick-bearded drifters and adventurers with spades over their shoulders. One picture showed a group of them sitting outside a barber's tent, having their whiskers trimmed.

When the mail service first started up between Southern Cross and Coolgardie, it had taken Cobb & Co. four days with a team of thoroughbreds according to a timetable fastened to the coach door.

'How long did it take you and Baz?' asked David.

'About the same I think.'

Later in the day, Colin Olderson took us to the Ghost Town Inn to meet a friend of his who rented a room there. The wood creaked under the worn carpet as we climbed the stairs to a landing on the first floor. Colin didn't bother to knock, but pushed open the second door he came to and we followed him inside.

A white kitten lay on a purple bedspread. A man who was losing his hair at the front got up out of a brown leather chair and came towards us.

'Colin mentioned you when I spoke to him earlier. He told me about the run an' all. My name's John Birch. I'd like to shake your hand.'

Like a good many intent on making money, John Birch was heavily in debt and on the run from the Inland Revenue. Not that he was dwelling on his misfortune too much.

'What's money anyway?' he said, soon after we had been introduced.

The room was not very large and it smelled of cat piss and whisky. John Birch sniffed the stale air and cursed the warped sash window as he struggled to manoeuvre it free. When he turned around to face us, his foot caught the brass casing of a shell from the Boer

War, and there was a loud thud as it hit the bare floorboards and rolled under the bed. The white kitten leapt on top of the wardrobe.

'Shit! The landlady will be after my blood again. She reckons there's more plaster than beer goes in the glasses since I took the room.'

'Colin tells me you met the two Americans when they came through this way on foot,' I said.

'I did. They were lookin' to buy a mule and so I took them to Charlie Wavers. The man was always owing money, so the horse sale helped him out. Not that I saw any of it. Poor bastard blew his brains out only the other week.'

69

We spent a damp, miserable day reaching Kalgoorlie, and a miserable morning walking through it. I wondered what the town would look like when the sun was shining, but it wasn't and we didn't feel like hanging around to find out.

In 1893 Paddy Hannan probably felt the same. After all, he was on his way out of the place when his horse went lame. Finding gold must have coloured his outlook no end. You can bet there would have been rainbow-coloured flashbacks for the rest of his life.

The broad drag through town is named after him, and the hotels on either side are monumental. As we approached, I watched an elderly resident teeter under a brolly on the edge of the pavement. She surveyed the wide-open expanse of the street as though it were a desert and shuffled forward to cross it.

'There are less deaths on wet days, on account that it keeps the dust down,' John Birch had told me when he explained what happened when it was hot and the wind swept over the slime tips and blanketed what was known as the "golden mile" in bone-dry deposits from the diggings. 'That's when the old folk get disorientated and step out in front of the roo bars.'

The grandiose buildings at the heart of 'Goorlie did not extend into the adjoining town of Boulder. When we turned off Hannan Street to follow signs for Kambalda, the corrugated walls of ugly shacks merged with a leaden sky as the rain sluiced down over the tin roofing.

'It must be deafening,' muttered Baz. 'How do they manage to sleep under all that racket?'

The black outline of the pithead gear and the flat-topped slime tips reminded us of the coal mines and slag heaps dotted around the towns we grew up in. The road past the tin shacks was busy. Workers from the nickel mines had just knocked off and were speeding home towards Kalgoorlie. A married couple in a patched-up convertible were heading in the opposite direction, back to Esperance after a shopping spree in town. They stopped their car and handed us a lemon each to suck on while we ran through the rain.

The bad weather cleared up overnight. Next morning there was a blue sky and a silvery sheen on the spiderwebs in the bushes. We set off early and met a hitch-hiker with a heavy pack and a sense of humour, who stuck out his thumb for a laugh as we ran up to him. The hitch-hiker was called Maurice. He was in a rush to cross the Nullarbor to see a woman named Stella who he had split up with five weeks earlier.

Stella lived in Sydney. Maurice said the journey would take about four days – five at the maximum, even if the lifts were diabolical. Getting back together with Stella was a different kettle of fish.

'Yeah,' he sighed, 'crossing the desert's one thing: crossing Stella's quite another … quite another!'

We wished each other luck and Baz and I jogged off down the road. Just as we eased up to hop across a cattle grid, a big truck thundered by bearing New South Wales number plates. Maurice was waving from the driver's cab. It was all down to Stella now.

On the edge of Widgemooltha, a Welshman was standing on a ladder hammering nails into the timber framework of a new building. When he saw us, he came down the ladder and hurried across the road, still holding the hammer.

'Don't often see anybody taking exercise in these parts.' He glanced down and rubbed his thumb along the head of the claw hammer. 'Unless they have to that is.'

The Welshman was of stocky build with a round stomach that jutted out from the rest of him to balance on the broad belt of his shorts. He wore a yellow shirt with different coloured buttons that were fighting a losing battle to hold the material in check at the front. Side on, when the dust swirled, he took on the appearance of a scaled-down JCB digger. But his voice had a generous lilt that carried all who heard it to the Welsh valleys. When he spoke it was like listening to sticky toffee and we hung on his every word.

Tom Harrison had last seen his native land twenty years ago and he knew he would never go back. He and his wife had left Cardiff to come to Australia in search of gold. They were still looking, but they had a teenage son to help them now.

'When we came here in the fifties we bought a house with land in 'Goorlie. Then one day we just sold up – quick as that – and decided to go bush. Been doing it ever since. Just moving from town to town, stopping off wherever … bit of carpentry, digging trenches, this and that; mostly manual stuff.'

Tom asked us back to his caravan. It was parked under gum trees along a track off the highway. When we got there, Mrs Harrison was relaxing in a rocking chair beneath a tarpaulin that stretched from the roof of the caravan to the top of a Welsh dresser. She tugged a hanky from her sleeve and placed it between the pages of the paperback she was reading. Then she put the kettle on.

Mrs Harrison's maiden name had been Mary Nightingale, but her voice was no match for Tom's and she was happy to let him do all the talking. Tom loved company. He told us of the old-timers camped in the hills all around – fossicking half for adventure and half for gold.

'We get together sometimes. I have a regular grocery run delivering supplies, and medicine too when it's needed.'

'Can they make a living out of it?' asked Baz.

'Most scratch one at best. A few are luckier. Of course there are those that dip into their savings or have a pension to fall back on. And the government provides prospectors with a weekly allowance of ten to fifteen dollars. But you could hardly feed a chook on that.'

When the kettle started to whistle, Mrs Harrison bustled across to the dresser and picked up a tin. The tea caddy had a picture of Caernarfon Castle embossed on the lid.

'It didn't come out with us,' she said, anxious to dispel any notions we may have had that they missed the old country or needed to be reminded of it. 'An aunt gave it to us when she visited. That seems some time ago now. When we had a house to visit.'

After we drank the tea, I told Tom we needed to press on.

'We're aiming for between thirty and forty miles each day. If we leave now we should manage the last ten miles before it gets dark.'

'Listen,' Tom said. 'Why not come back with the others when you're done? I'll take you all to meet Ted.'

Mrs Harrison raised her eyebrows. 'Ted's a gem alright. He feeds mice to the crows and when he has a campfire he can tell you which branch will still be alight next morning.'

70

We saw three emus goose-stepping between the trees on the last stretch of the day. The sun sat on the road ahead for a short spell, then dropped away. Faint pinpricks of starlight became visible in the sky soon after, and smoke, drifting up from a fire lit by an Aboriginal family whose car had broken down. The Aborigines seemed to know instinctively what we were about. They waved to us with big wide-sweeping arm movements, and no explanations were necessary.

When we reached the van, Chris and Lea looked worried. They were about to drive back to look for us and had just cleared the cooking gear from the top of the trailer in order to do so. I let Baz explain about the Welshman and his wife. Then we drove back to Widgemooltha in the dark. Tom was pacing about excitedly under the canvas lean-to. It was warm and snug inside the Harrison's caravan. Their son was there. He looked like his father and he was just as amiable.

'You can do anything in this country,' said Tom. His son nodded. 'Go up north and you don't need a thing to live – certainly not a house. Once we met an old guy stuck in the back of beyond. When I asked him how come he'd chosen such a remote spot, he told me he'd run out of juice where the trees were, and that he had chopped them down to build himself a house. Before long he'd started growing pineapples there. Next thing he knew, he had himself a pineapple plantation.'

'How long were you in Kalgoorlie?' I asked.

'Too long! 'Goorlie … what a dump. We were crazy to live there. Crazy! Our neighbours ran some kind of prairie brothel. Each time you went out to the dunny, you'd see naked sheilas through the fly screens. It was all cut-glass, dangling and glitzy behind the net curtains there.'

I stole a glance at Tom's son. His head was nodding involuntarily. He was miles away – dreamily peeking from the open door of that dunny to the neighbour's lit-up windows, while the mozzies buzzed around his bare legs.

Tom lifted the lid of an Esky and put a row of cold cans on the Formica worktop next to the sink.

'There'll be no grog at Ted's place so we'd best drink up before we go.'

Tom opened the cans of beer and then stepped outside to fetch something from the dresser. He came back in carrying a small cotton bag which he emptied onto the fold-out table in front of us. A handful of uncut stones rolled across the chequered oilcloth. The Welshman sorted through them, picking one out every now and then and holding it up under the yellow strip-light. The small stones changed colour when he did this and slivers of blue flickered through them like tiny trapped fish.

'Opals,' Tom said, still sifting amongst them with his big bruised fingers. 'Mary and me used a jackhammer at Lightning Ridge for these little beauties. We'd like you to have one each ... something to remember us by.' He finished drinking his beer and looked around to see if the rest of us had emptied our cans. 'C'mon, let's go and see what Ted's up to.'

On the way out of the caravan, Mrs Harrison wiped her hands on an apron and opened a tin of treacle toffee for Zhenka. His eyes lit up like the opals in our pockets.

Tom's station wagon took a little sorting out before we could all squeeze inside. His son had wanted to come with us but there wasn't room.

'I spent two Christmasses bogged down in this, up north, and I've been loath to part with any clutter ever since. You never know when it's going to come in handy.'

It was the first time we had driven through the bush in the dark and it was a rough ride with sudden dips and troughs that the headlights failed to pick out. We bounced up and down on the seats and hung on to each other as we tried to catch what Tom was saying to Baz in front.

'Ted's sixty-seven. He was a land inspector in Esperance for a good many years. He has a son in Perth, I think. A lad named David ... came out here once, but not his cup of tea at all. Ted would have liked him to stay though. He has this hunch you see, that he's on to some big find. Trouble is, the shaft needs to be sunk deep and he can't do it on his lonesome. Not many youngsters are up for it. Lot of digging and hauling, for what they say? I tell you, the bright lights and flash cars have taken the place of gold fever. The hills out here are full of old men whose dreams have taken root in the land they lease. I'll be one of them soon I suppose.'

The red dirt track went over a water pipe and railway lines, twisting through the spinifex and white gums. Stones clanged against the underside of the station wagon and sometimes a front wheel spun before it gripped.

'Moon's out!' shouted Tom. 'Keep your eyes peeled for dingoes, Zhenka.'

The moon was low and very nearly round. I pictured it next to the Staffordshire plates propped up on the shelf of Mrs Harrison's Welsh dresser.

Ted's camp looked like the ones we had seen in the sepia photographs at the Coolgardie Museum. The brown canvas tent was high enough for us to stand up inside, and the ropes securing it were looped around a tree at each corner. Outside the tent opening, a sheet of corrugated iron had been fixed to three fence posts. This was where Ted kept his digging gear – the spades, shovels and picks, and the crowbars and coils of wire. Everything was cleaned after use in an oil drum full of rain water.

There were empty oil drums all over the clearing, big and small. Some were used for seating and had thick circular wedges of foam on top to make them comfy. Ted had seen the headlights of the station wagon drawing nearer and guessed that it was Tom coming out to see him. But he was surprised to see the rest of us.

The prospector was tall and wiry. He wore grey moleskin trousers and a saggy cardigan over a green shirt that had shrunk in the wash. There was an evangelical air about him. He had long, thin hands that could have been waving from the pulpit. When Tom had introduced us, Ted dragged a few of the empty oil drums closer to the fire and invited us to sit down.

'Some people turn up at the wrong time and some come just when the embers are ready for toasting. Now Tom, there's butter and miso hanging in the bush safe. I'll look after the rye bread.' He laid the thick slices of bread across the metal graders that were arranged in lines above the embers of the camp fire, and started to talk.

'I'm a Staffordshire man too. From a village called Barton-under-Needwood. It's near Burton-on-Trent. My brother was born in Stoke. I've no idea what my mother was doing there. We never lived in the Potteries to my knowledge. The family sailed to Australia in 1911. I was three years old.

'A bush fire destroyed our first home. It was the making of us. We lost everything overnight and found we didn't need most of it. Suddenly there were no material attachments to the old country and we simply got on with it. We built the next house ourselves, right down to the last stick of furniture. I loved it.'

Ted spoke in short clipped sentences, pared down to the essentials. He moved about like a squirrel: hopping, then stopping to listen before making the next move; alert in the extreme to whatever was around him.

'We don't need to elaborate on what nature discards. The bed in my tent is made of branches that were already on the ground – no ropes or nails hold it in place. Simple logic does that.'

'And you sleep like a log,' Chris butted in, bringing a faint smile to Ted's face before he carried on talking.

'I first worked this site forty years ago. There were two of us. A bloke named Jack Hammond and myself. We found a little gold and made a small amount of money. But Jack thought we'd found all we were likely to find, and as the lease for the digging rights was in his name we split up and moved on.

'I had a hunch about this spot back in the thirties and I still think the same now. Soon after we left I heard that two other prospectors struck it rich just over the hill there. By then, I had a full-time job and a family to look after. Over the years the work I did often brought me out this way. Sometimes I'd stop off overnight and rig up a hammock between the trees – right where I'm camped now. In the mornings I'd be up before it was properly light. Mostly just mooching around, seeing where this hunch of mine would lead me.

'When I finally retired and the wife died, there was nothing to keep me under a regular roof any longer. So I've taken out a claims right for a one-year lease on twenty-four acres. Anyone can go prospecting, all they need's a licence, and that only costs fifty cents.'

Ted stood up when we had eaten the last slices of toast. He grabbed a hurricane lamp but said we didn't really need it as the moon was so bright. Then we followed him, tramping over the dry grass that had turned silver in the moonlight, up and down a few uneven mounds of earth to a spot called Horseman's Gully.

'This is where we sunk the first shaft.' He held the lamp up level with his head and it picked out a gaping hole in the ground at our feet. Zhenka threw a stone to see how deep it was and Lea pulled him back away from the edge and wrapped her open duffel coat around him.

Ted stared into the shaft for some minutes. He must have been thinking of Jack, and the gold that was down there, and the dreams they'd shared of one day bringing it up to the surface.

'Tell me,' he said when he turned around, 'did youz ever get to see the Loch Ness monster?'

71

We returned to Horseman's Gully the next morning. Ted wanted us to have a closer look at the patch he had staked out. It had taken him three months to sift meticulously through the surface of the pegged area. Almost every loam – or sample – of the clay and soil had left behind tiny traces of gold sediment in the pan.

'The real stuff can't be more than four feet below the surface,' he told us. Then he searched the bushes for the right sort of branch and broke off a thick forked twig.

'Now I'll show you something you won't believe!' Ted gripped each end of the forked twig in his hands and strode forward with his arms held waist-high in front of him. As soon as he stepped over the length of orange twine that defined his 'golden plot', the twig dipped down. It stayed that way – pointing to the ground – until he strode clear of the taut line on the other side. Then it flipped back up, level with his hands, just as it had been before.

'There!' the prospector said. 'What do you make of that? It isn't only water that can be detected by dowsing. Want to try it out?'

This time, Ted only held one end of the splayed twig, while each of us in turn grabbed the other end. The same powerful magnetic pull drew the twig sharply down whenever it crossed into the demarcated strip of land.

'What draws it down?' asked Baz.

'Oh, I wouldn't have a clue,' replied the prospector.

Whatever strange force was responsible, it clearly affected all rational thinking. For one crazy moment we thought of abandoning the rest of our journey altogether to pitch in with Ted and help him dig up what lay beneath our feet.

Later, Ted used the divining stick to get his campfire going so that he could boil a billy. White smoke preceded the flames: shooting into the air like a ghost gum and leaning over low when the wind changed direction. We did the same, warming our hands as the flames sprang up and the water began to spit out of the blackened can.

Afterwards, when we'd drunk the tea, Ted said he'd show us

Mount Morgan. We piled into the utility truck parked next to the tent, and he drove us to the top of the hill, bouncing over the red ruts. On the way, as the truck climbed higher, Ted waved towards the distant landmarks and gave a running commentary.

'Back there, behind Widgemooltha, that's Mount Mine. You wouldn't see it from the main road. You can just see the top of the headframe. A man got killed there. They'd had problems with the air underground but the shift went down thinking it was all clear. When they didn't come up the foreman said he would go down to find out what had happened. The men had been gassed so he dragged them one by one to the shaft. There were four of them and only four could fit in the lifting crib that was winched to the surface.

'As the air got worse the foreman realised he didn't have time to wait for the crib to be sent back down. He'd saved the others but couldn't get out himself. He tried climbing a ladder but passed out before reaching the top and fell to his death down the shaft.'

Ted stopped the truck and switched off the engine. The wind had dropped. 'Silence is golden. Is that right? Is that what they say?' He rubbed his ribs and took a deep breath. 'That's where the digging gets me. And across the pit of my back too.'

From the hilltop there was a fine view of Lake Lefroy.

'The salt lake provides employment for most of Widgemooltha,' said Ted. 'The rest of the neighbourhood have jobs in the nickel mines.' He indicated where the dense bushland had been ripped apart to facilitate large-scale mining operations now that nickel was on the agenda. 'People are coming back in trickles. They've spent a million dollars on sinking a shaft over there. Ten years on and the land will have changed beyond recognition.'

Ted spoke more fondly of the abandoned gold mines. To him it was like visiting sick relatives who could no longer pay their way. They had glorious names, still painted on pieces of wood or carved into the nearest tree trunks. Redmine, Celebration, Two Boys, Christmas Flat, and the one near Comet Hill called Gibraltar.

I asked Ted about the track we were on. 'Can we use it instead of the road to get to the next town on the map?'

'That would be Norseman, wouldn't it? I'm not so sure it stretches that far.'

From where we stood, the sandy trail through the bush appeared to run on and on, over the hills in a straightish line. It drew me to it with a pull just as strong and unfathomable as that exerted by the splayed twig.

'Better not chance it,' said Baz. Ted looked at me and winked.

'How long will you stay out here Ted?' I asked him.

He paused before he answered, scraping at the red dust with the toe cap of his boot.

'I don't think I'll be leaving for a long time yet, Kelvin. I've had spasms of civilisation … you can keep it.'

72

Norseman is scarred by mullock heaps, mineshafts and claypans. Zhenka spent his fourth birthday there on 21 June. It was the last town in the state. The last place at which we could post a letter or replenish any depleted essentials such as toilet rolls and toothpaste. There wouldn't be another town of this size for over 700 miles.

The township of Norseman is named after a horse whose hoof dislodged a gold nugget in 1894. Chris renamed it Nosebag, which somehow seemed more fitting since most of the gold had gone and the treatment works in town concentrated primarily on the less romantic production of agricultural fertiliser.

We ran only ten miles that day, then we doubled back in the van and parked up at the local caravan site. Lea baked a birthday cake and topped it with chocolate and four pale blue candles. I bought a few plastic farmyard animals from a general store where several packets of rat poison were encircled by a bright display of hoola hoops.

In the afternoon, Zhenka and I built a cattle station out of Lego. When it was dark Chris drove us to a drive-in. Two films were showing. The first of these starred Burt Lancaster in *The Crimson Pirate*. We hooked up to the sound system and settled down in the front seats of the van. Zhenka already had on his pyjamas and dressing gown but was allowed to stay up late.

During the interval, people would jump out of their cars and race up the concrete slope to buy ice creams and popcorn from a snack bar next to the entrance of the drive-in. This was where the teenagers without transport congregated – draping their arms around each other for pretend warmth, while they enviously eyed the steamed-up rear windows of the Holdens parked in front of them.

Lea lit the cooker in the back of our van and brewed cups of tea before the main film began. It was called *The Thief Who Came to Dinner* and it starred Ryan O'Neal. Rain fell before the film ended and everyone turned on their windscreen wipers. Chris thought it enhanced the car chases.

At Norseman, the Great Eastern Highway (Route 94) joined the Eyre Highway (Route 1). But for the change of name and number the road stayed exactly the same. We had been running along it for less than five minutes when a car drifted onto the hard shoulder and stopped. Gerald, the driver, was an off-duty policeman with a blond moustache.

'Not many people've done what you're doing,' he stated in a grudgingly appreciative tone that implied we had been caught red-handed. 'There was a couple of guys a year back – Tony Rafferty and George Perdon – made a race of it for big money. Plenty cycle across of course. And every once in a while some oddball will wander into the desert and never be seen again. That's what happened to Leichhardt. Mind you, he was a hero already. Patrick White wrote a book about him. Called it *Voss*. You should read it.'

Gerald bent at the knees to fiddle with his wing mirror, keeping a straight back like policemen do in comedy sketches and pantomimes, usually with their hands clasped behind them. As he adjusted the mirror he grew preoccupied with the view it contained: a thin strip of bitumen receding into the distance. Real distance, where it took hours of driving flat-out before you reached so much as a hint of a bend in the road.

Gerald was in the middle of his annual holiday but couldn't bring himself to leave the highway he patrolled each day.

'They gave it the name of an explorer you know. A man named John Eyre. But he never would have made it across the Nullarbor without the help of an Aborigine. You would have thought he'd go easy on the blacks after that. But years later, when he became Governor Chief of Jamaica, he did away with a black opponent of his.

'Back in England it caused him big problems. His effigy was burned in Trafalgar Square and there were riots. Charles Darwin and the chap who wrote *Tom Brown's Schooldays* demanded justice. But he had popular support too – Charles Dickens, among others – and he got off when it went to court. If you ask me, John Eyre was a lucky blighter all his life. Strange that a road so straight should immortalise a man who was anything but.'

The patrolman made as if to get back inside his car, then another thought occurred to him.

'Better give that book *Voss* a miss until you've reached the other side,' he said.

73

Eight thousand miles were in the logbook. But over 2,000 miles more still remained to be covered. Baz and I had never felt in better shape. We were both full of determination as we struck out for the great plain where no trees grew. I think the overnight stops had something to do with this: a renewed surge of energy brought on by the more relaxing periods of recovery. Each afternoon, Chris and Lea left us running and drove ahead to search for somewhere to camp – preferably a spot that would go unnoticed from the highway.

The sites they chose got better and better. But this could lead to confusion. Once into the last run of the day, we had to keep our eyes peeled for any signs of tyre marks leaving the highway, or Chris's shaving foam arrows underfoot. Sometimes we walked half a mile from the road before we found them. A fire would often be alight and water already on the boil so that we could take it in turns to stand in a bowl and sponge ourselves down as the sun set. These were halcyon days.

With little traffic using the Eyre Highway and no towns or other distractions on this part of the route, we decided to aim for forty miles a day. To reach this target we split the distance into four ten-mile runs.

The first of these was always before breakfast. It was our favourite run of the day and usually the period during which we would spot the most animals. We saw a wild cat, emus, and lots of red kangaroos. Dingoes too, at this early hour, and a fox on one occasion – transfixed by the sight of two humans passing by on foot.

Of course we saw more dead animals than live ones. Carcasses crawling with flies heaped about the orange shoulders of the highway. Baz called it 'a nasal catalogue of mammal and marsupial deaths'. It was certainly that.

One morning we met a Buddhist mining engineer from Switzerland still distraught three days after witnessing the total eclipse of an emu at eighty-five miles per hour.

We took a long time over breakfast. It was the longest break of the day. When bread was available Lea would make toast over the embers of the previous night's fire, before she and Chris set out to catch us up. Sometimes a cheese omelette would follow, and a couple of Weetabix too.

If it was dry and warm enough, we would sit outside and read or listen to the news on the radio. Zhenka would be in his pyjamas still – playing frisbee with the lid from a plastic tub, or some other energetic game that required Chris to dart around the van with him.

After the breakfast stop we set off on another run of ten miles. If we had eaten too much and found we could not run on a full stomach, we would walk to begin with and take a couple of paperbacks with us.

Baz and I didn't always set out together. Even in the desert we needed our own space from time to time. When we did run side by side and were both running well, anything was likely to happen. Once, after an hour's solid running – when we were both feeling competitive and attempting to break away from each other – we ignored the breakfast stop altogether and just steamed on past the van.

Neither of us seemed prepared to give an inch. The pace quickened. I looked at Baz out of the corner of my eye and caught him doing the same. Then we stared straight ahead, like blinkered racehorses, and stubbornly went for it – charging down the road as fast as we could. Chris and Lea didn't know what to make of this. At first they thought we hadn't seen them and Chris rushed to the van and slid open the door to toot the horn. When that had no effect they just stood and watched us disappear into the distance.

After a few hundred yards we knew we had to ease back. But we were reluctant to admit it and carried on a little further. Finally, we glanced across at each other again – grinning this time. The grin turned into gasping laughter and before long we were on our knees in the middle of the empty highway like two demented kookaburras!

A longish break for a late lunch separated the final two ten-mile stretches, and the last ten miles was always the killer. No matter how well we had been running all day, the aches and pains were unavoidable. Our feet blistered if we carried on. Our legs seized up if we stopped.

In three days we ran 120 miles. The road went up and down but the hills were neither too steep nor too long. There were trees amongst the bushes, and barren patches of dry red earth. But it was still a gentle landscape, lightly timbered and easy to look at.

One night we huddled around a small fire in the dark, whilst Chris tuned in the radio. A foreign correspondent spoke of massive arrests in New Delhi. After allegations of corruption it looked as if Mrs Gandhi would have her work cut out to remain in power.

The news item was followed by an arts programme, which included a review of a new volume of poetry by the Melbourne-based poet Kris Hemensley. Chris fiddled with the radio to get a better reception, and he turned up the sound. The book was called *Here We Are*.

'That's my friend,' I said to Chris and Baz. 'The poet I told you about. The one I met on a ship sailing to Australia in 1966. We shared a bedsit together in Melbourne, then fell out and didn't see one another for a long time.

'To entice us into taking the room the landlady had told us that the area was very cosmopolitan. I thought she was talking about Italian ice cream! Soon afterwards her daughter burst into the kitchen and started punching hell out of her lesbian lover. Kris said that he was calling his novel *Campfire*. The sound of his typewriter drove me nuts.

'On Sundays I would escape into the Dandenongs to run with Ron Clarke and the Glenhuntly mob. And in the week I'd catch a train out to Caulfield and lap the racecourse there with Pat Clohessy and Trevor Vincent.

'It was during a time when the government was conscripting more and more young people to fight in Vietnam. Even LBJ flew to Melbourne to meet Prime Minister Holt and drum up support for the US cause. Most of my new friends were draft dodgers and I joined them on protest marches and demonstrations. Kris met his future wife Loretta at an all-night vigil outside Government House on the King's Domain.

'I was returning to England on a boat bound for the Panama Canal when news reached us that Holt had gone swimming at Portsea and had vanished into thin air.'

We lay in our sleeping bags when the fire went low, and listened to Bob Dylan and Joni Mitchell.

By the end of the week we had covered 269 miles – the most we had ever managed in any seven-day period. Also, there was something else to get excited about. The prospect of a bend in a daunting stretch of highway known as Ninety Miles Straight.

When we reached the bend in the road we ignored it and kept running in a straight line. Ahead we could see where the tarmac swung out in a wide loop that we would rejoin after a mile or so across the dirt. The cars and caravans whizzed by in the distance. As soon as they were out of earshot the sound of our footsteps grew louder: magnified by the acute stillness all around us.

Two hippies were preparing to leave the roadhouse at Cocklebiddy. They were travelling in a hand-painted pick-up truck with a lemon-coloured roo bar. Alan wore red socks and braces to match, with only a pair of dusty blue jeans between. His girlfriend Beth drifted by in a tie-dyed skirt that brushed the ground. She was barefoot and chattered to herself – breaking into tuneless snatches of a folksong whenever her boyfriend spoke. The couple were from Adelaide, and the truck was playing up.

'Our friends will fix it for us,' said Alan. 'They're following behind somewhere. They can get anything moving apart from their butts.'

Baz asked if they were headed west and Alan shook his head and motioned to a rough dirt track across from the Cocklebiddy stopover. The track was wide but peppered with potholes, and the gravel that had been swept aside by the graders looked like piles of gold nuggets in the sunlight.

'They call it the Connie Sue Highway,' grinned Alan. 'It runs north for hundreds of miles deep into the interior. Eventually it links up with the Gunbarrel Highway. It's one of the bomb roads.'

'The what?'

'Our government bulldozed a network of dirt roads through the bush during the fifties when the atomic bomb tests were taking place at Maralinga. The British couldn't do it in their own backyard now, could they? Bob Menzies was only too willing to oblige. So … Bang!' The hippy stamped his foot on the ground and the dust came up and settled over his desert boots and the red ankle socks. 'There are still roadsigns out there warning about radioactivity,' Alan went on. 'My dad came out here twenty years ago. He was in the army. One of the volunteers who thought they were onto an easy number by observing a cloud in the sky. He talked about it to me when I was a child. Said he was proud to have seen something so important. It was the only time he went into the desert and he never shut up about it.' Alan paused. 'I've got his ashes in the truck. I might just scatter them in the desert. He would appreciate the irony in that. He was a funny old sod.'

74

On our way to the Madura Pass we met up with Alan's friends and told them that he and Beth were waiting for them at the next petrol stop. The hippies tossed organic oranges to us as they sped off in their truck and one of them shouted back: 'Hey, I've lived with Aborigines – they can outrun a kangaroo!'

At Madura, the highway descended from the Hampton Tablelands to the coastal plain 200 feet below. The road dropped sharply and we slowed to a jog and leaned back to lessen the jarring. The land skirting the foot of the perpendicular cliffs stretched for 100 miles along the coast. Horses were reared here until the turn of the nineteenth century. They were shipped out to the Indian Army for service in the cavalry regiment.

The saltbush was only knee-high on the treeless plain and firewood was difficult to come by. Even so, on 3 July we stopped running early and left the road to gather enough branches for a larger campfire than usual. It was Chris's twenty-first birthday, and a guest arrived to join the party.

All that morning, giant grading machines had thrown up dust as they scraped the gravel from the dirt shoulders of the highway. Through the dust we saw an orange speck in the distance – wobbling like the sun did when the waves of heat buckled the horizon.

The cyclist approached us with his head bent low over the handlebars. He wore his hair tucked under a fluorescent orange crash-helmet and when he got off the bike and removed it, a tangle of blond locks tumbled around his shoulders. The teenager said his name was Rowan and that he was pedalling after the pioneers. He had cycled from Melbourne and he was on his way to Perth.

Chris had parked the van half a mile from the highway, along one of the tracks that led to a microwave tower. These Meccano-like constructions straddled the powdery landscape at intervals of 25 miles. Beyond them, far to our left now, ran the flat ridge of limestone cliffs bordering the Nullarbor itself.

We ate baked beans and Ryvita for breakfast, followed by pancakes and beer. Rowan left at lunchtime, intent on grabbing a saltwater shower in the motel back at the Madura Pass. The rest of us spent the day adding to our meagre woodpile and got a fire going just before dusk.

The clouds were red and purple when the sun slid away from the plain. The blue saltbush took on the same colours, so that it looked as if the embers of our campfire had rolled in all directions for as far as the eye could see.

Lea prepared a curry for Chris's birthday meal. Then she produced a tin of Irish whisky cake that we had hidden in the medical box especially for the occasion. Afterwards, we played cassettes and drank more beer, and opened a bottle of port too.

Chris stayed up late. When I woke in the early hours and stuck my head outside the door I found him asleep beside the ashes of the fire. I took a blanket out for him, checked that the fire was safe, and went for a piss.

The moon was low and big, the iron girders of the microwave tower etched into it like black ink. Looking up at the stars, I began to wonder what would become of us all. What we'd do when we reached Sydney ...

I couldn't bear the thought of flying straight back to England. Chris and Baz had already spoken of perhaps sharing a flat together in Sydney. And Lea loved Australia too – the vastness of it. She said it hinted at infinity. But I felt I needed to keep on the move a little while longer. To try and gain some sort of understanding of how far I'd travelled on foot. Make comparisons I suppose, if it were possible.

There was a slow-moving speck of silver among the stars. A satellite!

'Russia,' I said to myself, aloud. 'We'll take a train across Russia and stop off at Zima.'

'Zima Junction' is the title of a long poem by Yevgeny Yevtushenko. It is also the name of an important halt on the Trans-Siberian Railway. The Russian poet was born there and the autobiographical piece describes the childhood he spent in a town surrounded by dense forests. A translation of the poem by Peter Levi had appeared in a slim volume I had packed into the box of books we had brought with us. I had first read it just before our son was born. In one line, Yevtushenko's uncle called him Zhenka. It was a made-up name but Lea and I liked the way it looked when we wrote it down.

When I lost sight of the satellite I went back to sleep.

75

For the past few days we had noticed how all the oncoming traffic was coated in orange dust. When we crossed the state border into South Australia we found out why. Halfway across the desert, the Eyre Highway ran out of bitumen. In its place lay a two-laned strip of dirt and stones: the worst surface on the entire route.

Despite regular attempts at maintenance, the road crew manning the graders were faced with an impossible task. The longhaul freight carriers did the most damage. These trucks were scary beasts at the best of times. Whether approaching head-on or thundering up from the west, their enormous tyres showered pebbles and gravel in all directions.

The only sure way to avoid being cut up by flying debris was to make a run for it into the bushes and stay out of the way until all the trucks had gone by. But this was tiring and wasted time. Suddenly it felt as if we were going nowhere fast. There was nothing for it but to chance our luck and stay with the road.

Even without the big trucks our progress was slow. When the stony ground between the low ribbons of bush lay empty it was no less of a minefield to negotiate.

'I gave up cross-country running because of two bad ankle sprains ten years ago,' I told Baz, looking sideways momentarily, then quickly down again to watch where I was putting my feet. Baz said nothing.

We crossed from one side of the dirt to the other, then back again. For a few strides one lane would seem alright and then more stones and lumps of gravel would appear underfoot, and we'd go through the same procedure – glancing ahead to see if we were approaching a smoother patch. It was exhausting to run this way and before long our knees and ankles were aching due to the sudden twists and split-second changes of direction.

Fewer stones flew up from the cars towing the caravans since they were also forced to reduce their speed. But the orange veils of dust that floated in their wake were almost as menacing. We ran with cloths tied over our mouths to keep out the dirt and grit, and we put on sunglasses to protect our eyes.

A man who had been a passenger on the *Chidambaram* got out of his van and took our photograph. We'd last seen him in Singapore, hurling abuse at immigration officials.

'Did they let me in? Did they fuck! They put me on the first plane out because I wouldn't get a fucking haircut. Bastard country that. Oz is only a tad better. Don't know where the fuck to go next. There's a blowhole down the road. Have you seen them? Bloody weird things they are. Tell you what though, you pair, rigged out like that ... My lady saw you first, "Don't stop," she says, "they're nutters!"'

Chris and Lea were waiting for us at the first of the blowholes, just north of the dirt road. Zhenka ran across the pale sand to tell me what he'd seen. 'Chrissy threw an empty packet down the hole but the wind blew it back every time!'

The limestone plateau was riddled with natural tunnels and passageways, some of which led back to openings in the cliff-face many miles away. When the wind blew in from the Southern Ocean, the air was sucked underground and funnelled through the earth until it surged up out of the holes with a great whoosh.

Rowan had told us what a strange and timeless place this was, and that nowhere else on earth had the outer crust of the planet remained so little changed. Although the Nullarbor was bone-dry for much of the year, there were vast lakes beneath the surface. In their search for water, coastal tribes of Aborigines had discovered these subterranean catacombs 25,000 years ago. One of their most sacred sights lay close to the Koonalda homestead a few miles down the road.

Chris filled up with petrol at Koonalda. The homestead was built out of old railway sleepers plundered from the intercontinental line over a hundred miles away. A pile of rusty rabbit snares lay in a jumble on the ground in the direction of the cave. When we got there we found a gaping hole on the surface and a rickety steel ladder leading down to the entrance. Chris and Lea descended the ladder for a closer look but turned back at the bottom. The mouth of the cave was 120 feet wide but it was off-limits to non-Aborigines.

Back on the road Baz and I were overtaken by a vintage yellow Citroën. It was the very same vehicle that had first circumnavigated the continent fifty years earlier, and the man at the wheel gave us a wave.

The rest of the team were travelling in close attendance. They had a four-wheel drive jeep and a roomy caravan bristling with colourful stickers of their sponsors. The back-up group stopped the jeep when they saw us running and a big man wearing clean blue overalls made as if to stretch his legs and asked where we were going.

'Sydney,' Baz told him.

The man studied our legs and the state of the road. 'Well fuck my black cat!' he muttered. Then he grabbed a thermos from the jeep and gawped into the distance to where the receding Citroën was now no more than a cloud of dust.

'Better not let on where we've run from,' whispered Baz. 'He thinks we're just crossing Australia!'

East of Koonalda, where the open plain was at its barest, we ran past an empty wheelbarrow and wrecked cars daubed with names, dates and states. Messages were scrawled everywhere. It was as if once faced with nothing, most travellers seemed compelled to leave some trace of themselves behind. All that one trashed water tank contained were the words: 'Stoned is beautiful!' and 'Jesus is alive!'

Two furry wombats had met their end there; copped by someone's roo bars, they lay on their backs with their small legs rigid in the air.

The Nullarbor homestead was the next place we stopped at. It probably started out as a cattle station, but then as more people began to use the road, it turned into a no-frills motel with prefabricated cabins and petrol pumps out front. A light aircraft was parked on a landing strip nearby when we arrived. A red-faced man was warning the pilot to watch out for the Aborigines who were trading boomerangs for booze. The man had a rasping cough and a loud sneeze that seemed a strange thing to be listening to in the middle of the desert.

'I got nothing against 'em,' he went on, 'but they can't hold their drink like you and me. They don't belong here really ... not at Yalata anyway.'

The pilot peeled off a tartan sweater and undid the top two buttons of his shirt. 'Sam,' he said, smiling. 'Always remember: there are no strawberries on the Nullarbor.'

The Lutheran church at Yalata had chosen a picture of the altar in their green-walled chapel for the cover of the leaflet they had recently published. There was also a photograph of an Aborigine kneeling in the silver grass outside his wurley shelter.

The postcard-sized pages of the leaflet unfolded from top to bottom like a concertina. Half a dozen black and white snaps chronicled the making of various artefacts that could be purchased from the mission storeroom. A potted history in tiny print on the reverse side of the photographs told how most of the Pitjantjara-speaking Aborigines came to be at the reservation.

No mention was made of the atomic bomb tests over their ancestral grounds in the Great Victorian Desert. The pamphlet stated that the old mission at Ooldea was forced to close 'for various reasons including serious sand-drift problems'. The first of the bomb tests had taken place in 1952 – that same year, the South Australian government purchased land for the new reservation at Yalata.

'Where did you find this?' asked Baz angrily when I showed him the pamphlet. 'It's bullshit! Alan told us how his dad had driven a truck all over the place picking up stray Aborigines who didn't know what the fuck was going on. According to him, the army sent trucks out round the clock to try and clear the land, but they had a limited amount of time in which to do it.'

The mission at Yalata was not a pretty sight. But then neither was stripping away the cultural beliefs of the Aborigines and introducing them to booze and syphilis. Dogs ran loose everywhere, yapping and scratching at the perimeter fence. Inside, there were cars with no wheels or doors, and some were tilted on their sides to form windbreaks where groups of women sheltered on plastic sheeting.

A foodstore and canteen stood in a clearing, and boomerangs and spears lay on long trestle tables in a room at the back, where a sign read: 'No return on empties.'

'The last time I was in Australia, in 1967,' I told Lea, 'it happened to be the same year that the Aborigines were finally granted citizenship. It's not long at all is it? Not when you think that the first settlers came here over a hundred years earlier.'

76

It rained for two days after we left Yalata. Not continuously, but it felt that way. At first we didn't care because the rain helped to keep the dust down. And anyway, we had just crossed the Nullarbor and felt that we had something to smile about after the scaremongering back in Perth. But it was blustery too, and when we stopped running there were no campfires to sit beside and dry our wet clothes. Everyone's high spirits took a nosedive when it grew damp inside the van. Worst of all though, was to wake up and lie in our sleeping bags listening to the rain ping on the metal roof, knowing that we'd be soaked within minutes of leaving the van.

Outside the reservation we began to see green fields again. Pasture lands with scattered homesteads. The signs for water beside the highway rolled off the tongue: Pitumba Well, Tallala Tank … and I recited them to myself as I ran.

Near a place called Bookabie the dirt road began a long straight climb. At the top we stopped to take in the view below. Ahead lay a broad plain. Halfway across it was a strip of bitumen.

'Thank God for that!' said Baz. 'You know, I've been thinking – it's like joined-up writing isn't it, this highway? They haven't quite got the hang of it yet.'

It was good to plant our feet down onto a firm surface again and not have to weave between the potholes or swap lanes to avoid the stones. We splashed our way along the straight while blankets of mist rolled across the plain; rain, road and sky merging into one leaden weight. The sea was hidden from us but we heard it booming as it struck a reef, ten miles distant.

Penong was the first real township we had seen in the past three weeks. It was a tiny place, nothing to get excited about under normal circumstances, and I doubt whether most overland travellers even noticed that there *was* a town. But our food stocks had dwindled to one jar of peanut paste, one tin of beetroot, and a packet of crackers. Baz's stomach was beginning to rumble.

We found a cricket pitch, a small rural school and several stone houses. We even found two surfers: city boys with sun-bleached hair, who had dropped out of college to live in a shack eight miles away on Cactus Beach. But there was no shop open.

'Don't worry,' one of the surfers said. 'You'll be at Ceduna tomorrow. There's everything you could possibly want there, except for a decent wave.'

'Pie and chips even!' added his mate.

'Strawberries and ice cream?' asked Zhenka.

'That too.'

Soon there were pavements on each side of the road, and shops. The others had driven ahead to a caravan park close to the beach. Chris took Zhenka for a walk along the wooden jetty, past the fishermen who told him all about how Gulliver had met the tiny people of Lilliput on an island just off the coast.

Meanwhile, Lea collected our mail from the local post office. Amongst the bundle of letters there were birthday cards for Zhenka and Chris, and she taped them up on the inside of the van. Later, we all took cold beers and Coke down to the jetty.

'Dad,' said Zhenka. 'The 'riginals called where we are now Chedoona. Do you know what it means?'

I shook my head, 'No, do you?'

'It means a place to sit down and rest. The men fishing told me. That's what they were doing.' He pointed to the end of the jetty. 'See out there. That's where there's an island. It's got the same name as Aunty Vi's budgie and it's full of little people, but Chris says we can't go.'

There was a brief pause for breath, and also for the look he gave me whenever he was after something really badly. 'Can we go?'

The caretaker from the caravan park saved my bacon. ABC television had just phoned from Adelaide. They were flying out to film us tomorrow, but would I ring back to confirm that we'd still be around?

The light aircraft touched down exactly on time. An estate wagon hired by the TV company was waiting at the airstrip. As soon as the camera crew had loaded up their equipment we drove into the bush.

The filming lasted all afternoon. They shot footage of Baz and I running along a red dirt road. The sound engineer taped a mike to my waist underneath my singlet so that he could record our footsteps. Then they filmed Lea and Chris, who pretended to set up camp in a clearing. They asked Chris to empty the tin box of worn running shoes onto the ground and filmed those too.

ABC were not alone in their sudden interest. Before we moved on, a Sydney-based national – *The Australian* – caught up with us at the caravan park. Other calls followed. Most reporters asked us about the Nullarbor. They didn't seem all that interested in how we'd managed to get there. Baz put it down to the scale of the country.

'It's so blasted big they're nervous of what they'll find out there,' he reasoned. 'Crossing some desert in Afghanistan is too remote for most people here to comprehend. They've only just come to terms with the capture of Ned Kelly!'

Beyond Ceduna, large areas of mallee scrub had been uprooted and replaced with fields of wheat. We passed through cattle country too. Cows stared after us over the wire fences.

The TV programme *This Day Tonight* had been shown nationwide the evening after they had filmed us. Cars and trucks now began to pull in more frequently, while the occupants scrambled out to take photographs and hand over steaks, fish or dollars.

Depending on where Chris was at the time, some of the people who stopped also signed our logbook and scribbled comments about their own travels: 'Charlie Anderson – drove overland in a Klute with Frank Foster', 'Jane Bushell – I took the easy way and drove here in seven months', 'Sarah Frazer – I flew'.

The wind stayed behind us for a few days, whipping the loose topsoil from the fields so that it still felt dusty. At Wirrulla the road joined a railway track. Grain silos threw giant shadows over the sidings at each of the small towns along the way.

On 23 July I notched up 9,000 miles. The aches and pains were back: sore knees and a dodgy ankle. Baz welcomed the opportunity to press on in front. The distance he gained – however slight – meant more time to himself. And there had not been much of that for over twelve months now. Even the open spaces looked less empty. Oddly enough, the first sure signs that we were moving back into sedentary communities turned out to be the growing number of caravan parks we came across. Not that we used many of them. We still preferred to camp in the outback and to build a campfire whenever we could. But our journey was changing, albeit slowly. And we all knew it – though none of us could understand precisely what was happening. Not until Chris happened to mention Sebastian Snow ...

In February 1973, this man had set out to walk from Cape Horn at the tip of South America all the way north to Alaska. He had no back-up team. Just a pack of supplies and a lightweight tent. He never left the road – saying it broke his rhythm – and he averaged 15 miles a day for over a year and a half.

With the toughest part of the long trek behind him, he called it a day when he reached San José in Costa Rica. It wasn't the lonely stretches that caused him to quit when he did, but rather the opposite. He simply couldn't cope with the volume of traffic, the roadside billboards, and the gruesome evidence of what America had done to itself, staring him in the face day after day. His sudden re-emergence into a supposedly progressive environment scared the shit out of him and so he hung up his walking boots after 5,110 miles.

'This is the hinterland,' said Baz. 'They've not fucked it up yet but they will do – like Ted said they would. From here on it's going to get busier.'

'Chris was looking at the maps this morning,' Lea said. 'He found a route that bypasses Adelaide.'

'We don't have any special reason to go there, do we?' asked Chris.

'Only to collect our post.'

'Couldn't that be forwarded to Melbourne?'

'I suppose so. Let me see this route of yours, Chris.'

From Port Augusta, Highway 1 ran due south to Adelaide. But there were other roads shooting off east that eventually linked up with the Murray River in the state of Victoria. Chris's alternative was probably hillier, but the names of the places it passed through – Wilmington, Melrose, Laura and Clare – suggested dawdling jalopies and sleepy country stops.

'Let's take it,' I said.

First of all we had to reach Port Augusta. On the way we watched a distraught homesteader rounding up his sheep on a Yamaha, with his dog riding pillion. The land on this side of the Middleback Ranges was parched and what grass there was looked straggly and yellow. Everyone we met said 'it must rain soon or else ...' One farmer had already replaced his stock with a go-kart track.

A few families were living in orange railway carriages in disused sidings on the edge of Kimba. We strode past them at dusk and glimpsed the yellow glow from their oil lamps. That night at the local caravan park, Baz gave Zhenka a swing in the dark.

'Stop the swing a minute Baz!' he shouted. 'Have you ever been to England?'

'Yes.'

'Really?'

''Course I have – that's where I come from!'

'This is a big country, isn't it Baz?'

77

The quieter road Chris had chosen followed the same direction as the busy highway we had abandoned outside Port Augusta until it reached Auburn.

Every day now we passed through at least one country town, sometimes more. They were all arranged along the same neat lines with broad streets and a central crossroads. Most of the single-storey houses along the route had iron roofing and weather-boarded walls.

Suddenly there were complicated intersections to puzzle over and our road maps came out more often than the kangaroos did.

Campfires were a thing of the past too. And Chris found that he couldn't just pull off anywhere to park up for the night without first asking permission. It seemed odd to read an entry in our logbook stating 'D. K. Prior – Very happy to have you camp on our property.'

Without a fire to look forward to, our evenings were hardgoing. Baz reckoned that a cold van led to heated arguments. He was right. And so we turned in soon after we'd eaten, both to keep warm and to keep the peace. Chris reasoned that our true temperaments were resurfacing – coming out of hibernation as it were – after a sleepy lull in the outback.

But at the root of it all I sensed a growing anxiety about what would happen to us all when there was nowhere else to run to. Whatever hardships we'd faced, life had never been so uncomplicated. On waking, Baz and I were geared up for ten miles' running. We had no idea where exactly that would take us, simply that it was somewhere ahead – a place that we had never seen before and were unlikely to pass through ever again.

When we got there we would eat the breakfast that Lea had prepared for us. Then we would both look down the road – if Chris had pulled in by the roadside – to try to determine what the next hour's running held in store. After breakfast we strode off again into the unknown. It was a safe bet to assume that we were unlikely to bump into anyone on the planet similarly engaged. Everyone else seemed to be scurrying around like ants for all kinds of reasons.

Soon it would be our turn. Baz said that it couldn't come soon enough for him. But he was feeling tetchy at the time, having found a toenail in his underpants.

'Fuckin' hell, Kel!' he stormed. 'You were the last one using the nail clippers!'

On 5 August we reached the Murray River where it flowed east at Morgan. The water was brown and wide and there were red gum trees on the riverbank. But the sky was grey, the weather having changed for the worst.

An elderly river skipper was talking on the local radio as we ran up to the van. 'The wife, she navigated these waters … our life. The children learned their sums and spelling on a liquid slate when condensation formed on the cabin roof. They fell overboard often, but they could all swim like fish. We carried wool and sometimes teams of shearers. One time my youngest said we were carting clouds downriver to where it hadn't rained enough. She would race barefoot across the bales of wool after they'd been loaded into the boat and she told me that that was what it was like to be up inside the sky.

'Captain Charles Sturt first charted the river in a whale boat. The same fella that got the highway named after him. When he ran short of tucker he ate ten parakeets and a swan. Do that now and yer wouldn't get much named after yer.'

We kept the river on our right all the way to Renmark. It drizzled off and on as we ran along the valley. The rainwater cascaded down the empty crates and mesh cages which had been stacked high beside the fruit trees that would fill them when the picking season started. Fallen oranges glowed luminous in the long grass.

There were locks at intervals along the river, grey concrete and green rails; hard to distinguish from the same coloured clouds pressing down onto the treetops. Mist was slow to clear wherever the overhanging willows cradled the water's edge. One morning we heard hidden wings beating where the brown river was shot through with white. Suddenly a flock of pelicans rose out of the mist and wheeled away over the Murray.

At Renmark, a circus family were putting up their big top, hauling guy ropes and hammering tent pegs on a bumpy expanse of grass that reminded me of a village green. We camped beside their caravans and took Zhenka to the evening performance. He'd never seen candyfloss before, and we could hardly see him when he was eating it. The kids in the row behind wanted some too, but their uncle came back empty-handed.

'The lady who makes the candyfloss is dressing up to go into the lion's cage,' he told them, promising to return to the goodies kiosk in the interval for another try.

A Shetland pony stampeded before the show began and the ringmaster's whip got tangled up between his legs. I stole a glance at the family behind. The kids were laughing, but the slapstick beginnings did not bode well for the candyfloss, and their uncle's face was wracked with anxiety.

Zhenka enjoyed the clowns most of all. One of them limped towards me, slapping his long flat shoes up and down across the sawdust as if he were in pain.

'I've got a sore toe, boys and girls. Boo hoo hoo! And I know another man whose feet are sore – he's just run across the Nullarbor!'

At that, two other clowns ran down the nearest aisle and lifted me out of my seat. I was hoisted onto their shoulders and carried into the ring. The limping clown handed me a giant-sized sticking plaster and asked if I'd tell the audience what it felt like to run so far without being chased.

So I told him that we had been chased for some of the way – but not in Australia.

One morning, Chris waved a newspaper towards me and pointed to a paragraph.

Percy Cerutty – who made the sand dunes at Portsea and a young West Australian miler called Herb Elliott famous around the world – has died at his Portsea home. Cerutty was often heard to say: "What's the use of a body that can run a four-minute mile if the brain can't appreciate the beauty of a sunset across the sea?" On hearing the news, Herb Elliott commented: "Ninety-five per cent of what Percy taught me at Portsea had nothing to do with the sport of athletics."

He was eighty years old and had never fully recovered from a bad fall nine weeks earlier.

I thought about the first shack he had built at Portsea and Landy's bunk inside. Remembered him clowning about with Nancy at mealtimes when the weekly pop slot was on TV. And how she pretended to be annoyed with him, but wasn't really. How could she be? How could anyone be? Even when Perce set out to be awkward or goaded you into doing crazy stunts …

Like running all this way for instance.

'I wonder if he knew?' asked Chris.

'Knew what?'

'About your marathon.'

'Perce's marathon, Chris. It was his idea. Know what he said the last time I saw him, nine years ago now? That if I wanted to leave, then it was up to me. But he and Nance were like a river. They'd still be there if I ever went back.'

78

The postmistress stamped our logbook at Echuca. It was 18 August, 1975. Melbourne was three hours' drive away. We planned to travel there and back in the van before resuming our run along the Murray. I had last seen the state capital in 1967, when I was twenty-one. My friend Kris, the poet, still lived there somewhere.

Nostalgia got the better of me as the mileposts along Highway 75 zipped by. I talked too much and the others grew tired of listening to me drone on about the merits of the city we were making for. Not surprisingly, by the time we arrived on the outskirts everyone was already thoroughly sick of the place.

When Chris asked for directions I scrambled eagerly into the passenger seat. 'We should be able to park off Domain Road outside the Botanical Gardens,' I told him.

The closer we got to the city centre, the more trams we saw. Zhenka sat up and suddenly began to take notice. Our stay might be too brief to allow a trip to Luna Park – the fairground by the seaside at St Kilda – but a few tram rides were definitely on the cards.

'They're the same colour!' I shouted, pointing out of the windscreen. 'Green and yellow ... just as I remember them. Isn't that wonderful?'

'Don't forget to navigate,' muttered Chris.

'Turn right at the next set of lights,' I quickly instructed. But a new one-way system dictated a different route and Chris drove on.

'Over the grassy hill there, see? That's the King's Domain. The Myer Music Bowl's in a dip behind. It's an open-air concert venue. I saw The Seekers there in sixty-six. I used to have to cross this road on my way to work each morning. God, it's busy isn't it?'

After a short detour, Chris managed to find a parking space outside the Botanical Gardens directly opposite Domain Street where I'd once rented a room. I slid back the door of the van and leapt out. The fallen leaves on the side of the road crunched underfoot like shards of stained glass and my feet sank in and disappeared. Already I wanted to be racing off down the streets revisiting old haunts in South Yarra and Prahran. But the others were dragging their feet. Baz was first to warm to the place.

'Lots of runners, Kel.'

'Yeah, this is known as the Tan Track. Toorak's well-to-do used to exercise their horses here when the gardens were first laid out. A sort of Hyde Park. There weren't as many fitness freaks using it when I was last here though.'

We moved aside to let a group of joggers go by.

'The outer loop around the fence measures a mile and a half, I think. The far side, in the direction of the city, borders the River Yarra. It's mostly flat with one steep gradient towards the end. I'll show you later; we can stretch our legs. Elliott used to train around this circuit when he wasn't out at Portsea. Perce would clock him doing repetitions up the hill.'

We had come to Melbourne to collect our mail from the British Consulate and also to attend a press meeting they'd arranged. First, we contacted the mayor's office at the town hall in Sydney. Next, we made a few rough calculations. The distance from Echuca to Sydney was 550 miles – no more than two and a half weeks' running. Providing that we could be back at Echuca by 22 August, there seemed to be no reason why we couldn't reach Sydney by 9 September. That was the date I announced to the press.

Afterwards, I decided to find Kris Hemensley. The only telephone number I had on me belonged to his mother-in-law. I gave it a try.

'They're at Westgarth, Kelvin. They bought a house in Urquhart Street – just a few doors up from where Kris used to live. You remember? Des and Margaret's place?'

That same night I caught a train out to Westgarth. It was a twenty-minute ride.

'The winters here can be so damp,' Loretta's mother had grumbled – reminding me of how often everyone in Melbourne complained about the weather. *Just like back home*, I thought.

It wasn't much of a walk from the station to Urquhart Street, but it was wet and I wasn't wearing enough to keep out the cold.

Their small front garden was tropical and overgrown. A ti-tree leaned against the tin roof of the porch. Blobs of rain collected on big leaves where the letter box was stashed. The waist-high gate was made of iron and the rust had been painted over. It opened only as far as the bushes allowed.

Kris swung open the door before I could press the bell. He had seen me from inside. 'You're here then, mate!' He gripped my arm tightly. 'C'mon through. We've been expecting you. Retta's mother rang to tell us. She couldn't keep a secret for five minutes.'

Loretta was in the kitchen, opening a bottle of white wine. We all had tears in our eyes and didn't know what to say, so we hugged instead. Then Kris led me into the front room and sat me in his favourite red rocker, in the arc of the bay window.

'I only got back myself the other day.'

'From where?'

'England – a three-month visit. My brother Bernard told me about your journey. He has a pile of newspaper clippings. Last I heard, you were in India.'

'Kris phoned me up when he found out,' said Loretta, following us into the room with the uncorked bottle in her hand. 'He said, "Guess what? Kelvin's running to Australia!" I thought it was just a bad line. "What, coming to Australia?" I asked. "Running," he said. "With his legs."'

Loretta poured out the wine and Kris raised his glass and gave a slight cough – the way he did when he was about to read out a poem.

'Well,' he beamed, 'here we are.'

'The title of your new book,' I grinned.

He looked puzzled. 'That's right, but ...'

'We were in the middle of the Nullarbor one night, listening to the radio. They were reviewing it.'

'Kris told me you had a little boy. How old is he?'

'Zhenka's four now. He had his birthday here in Australia, in June.'

'Timothy's just four months younger. He's asleep in his room. You must take a peep at him before you go.' Loretta refilled my glass and carried on talking. 'It must have been difficult for Leona, trying to keep Zhenka occupied. And what with the flies and the heat. How on earth did everyone cope?'

'Let me put it this way – living in the van is much harder than running down the road. But we've been packed together like sardines for too long now. I don't know how Chris and Baz have managed to control themselves for all this time and still be able to switch off whenever Zhenka throws a tantrum. It's different when it's your own child, isn't it? Even then it's bad enough.

'We owe a great deal to Chris. He's the driver, and the most easygoing bloke you could ever meet. He caught typhoid in India and started to dehydrate. Luckily, we met someone who got him into a decent hospital in time – that was in Singapore.

'As for Lea – you should have seen her in India, trying to cook outside with half the village surrounding her and asking questions ten to the dozen. It was the same in Iran and Turkey too. The outback has been sheer bliss but now that we're threading our way through more populated parts we've started to crack. We were meant to come to Melbourne on foot but we changed the route.'

'How long will it take you to reach Sydney?' asked Kris.

'Just over a fortnight.'

'And then?'

'It depends. I have this idea about travelling across Siberia. This has been the longest run in history, so it would be fitting if we were to take the longest train ride home.'

'You still have it then,' said Kris.

'What's that?'

'That English impulse to be somewhere else.'

Kris got up from the long sofa and went into the kitchen to fetch another bottle of wine.

'How are things then Retta?'

'Not so bad. I'm teaching at a primary school. I've been there a couple of years now. Kris is still writing of course. This government has been kind to young writers you know. He's already received two fellowships.'

'Does La Mama still exist?'

'Oh yes. Kris still reads there every once in a while, and they put on his plays. Remember the first time it opened?'

I nodded. 'A poet named Ken Taylor read a long poem and Glen Thomasetti sang folk songs. They sold Danish pastries during the interval.'

'She was in the Ned Kelly film playing her guitar. Know the one I mean? Mick Jagger played Ned Kelly.'

'Terrible film,' added Kris, as he came back from the kitchen carrying a platter of various cheeses and another bottle of wine. He cleared a space on a low table, pushing aside a pile of typewritten pages.

I looked around the room. The ceiling was high. There were shelves full of books reaching almost to the picture rail. A Charles Olson poem on a poster was pinned to the back of the door. Two more posters hung one above the other on the main wall: a Sydney Nolan painting from the 1940s and a photograph of Samuel Beckett's face. Notes, letters, and pages torn out of magazines covered the floorboards around the edge of the carpet. Behind me, a large sash window was propped open with one of Tim's wooden trains.

'Percy Cerutty died, Kris. Did you hear?'

'Retta told me. Quite recent wasn't it?'

'Yeah.'

'Can you recall my visit to Portsea? When we stood under that incredible rock formation called London Bridge and the *Fairstar* was leaving Port Philip Bay.' Kris looked at Loretta. 'Two years earlier Retta, I'd gone down to the Labour Exchange in Southampton and they'd found me a job as a steward on board that very same liner. I sailed around the world on the *Fairstar*, and then met Kelvin on the *Fairsky*.'

'What about our meeting? The three of us,' said Loretta, 'on the King's Domain during that all-night vigil to protest about the Vietnamese leader's visit to Government House. And you Kel, said it was too cold and went home early to your place across the street.'

'That's where we've parked our van.'

Much later, when we'd drunk more wine and it was time for me to catch the last train into the city, Kris said he'd walk to the station with me. Outside, he gestured to the ivy dangling from the porch. 'It all needs attending to, cutting back. That's a bottle bush over there in the corner. And jasmine and more ivy on the trellis. When I look out of my window the suburban strip of asphalt is hidden and it smells as if we're in the country.'

On the platform, before the train came in, Kris unrolled a sheet of paper.

'Take this drawing of Tim's for young Zhenka. It's a lion. Look at the way it roars – filling the page, eh! And you, off to Siberia.' He placed his hand on my shoulder. 'I'm glad you looked us up. It feels like the past and present are here with us now. Spiritual kinship and continuity, that's what it's all about.'

79

We crossed the Murray River for the last time at Cobram, two days out from Echuca. Again we were on the lookout for dirt roads through one-pub towns. But to begin with the sealed highway leading to Berrigan, Urana and Lockhart was quiet and no deviations were necessary. The short break in Melbourne seemed to have helped us patch up our differences. Baz and I ran side by side – talking as we used to – while the miles drifted by. I told him about my visit to Kris and how it had stirred up old memories.

'One time we went to see a stuffed horse in the state museum. The Aussies are nuts about horse-racing and Phar Lap was the best racehorse ever. Perce said I should study its legs. I even went to the Melbourne Cup. Ended up coming away with photographs of Jean Shrimpton.'

On the far side of Wagga Wagga we joined the Olympic Way. 'Wagga' is an Aboriginal word that means crow, so perhaps Wagga Wagga means two crows or at least more than one bird. We were thinking about this as we meandered along a country track that would eventually run parallel to the main road. Suddenly a magpie plummeted out of the sky and flew straight for us with its beak open. We ducked and waved our arms about to scare it away, but it kept flying back at us. Then the first bird was joined by another.

'Magpie, magpie!' cried Baz, while they dived and swooped down inches from our heads. 'The mating season, that's what this is all about. Better grab a branch.'

Baz knew lots about birds. I snapped off the nearest branch. Once they saw that we were armed, the magpies flew into the trees.

'Hope they're not fetching reinforcements,' I half-joked, recalling that Hitchcock film I'd once watched in terror.

It was dusk when we reached the van. Chris had parked at a place called Shepherds Sidings. The moon was full and bright. Everyone laughed when we told them about the birds, and Zhenka asked what would have happened if they'd flown off with us.

Next morning, Chris said he'd dreamt he was back in England attending an interview for a job as an astronaut. 'In which direction would you say your strengths lay Mr Baxter?' an officer from the Space Academy had enquired.

'I can recognise moonlight,' answered Chris.

For the next week we averaged 35 miles a day.

'One down and one more to go!' said Chris, trying to muster up some enthusiasm.

We ran harder to get it over with, but couldn't quite convince ourselves that Sydney lay somewhere beyond the mountains we were approaching.

It hailed on the first day of spring. Not small hailstones, but big ones that clattered onto the black road and left it white.

After running through Young and Cowra, we had just turned off the Mid-Western Highway at a small place called Mandurama, and were heading for the hills. Nearing Neville – a tiny village overshadowed by a 4,000-foot high mountain in the Stringy Bark Ranges – the sleet turned to snow. We shook our heads in disbelief and strode on, hoping that the snow wouldn't stick. When the van drew alongside us we waved it down and reached for hats and gloves. Chris had been listening to the local news.

'A woman skier just froze to death in the Snowy Mountains,' he told us.

We carried on, but the snowclouds shortened the hours of daylight and visibility was down to a few yards. The next time we saw the van we made up our minds to stay put. A flurry of snow blew in when I opened the rear door, powdering the foam cushions on top of one of the bunks. Lea was sitting in the front huddled under her duffel coat. Zhenka was standing on the seat leaning back against the steering wheel screaming.

'Where's Chris?'

'He went to ask if we could pull off the road. There's a homestead up there, see the lights?'

I stared out and saw a faint glow on a hill that overlooked an apple orchard a few hundred yards away. Smoke was rising from two different chimneys. *Maybe they'll ask us in*, I thought.

'What's the matter with Zhenka?'

'He's been throwing snowballs. His hands are freezing cold.'

'Mine too,' said Baz. We tried to dry ourselves off – first wiping the wet snow from our faces and then rubbing the sweat from our shoulders and legs with damp towels. Then we draped our wet clothes over a bit of washing line and stuffed our shoes in a corner out of the way.

'I'll get the stove going in the back,' said Lea. 'It'll help dry things out and warm us up.'

We swapped places, climbing over the seats so as not to venture outside again. Zhenka had stopped crying.

'Chrissy's back!' he pointed. I looked out through the windscreen.

A figure wearing flip-flops came stumbling downhill through the snow.

'Baz, quick,' I said. 'Take a look at this.'

'Oh no!' he gasped. 'He hasn't, has he? Not dressed like that.'

We tried to imagine how it must have appeared to whoever was inside the building. An isolated homestead in the Stringy Bark Ranges where a blizzard raged outside. Suddenly a knock at the door startles the occupants. Who on earth in their right mind is going to be out in this weather? They get up, walk over to the door and slip back the latch, peering outside into the swirling snow.

A young man is grinning up at them on the porch steps. He is wearing a black leather bomber jacket, unzipped at the front to reveal a paisley-patterned cardigan over an orange shirt. He is also wearing Ma Mistry's striped pyjamas. And, on his feet, thick Afghan socks crammed into rubber flip-flops.

'Sorry to trouble you,' he says, still grinning but by now unable to see who he is talking to because the snow has plastered over his glasses and a torch is directed in his face. 'My friends are running from England to Sydney and I drive the support vehicle. Would it be possible to park in your paddock overnight?'

In the morning, Midge Rider brought a flask of hot soup down to us. He had thrown a yellow cape on over the long johns he was wearing and he was chuckling to himself.

'Thought yer mate was a leftover from the Cowra break-out, I did. Yer hear about how the odd soldier goes astray in the jungles and doesn't show for years, and then when he does, he's no idea it's all been sorted? Well, it got me thinking. 'Course, I was just a teenager when it happened, when the Japs got loose. They were prisoners of war see, close on four hundred of them. Some came through this way, over the hill from Kangaroo Flats. I hid in the barn, I did, until they'd all gone. Biggest thing that ever happened in Stringy Bark. Not something you forget in a hurry.'

80

The country road we were on stayed empty, twisting in and out of the hills and sometimes straight over the top of them. Every creek we crossed was full and fast flowing. Chris and Zhenka raced twigs down the rapids. Baz and I became competitive too. It was the only way to keep warm.

There was a time, earlier in the run, when I could have been sure of outpacing him to the top of any hill. But Baz was stronger now, and wiser too. He had learned how I accelerated uphill to demoralise him: surging as hard as I could at the foot of each climb. And all the better if the hills were steep. I couldn't run downhill to save my life though. Of course, Baz knew this too. So, when I took off at the bottom, he would do everything to hang on, and if he was anywhere near me at the top he would swoop past as we descended. This was the way we trained in England where we had constantly been plagued by injury. It was not the way we had been running for most of the journey.

We ran through Locksley, Gemalla and Tarana. Then on to Sodwalls and Old Bowenfels. One afternoon we heard gunshots in the trees, and saw a skinned fox hanging from a barbed wire fence by its hind legs.

From Lithgow, a switchback route called Bell's Line of Road took us to the top of a long sandstone ridge. The Blue Mountains really did look blue. So did the sky. Dry weather had coaxed most Sydneysiders out for the day. The roads were full of them. Each man, woman and child, straining at the suburban leash for a heady whiff of eucalyptus. Fine views for Baz and I came once in a Blue Mountain, so to speak – whenever we could sneak a look between the bumpers.

The one view we had not counted on seeing from so far out presented itself to us at a lookout point called Kurrajong Heights. Chris had parked the van nose to kerb in the wide lay-by, and he, Lea and Zhenka, were taking turns to look through the binoculars. They waved us over.

'Luna Park!' giggled Zhenka. 'I can see Luna Park!'

'Which rides?' asked Lea.

'The ghost train! I can see white skeletons scaring everyone inside the tunnel!'

'Wonder if they ran from England?' laughed Chris.

I grabbed the binoculars and began to adjust the focusing mechanism. When it looked right I steadied my hands and tried to hold my breath so as not to mist up the lenses. The high-rise office blocks in downtown Sydney stood out like a row of far-off skittles.

'How far d'you reckon?' asked Baz.

'Can't be more than fifty miles can it?' I said. 'We have to be there in two days, anyway.'

We told Chris we'd run a few miles more and turned around to face the road again. Just then, a woman and her daughter asked if they could take our photograph.

'We saw it on the television when you were running through the desert. To think you came all that way. Could you see the city through your binoculars? You can't often see it – hardly at all during the summer.'

'We've been promising my son he could go to Luna Park for the past seventeen months now – and he just saw the ghost train!'

Pearl Rainey was Irish. She wanted to know where we would be staying on the eve of our arrival. When we shrugged our shoulders, she said we were all welcome to stop overnight at her home in the suburb of Fairfield. We had to pass close by on our way into Sydney. It would give us a chance to freshen up before we met the mayor, she said. And we could use the telephone to make any last minute arrangements.

A bed! With clean sheets. A bathroom! Hot running water. We jumped at the chance. Pearl scribbled her address on a notepad and she and her daughter walked across to the van, while Baz and I proceeded down the road.

All the way across the Nullarbor, whether we were shaking the red dust from our blankets and pillows or wiping our backsides in the bush – so stiff it hurt to crouch – I'd be telling the others: 'You wait till we get to Sydney. We'll be put up at the best hotel.'

This was only the beginning.

81

Our elation was short-lived. For some reason everyone slept in late the following morning. Baz 'the clock' was grinding out a path in the dust with his heels when I unzipped my sleeping bag.

'Why didn't you wake us?' I asked.

'I did, but you turned over and went back to sleep.'

'Might as well eat breakfast here now, I suppose. It's a good quiet spot.'

Baz was not happy with any change of routine. Also, he knew how much food we would eat, and that it would probably play havoc with our digestive systems when we tried to make up for lost time.

'I thought you'd want to make a decent start, today of all days,' he said.

'This way we'll miss any rush hour traffic. We can do without that now, can't we?'

Lea sensed the tension when she woke up. Even Zhenka seemed grizzly. He climbed on top of the bunk lid and refused to jump down when Baz asked if he could get to his trainers. Baz raised his voice and Zhenka started to cry. Chris, noticing the look on my face, hurried Zhenka off to boot a plastic ball around the dry ground. The second kick of the ball landed in a bowl of cornflakes. Baz grunted, and once he'd laced up his shoes, set off along the road without me.

I should have let it go. I had done before, countless times, and so had Baz, but time had run out. If we were going to vent our grievances we would need to do it soon. I crammed the last of a peanut butter sandwich in my mouth and set off after him.

It was a beautiful morning. By now, the up-country commuters would already have reached the inner suburbs. They'd be tapping steering wheels in frustration as they sat in their vehicles at the far end of the tailbacks. We had the road to ourselves, near enough.

Baz had not hung around. We were halfway to Windsor before I caught him. We had both run fast. Because I'd run faster, I figured I must be angrier. But I was mistaken. Now, a combined rush of adrenaline threatened to push our friendship to the limits. I began to tell him some of the things I'd been thinking about as I'd chased after him. Once I opened my mouth – that was it! The catalogue of his shortcomings flowed out like a burst dam. Resentments that I'd stored away inside my head for over a year suddenly received a calamitous airing.

Baz listened. For one long bewildering minute he stood in the middle of the road and heard me out. Even the demented kookaburras fell silent. Then, from nowhere, his clenched fist slammed into my right eye. Another punch followed. And another. Each one on target. I reeled across the road, clutching my head. Blood dribbled from a cut lip, and my singlet was torn. Baz stayed where he was, his arms hanging limply at his sides. We were both crying.

We were still upset when the van drove up. Chris and Lea looked astonished to find us standing in the road in such a state. We mumbled something about having had a bit of a disagreement, then climbed slowly into the back of the van. My right eye was swelling fast. Lea emptied a plastic container of cold water into a bowl and bathed my lip with cotton wool. I wrapped a wet towel around my head. None of us said very much. The words 'stunned silence' sprang to mind, and also 'thumping headache'.

I stretched out on one of the bunks and closed my eyes. It helped a little, even if only to blank out the pained expressions on everyone's face. After a while, I knew we had to make a move. It was vital to get as close to the city as we could so as to reach the town hall in good time the next morning.

We set off at last, jogging together. In my case it was more of a stumble than a jog; a stumble that soon turned into a walk as the sun beat down and the sweat stung my eyes.

When we reached Windsor, Lea bought an eye-patch for me from a chemist's. Zhenka thought I'd look like a pirate if I wore it. I said I felt like I was already walking the plank, so what did it matter. At this, he said he'd like one too, and a cardboard cutlass that Chris could paint silver.

We stopped beside a park at lunchtime and sat on a bench to eat cheese sandwiches. Baz turned to face me for the first time since the fight.

'Fuckin' hell, Kel! It looks a mess.'

'I don't like to look,' I told him.

'I'm sorry I lashed out like that. I can't recall hitting anyone before. Not even at school. No one except my older brother and that doesn't count, does it? I just need you to know I'm fucking sorry it ever happened.'

'It was my own fault, Baz. We both know that at least. It was bound to happen sooner or later – cooped up like battery hens. I'm surprised we lasted this long.'

'One day away from Sydney though. Only one measly day and we go and balls it all up.'

'I didn't mean those things I said about you Baz. My tongue runs away with me when I'm riled. It can do more damage than a fist.'

'What shall we tell everyone when they ask how you came by your black eye?'

'Well, I'd sooner the press thought it was an accident,' I said. 'One sniff of a punch-up and all the running in the world won't get a mention. I can just see the headlines: 'A Black Eye in the Blue Mountains – Marathon Men Scrap It Out On Their Way to the Pacific'. We'll think of something before the day's out.'

When we got up from the park bench we walked for several miles. I tried to jog, but each time the extra jarring increased the throbbing pain around my eye after only a few paces. Early in the afternoon, the inevitable build-up of traffic began. It was safer to keep on the pavements but my eye-patch made it difficult for me to judge where the kerb was whenever we crossed a junction. Baz helped me out, as if he were escorting a blind man along the highway.

'Watch for the kerb,' he would call, and I'd wipe the sweat from my one good eye and stare down at my feet.

It was slow going all the same. The traffic became worse when we hit McGrath's Hill and Vineyard. Even when we found a few unmetalled back roads running parallel to the main one, their white dusty surfaces threw back a blinding glare. Both my eyes were watering by this time, but I couldn't be sure if it was sweat or tears. Step by step we made our way sadly along Railway Terrace, plodding on through Riverstone, Schofield and Quakers Hill.

In the middle of the rush hour we arrived at the junction of Old Windsor Road and Hammers Road, approximately 18 miles from Sydney Town Hall. Chris was waiting to drive us to Pearl's home in Fairfield. When we got there she took one look at my bruised face and said that we ought to call a doctor. Instead, I persuaded her to fix me up with an ice pack and we all went inside.

'How did it happen?' asked Pearl's daughter.

'My son poked me in the eye with a branch when he was collecting firewood just after we met you, up at Kurrajong.'

In the lounge, Pearl had laid out a buffet on a wide table: plates full of cooked meat, little delicacies on sticks, different coloured slices of salami and wedges of cheese, and fish kebabs marinated in spicy sauces and arranged in rows. Cakes and ice cream too, and mounds of crisps. All afternoon my eyes had watered. Now it was the turn of my mouth.

'There's Newcastle Brown in the kitchen: go ahead and help yourselves. My brother and his family said they'd stop by. I hope you don't mind.'

I think I drank more than I ate. Halfway through the evening a local newsman found us. By then I was wearing a paper hat above the pirate's patch. When Pearl had first offered to put us up for the night, she had also kindly agreed to telephone the press office at the British Consulate to let them know where we could be contacted. Now the calls came through one after the other. Some were live interviews on air, with the BBC's *World at One* and Granada Television. Others were taped interviews for national newspapers.

One reporter rang from Scotland. 'Are your feet swollen yet, laddie?' he asked. I glanced at my battered reflection in the hall mirror and grinned.

'No,' I told him, 'they're in good shape.'

Towards the end of Pearl's party, Baz and I borrowed her road map and retired to the patio to plan the complicated last couple of runs from the outer suburbs to the town hall. We each took a swig from the last remaining bottle of Newcastle Brown, and stared out across the long grass in the back garden where Chris had parked the van. There were red-brick bungalows all around, and ugly tanks that people took dips in when it grew hot. But the dark helped to keep them hidden.

'Listen to those cicadas, Baz. They sound really loud tonight.'

'They do, don't they?' He gave a chuckle. 'It's not like listening to a telephone ringing is it? I mean, you don't have to pick the buggers up and answer them do you?'

'Is that what we'll be doing?'

'Well, I will if I go back to my old job.'

'Mustn't let it go, must we? All we've seen.'

'I don't know what it's like for you, Kel. But for me it's like a constant running film. It's in my head all the time. Just a sound, a smell or a word and I jump into the film. It worries me when I think about what Peter Taylor said though – that everything else we did in our lives would be an anticlimax.'

'Peter had his big climb in the mountains and he peaked at that point in time but it never stopped him going after other things – quite successfully too. It's all down to how badly you want something. The Aborigines have their dreamtime: why shouldn't we have ours? It could be like the film in your head. Something you carry with you into different phases of your life – adding layer upon layer as you go.'

A light came on in the window of the room Pearl's daughter had vacated for us. Through the blinds we saw Lea putting a sleepy Zhenka to bed. As she tugged his bright blue jumper over his head he opened his eyes and pointed to a desk in the corner. Lea lifted him up and traced her finger around the globe of the world that had caught his attention. Then he slid back to sleep again in her arms, whilst the globe went on spinning.

82

When I opened my eyes I wasn't sure if my sore head was due to the drink or the previous morning's pounding. I asked the others how they felt.

'Fine,' they told me, 'but then we didn't empty as many bottles of Newcastle Brown as you did.'

Pearl had been up for an hour already and it was only six a.m. There were steak butties wrapped in kitchen foil on a Formica worktop next to the electric cooker.

'Can't have you sipping champagne on an empty stomach,' she smiled.

After coffee, we said our goodbyes and promised to keep in touch and to return for a barbie as soon as the weather hotted up. Pearl said that she was going straight back indoors to sit by the TV screen.

'I'm not budging from my chair until I see you run up those steps at the town hall.'

Steps? Shit! I hadn't counted on that. You need two sound eyes to go running up steps. Only the day before I'd been stumbling over the kerbs! Even if I removed the eye-patch it made no difference. I still couldn't see anything out of my right eye because of the swelling. Besides, it looked hideous.

'Bruised to buggery,' Baz reckoned.

And so the only vision remaining, in my mind's eye, saw me suddenly come a cropper at the bottom of the town hall steps, in full view of the media. What a drama queen's dream of an entrance that would be. Echoes of Pheidippides collapsing at Athens.

Chris drove us back to Hammers Road, on the edge of Parramatta. We agreed to meet him at the Gladesville Bridge, about twelve miles away. It was early, but people were out and about, hurrying to catch buses and trains into the city. The wide pavements were filling fast. Overhead the sky was clear and blue. Bright sunlight bounced up from the white concrete.

The men and women on their way to work stared at the lettering across our singlets. 'England to Australia,' I heard them say to one another as we weaved between them. A popular DJ with an early morning radio show had told his listeners we were on our way. He had neatly linked our arrival with that of a famous film star – joking that some people would run halfway around the world just to be in the city at the same time.

Further on, a few people in a bus queue parted to let us through, and called out 'Up the Poms!' One car cruised alongside us for an entire block with a big Union Jack tied to the bonnet. When we reached a busy intersection that required both eyes, Baz had to lead me across it. Soon after, we turned left into Victoria Road on the north bank of the Parramatta River.

We ran steadily on through the suburbs, past the wide streets of terracotta-roofed bungalows, and the shops, banks and post offices. As the morning advanced, new lunch menus were chalked up on the blackboards outside the street corner hotels. The pedestrians changed too, from factory hands to office staff in light blue shorts. There were straw-hatted schoolgirls giggling outside a milk bar, and mothers escorting their toddlers across a zebra crossing in Ermington.

It was no easy twelve miles. We jogged in and out of the slow-moving pedestrians – up onto the pavement then down and off across the road. The jarring hurt and the traffic was heavy. I stuck to Baz's left shoulder like a limpet to safeguard my blind side. Every so often he would ask if the pace was alright and I'd nod my head, even if I was hanging on.

Chris was sitting on a bench at the roadside waiting for us. The van was parked in a quiet riverside lane close to the bridge. As soon as we arrived he went off to telephone the British Consulate.

'Ask them to give us half an hour before they contact the press,' I told him. 'Just enough time to relax a little. You know how it is.'

Under different circumstances I expect we would have tidied up inside the van, in readiness for the cameramen – as one would at home for instance. Well, this small vehicle had been our home for the past seventeen months. It wasn't spick and span inside and it would have been misleading to present it that way. Far better if everyone saw how we had really lived whilst on the road together.

One look at the interior would go a long way in explaining how I got my black eye.

A grass embankment sloped down to the river, bisected by the little side road lined with trees. The sun was already strong enough to have dried the dew on the grass and so we lay there next to the trailer and rested for a few minutes before breakfast.

'Wonder where we'll be having breakfast tomorrow,' said Lea, 'and who'll be cooking it?'

'It'll be breakfast in bed tomorrow!' I said. 'In some swanky hotel I shouldn't wonder. My mother's throwing a party to celebrate back in England. All our parents are going to be there, waiting for us to call, remember?'

Lea nodded. 'You wouldn't think we were so close to the city centre would you? It's a lovely spot.'

We ate the steak butties while we waited for Chris to return. Zhenka rolled down the grassy slope pretending to be a felled tree like the ones he'd seen on the big trucks outside the lumber camp at Wirrabarra.

'Amazingly enough, the sun was shining just like this on the day we set out from the town hall in Stoke,' Lea said. 'And you Baz, met up with us at the Walton roundabout on the A34, and handed us an envelope with a good luck card inside and thirty pounds "to spend somewhere along the way". Who'd have thought then that one day we'd all be over here, together?'

Baz looked ruefully at my eye-patch. 'Are we still together?' he asked.

'I hope we are,' I replied.

Just then Chris returned, and soon afterwards several vehicles pulled into the lane and stopped close by. Suddenly, there were cameras and recording equipment everywhere.

'Is this what you lived in?' asked a TV reporter, trying to tone down his incredulity.

'That's it,' I said.

'No caravan then?'

'Only what you see.'

'So small!'

'It gets smaller when we're all inside.'

'And you lived this way for how long?'

'Seventeen months.'

'Really? A long time.'

'That's right,' I said, 'too long.'

'Of course we won't be concentrating on the living conditions during the actual interview. We don't have the time and it's not what the viewers are interested in. Our main concern is that we keep it simple. We'll ask you what you were thinking about as you ran across the Nullarbor, how many pairs of trainers you got through, how far you ran each day. That sort of thing.'

'What about Afghanistan?' I asked. 'And India?'

'Oh yes, that too.'

The camera crew intended to film us from their car as we ran into the city. We had also been provided with a police escort: two cars with flashing blue lights, one driving ahead of us and the other trailing close behind our van. When it was time to leave for the town hall, the lead patrol car swung out across a four-lane highway and stopped the traffic.

Quickly, we strode past the waiting cars and on up the gentle slope of the bridge over the Parramatta River. We ran side by side in the centre of the near lane and well away from the kerb. Briskly too, so as to make it evident that we were no mere joggers. Over to our left, out of my good eye, I could see the harbour spreading its blue tentacles all about the white coves. There were sailing boats below us and we could feel a breeze coming in off the sea.

'What do you think about it, Baz?' I shouted.

'Beaut!' he roared. 'She's bladdy beaut!' And his long blond hair bobbed like the sails.

I wanted to turn around and share the moment with the others, who were sitting in the front of the van, but our pace had quickened, and anyway the eye-patch prevented even a casual glance over my shoulder. Instead, I pictured them waving excitedly and pointing, Zhenka's eyes glued to the windscreen for his second sighting of Luna Park.

We passed a signpost pointing the way ahead to Sydney, with

Balmain on the left and the Great Western Highway on the right. At a major crossroads the traffic lights were held on red, and a police motorcyclist halted the flow of vehicles while we surged across.

When I first spotted the Harbour Bridge it reminded me of a raised eyebrow. Later, I reasoned that this was simply because I'd become paranoid about my black eye. When I looked again, I saw a distant rainbow of steel and dripping misty grey girders.

We lengthened our stride down an incline towards the tall chimneys of a power station. The road wound between dockland loading bays, warehouses and jetties, to a bridge over Johnston's Bay. We were closing in now on the Harbour Bridge itself, although that wasn't to be part of our route to the town hall.

The 'Coathanger Bridge' towered above the spindrift of swinging cranes, dwarfing the huge containers and adjacent machinery along the waterfront. Directly ahead of us, skyscrapers loomed above the funnels of ships in Darling Harbour.

At Pyrmont Bridge we split up from the two police cars and the van. A police motorcyclist took over to guide us along the last few streets. We kept as close as we could to the motorcyclist, but it was too busy to run fast in downtown Sydney, where the shoppers and office workers were constantly stepping off the pavements and into our path.

At last we turned a corner and there, at the end of the block – lit up by sunlight – stood a grand building with a clock tower and window boxes full of red flowers. The clock read 12.15 p.m. and the policeman in front gave us the thumbs-up sign. A second policeman was on duty outside the town hall to direct us to the front entrance.

When we reached the foot of the steps, I adjusted my eye-patch and looked up. The Lord Mayor-elect of Sydney, Alderman Leo Port, and the New South Wales Minister of Sport, were on their way down the steps to greet us. Pearl had made a phone call to ensure that nothing spoiled our big day.

'Helluva way to get a suntan!' someone piped up from the back of the crowd.

83

The alarm clock sounded as if it was ringing inside a large tin can – which, in a way, I suppose it was. The clock had been a parting gift from the Satur family in Madras and until now we hadn't used it, choosing instead to rely on Baz, who seemed every bit as punctual.

The phone call! We had to make the phone call to England. I had promised to ring them. Everyone would be there, crowded into my parents' front room. Friends and relatives partying and waiting for the call to come through.

I sat bolt upright like a cocooned mummy and struggled to unzip my sleeping bag. When my arms were free I reached across and fumbled to switch the thing off.

Lea groaned, and muttered something about how early it was. But there was a promising rustle from the front seat where Chris appeared to be at least partially awake. Even in that state he wasn't entirely bereft of the odd witticism: 'And how many stars will you be awarding this splendid establishment Mr Bowers?' he asked.

'Alright, alright,' I acknowledged. 'I was wrong about the hotel.'

'I'm waiting for breakfast in bed this morning – remember?' came Lea's half-muffled voice from under her sleeping bag.

The posh accommodation I'd envisaged so many times had not materialised. Here we were, on the day after a grand civic welcome, back in our humble van on a beachside caravan park. The telephone kiosk stood on a windswept drag facing the sea, about fifty yards from the campsite.

Chris, Lea and I crammed inside to shelter, having left Baz and Zhenka asleep in the van. I got through to the operator and requested a transfer charge call to the United Kingdom. When my mother answered I didn't let on that we were calling from a phone box. I could hear their party in the background, and everyone hushing everyone else.

At a pound a minute, we spoke in turn as quickly as we could. Rushed congratulations from everyone ensued, including Jeff and

Sue, and even Chris's dad – up from his sickbed to let his son know that he was proud of him.

'We're taking Zhenka to Luna Park tomorrow night,' Lea told her mum. 'It's all he ever talks about.'

It was a tight squeeze inside the phone box. Chris wedged open the door to give us more room. Fred Berrisford, the one-armed bandit, had the last word: 'I knew you wouldn't let us down. But remember, you'll be a hero today and forgotten tomorrow. Don't let anyone jump on the bandwagon.'

The wind whistled past outside.

'What bandwagon Fred?' I asked.

Later that morning, Lea, Zhenka and I were scheduled to appear on *The Mike Walsh Show*, an hour-long TV chat programme in front of a live audience. A taxi took us to the studios. In the make-up room an assistant powdered my face to pale out the suntan, after complaints from the lighting engineer. A couple of transvestites went on first and we watched them from a TV screen backstage.

It was a light-hearted show and the interviewer made everyone feel relaxed. When it was our turn, Zhenka talked about bandits and Luna Park, and how his potty had been stolen in eastern Turkey. Mike Walsh mentioned that vehicles carrying equipment for an Everest expedition had recently been fired at by tribesmen in Afghanistan and asked if anything like that had happened to us? I told him about being threatened with guns and pushed inside a small hut. How the women in the mountains of Turkey and Iran had screamed at the sight of our bare legs, and hurled stones at us.

At this, he smiled. 'I don't think any of the ladies in this audience would react in that way. Would you like to see a bit of leg, ladies?'

Everyone yelled yes, so he rolled up his trouser leg to the knees, and I unbuckled my belt and pulled down my jeans. There was a roar of laughter. The transvestite sitting next to Lea turned to her and said, 'Marcia would kill for pins like those.'

Mike Walsh then suggested that the lack of privacy in our tiny van must have dampened any ardour. 'I think we owe you a night out in one of Sydney's best hotels. What about the Sebel Town House? How does that sound?'

The Sebel overlooked Rushcutters Bay. It was where all the showbiz people stayed and there were said to be spectacular views over the water from the most expensive of the suites. As things turned out we never got to stay there. After the chat show we were driven to the British Consulate to collect the many telegrams of congratulations that had been sent to us.

There were letters there too, from all over the world, including one from Balmoral Castle, in which the Queen referred to the marathon run as being an impressive achievement and added her congratulations. We were also given a message to contact a Mr C. Moreton.

Chris Moreton had at one time been my best friend. He was yet another globetrotting ex-member of the North Staffordshire Harriers – a talented 800-metre runner who had represented Great Britain as a Junior. Chris and his wife Wynn, immigrated to Australia in 1972, and I'd not seen them since.

When I called his number he sounded excited to hear from me.

'Kel!' he cried. 'I switched on the TV yesterday to catch the evening news, and there you were – striding along the bloody street with a patch over one eye. Listen, we're over at Faulconbridge. It's in the Blue Mountains, about forty miles out from Sydney. Why don't you all come over? You can stay here, there's plenty of room.'

I explained that we were booked into the Sebel Town House for the night but told him we would far rather grab some wine and travel into the hills for a reunion.

The reunion lasted for two months. And fame – only for as long as I continued to wear the eye-patch.

Epilogue

Faulconbridge was situated on a high ridge against a vast backdrop of the bush. My friend's back garden sloped away into the wilderness and we were grateful to have such a quiet place to stay. Chris and Baz were still talking of sharing a flat and seeing more of Australia before their visas expired.

But one morning Chris received a telegram. His father had died while on holiday in Scotland. He flew home the very next day. After a couple of weeks Baz moved on too; heading for Western Australia again, where he intended to stay with Derek and Rita Hoye.

In the meantime I looked up Sundowners Travel Company at their headquarters in Bligh Street, Sydney. Somewhere along the line they had featured our journey in one of their overland adventure newsletters. They were the only Australian company operating on the Trans-Siberian Railway. The meeting went well and as a result I was given the job of tour leader on the next trip out. If I could maintain peace between a motley band of Western tourists and the official Russian Intourist guide, then my free passage all the way from Yokohama to London was assured. In the intervening weeks we shopped in Paddy's Market for cut-price woollen long johns and mittens, while everybody else was bargain hunting for beachwear.

One day, I glimpsed a dusty bicycle chained to railings outside the main post office. I tugged Lea's arm.

'It isn't, is it?' she cried.

'Oh yes it is! He's there look, coming towards us. Do you remember him Zhen?'

'Yes. I had a ride on his bike, didn't I?'

We had last seen Stan when our ship docked in Penang. He still wore the same big smile: it hadn't frayed at the edges. We yelled loudly and slapped each other on the back and tried to swap as many tales as we could there and then.

'Where's Barry?' he asked.

'He went back across the Nullarbor. Look, this arrived two days ago.' I slipped a postcard from between the pages of my passport. The Dutchman's grin widened when he read it:

> I was sitting in the dunny in some outback nowhere-town, when I pricked up my ears at the sound of the bladdy coach starting! I yanked up my kegs and hotfooted it outside – but there was only rising dust. Everything I owned, gone, disappearing into the sunset. So, it's no money or passport and only what I stand up in! I rush to the cops to tell them what happened. In the end, some wild-eyed cabbie on speed comes to the rescue and we set off in pursuit. It took 100 miles to catch up! I thought of Neal Cassidy in *On the Road*. I've never travelled so fast in my life. It cost me nothing too. Just a few grey hairs. Of course, this is what we have to contend with now that the run is over – SPEED! Anyhow, keep yer bunyips warm in the frozen wastes. Love, Baz.

When I asked Stan about the next stage of his trip he consulted a ragged little notebook which looked familiar. Inside – highlighted by inky asterisks – were the places he'd heard about along the way. His 'must-sees' he called them.

'Jenolan Caves,' he said. 'I have this ride up into the Blue Mountains planned.'

'Listen Stan, we're staying with friends of mine at a place called Faulconbridge. It's out on the Western Highway – the very road you'll be taking to get to the caves. My friends are having a barbecue this weekend. Why don't you stop by then and meet them?'

So, at the weekend, Stan cycled into the hills. He stayed at Faulconbridge for a couple of days and then set out for the Jenolan Caves. We were to meet him one last time, over a year later, in England. He was still on the bicycle and still itching to cover new ground.

On 11 November, the party of travellers I was to lead across Siberia had a get-together in downtown Sydney. There were twenty-seven people in all. It was to be the largest group that Sundowners had ever let loose on Russian soil. I was introduced to them as a seasoned traveller, in order to dispel any fears they may have harboured about their forthcoming adventure.

My fears multiplied when confronted by such a diverse range of faces. I had spent the previous evening engrossed in a red-covered dossier supplied by the travel company. It made interesting, if not alarming, reading: '*The Trans-Siberian Railway is the world's longest, the equivalent of travelling from Perth to Sydney, back again and back again.*' Always supposing anyone was crazy enough to make that sort of journey – although Baz was having a good try, with only one lap to go now.

What gripped my attention most was the extraordinary number of stops the train made before it reached Moscow. These varied in length from a mere two or three minutes to half an hour. I had worrying flashbacks of school trips when a frazzled Mr Collier, my geography teacher, counted in the raucous pupils after the school bus had earlier disgorged them into unfamiliar territory. What would happen if someone went missing in Siberia?

After a stopover in Bangkok, we flew to Japan and boarded the *Baikal* for Russia. The tugboats towed us out of the harbour and into the Pacific. Lea was pleased as Punch that we had a cabin to ourselves, even if it was hot and stuffy inside. Zhenka set about making comrades with the ship's crew. When the band struck up in the evening, he was first on the dancefloor.

The *Baikal* sailed up the Pacific coast and through the Tsugaru Strait, which divides the islands of Honshu and Hokkaido. It soon grew cold outside on deck. We wrapped up well in our winter clothes and strode briskly up and down the boat, killing time between meals.

On the second day we got talking to one of the sailors who played a squeeze-box in the band. His name was Boris and he spoke good English. I told him how we came to be travelling back from Australia.

'I sometimes run in the birch forests,' said Boris. 'I even go through the snow and sometimes on skis. When at school I watched Vladimir Kuts run. He was a hero of everyone.'

'I admired the way he ran,' I said.

'From the front. Always from the front. And sudden bursts of speed to upset the rhythm of the other runners,' added Boris. 'But last year, one of our athletes made a great run across Russia. All the way from Riga, on the Baltic, to Vladivostok. It is a distance of 6,800 miles.'

This news surprised me. It meant that at one time, in 1974, three very different long-distance journeys were being undertaken on foot. While Georgyi Bushuyev, of the Soviet Union, was running across his own land, and Sebastian Snow was trekking through South America, Baz and I had been making our way east.

The next day the *Baikal* docked at Nakhodka. Women and children were standing at the dockside. They were bundled up in fur hats, scarves and thick coats, and they reminded me of a row of plump matryoshka dolls. It was minus 10 but it hadn't yet snowed. An armed guard and a piercing wind greeted us at the foot of the gangplank. We hurriedly changed some money into roubles and then left for the railway station.

The boat train pulled out of Tikhookeanskaya (Pacific Ocean) Station and dinner was served in the rattling dining car. We chose a table on the left-hand side of the carriage so that we could see the Chinese frontier through the window. But it was already dark outside. After we'd eaten – the unleavened brown bread was Lea's favourite – we returned to our compartment. It had three bunks inside, one above the other. Lea and Zhenka decided that I should have the top bunk. It was quite some way from the floor and I worried about rolling off when the train lurched.

Before I went to sleep I spent a long time looking out of the window. The line skirted a wide river. I guessed that China lay on the other side. We passed through villages and towns that were no more than twinkling lights. The frontier was fenced, with watchtowers at regular intervals. Once, I caught sight of slag heaps and thought of Stoke-on-Trent.

The topmost bunk seemed narrower than the two below it when

I finally hauled myself up to bed. The train rocked to and fro through the night as it sped along the branch line to Khabarovsk. I fell asleep thinking of what Baz had written in the postcard he sent from Perth: *This is what we have to contend with now that the run is over – SPEED!*

Dawn came, dragging something resembling daylight after it. I scrambled down from my high perch and pushed my face against the cold grubby window to see more. It was like peering into a cement mixer. Outside, a patchy fog swirled through the small allotments that backed onto the railtracks. Beyond them, factories spewed corn-coloured smoke from their black chimneys.

The boat train had a reputation for being a bumpy ride, but most of the passengers said they'd slept well. Our journey had lasted just fourteen hours. In that short time we had travelled 569 miles – a distance that would have taken me almost three weeks to cover on foot.

When we arrived at Khabarovsk station, the Intourist guide who was to accompany us to Moscow stood in wait on the platform. She wore an expensive fur hat and a stylish coat, and she came from Khabarovsk where it is 'not possible to buy such clothes'. Her name was Irene, and to break the ice she produced a dutiful Intourist smile and patted Zhenka's head with a gloved hand, as if she were making a snowman. Lea and I stole a quick look at one another to see if either of us had warmed to her. The answer was *'nyet!'*

'Kelvin and Leona, I will be sharing with you your compartment on board the *Rossiya*. I hope we are good at travelling companions. Yes? All the way to Moscow. Only the tour leader enjoys this privilege. It is an education. Anything you wish to know, you will ask. Yes?'

We had time for a short sightseeing tour of the city before we joined the Trans-Siberian Express. Irene directed our attention to a statue outside the railway station.

'He is Yerofei Pavlovich Khabarov, and you may photograph. He was a leader of Cossacks and he is here in 1649.'

Already intimidated by this new Intourist addition to our happy band of overlanders, a handful of the Sundowners grabbed their cameras.

'All aboard the bus please next,' instructed Irene.

We were driven along an empty boulevard lined with trees.

'I am taking you to the banks of the river Amur,' Irene informed us.

Through the windows we could see wide streets where grey concrete apartment blocks stood side by side with small wooden buildings painted green and brown. At the riverside we were let out. The Amur was frozen solid. A dozen or so figures wearing dark clothes were huddled over holes they'd made in the ice, fishing.

'You may walk on this ice if you wish. It is not thinning on top,' smiled Irene.

But no one trusted her. Instead, we hung about at the edge of the frozen river until Ron alighted from the bus. Big Ron from Wimbledon weighed twenty stone and was wearing a heavy greatcoat and thick-soled climbing boots. He would do anything for a laugh and sensed straight away what was required of him. Like a knight in armour he gallantly handed Irene his woollen balaclava. Then he bounded across the ice with big exaggerated movements.

Within a few moments most of us had joined him. No sooner were we sliding about, enjoying ourselves, than Irene began to wave her arms.

'Quickly, back to the bus. We can be fitting in a Siberian tiger and a hairy mammoth. Then we must eat.'

The Museum of Local History was less than a hundred yards along the frozen waterfront, but Irene took great pleasure in herding us on and off the bus in order to get there. Afterwards, in exchange for the luncheon vouchers relayed between Irene, myself, and a stout-looking dinnerlady, we were served a hot meal and apple juice at the railway station cafeteria.

Then it was time to catch our train. We were travelling second class as opposed to the soft-class carriage, which the majority of foreigners plumped for. Soft-class compartments had only two berths and were roomier: the ideal arrangement for honeymooners or couples who'd seen *From Russia with Love* one too many times at the cinema.

Second class meant four berths, with a folding table in the middle and the essential prerequisite of seeing eye to eye with your sleeping partners, even when they were complete strangers. It should have been luxurious accommodation compared with how we had lived during the past year and a half. However, no one back at Sundowners had prepared us for life on the rails with Irene.

Our cold war with Intourist began in the buffet car that first night. To save time Irene ordered our food for us, and when Zhenka turned his nose up at the raw fish, she gleefully spooned a couple of mouthfuls down his throat – insisting that he at least try it out.

When we got back to our compartment, Irene removed her fur hat and placed it on the fold-down table. Lea told her how beautiful it looked.

'The fur of silver foxes is making this hat Leona, and I was saving up to buy it for a long time. Now I am visiting the lavatory and the wash basin. It is at the end of the corridor. You will follow when I am finished.'

As soon as the door was shut I chased Zhenka from bunk to bunk, whilst the train swayed and clattered over the points. When I caught him I swung him upside down and tickled him. He giggled, held his tummy and then suddenly threw up over the fabulous fur hat.

I stayed under the sheets and wriggled into my jeans before I swung down from the narrow upper berth. Zhenka, Lea and Irene were still asleep. A chink of dawn showed through a slit at one side of the window blind.

Out in the corridor the light was blinding. I lowered one of the jump-seats with my knee and sat beside the window for a few minutes. Outside, the snow looked deep and was tinged with pink where a feeble sun flickered between the birch trees. I was here to keep a watch over distance so that it might relay to me what I had done. But this was a side-on view of miles sliding away from me, and I couldn't get to grips with it.

Perhaps I should have confronted the journey head-on and clung to the big red star mounted on the nose of the locomotive pulling us along, like Turner lashed to a mast to paint the full force of a storm. Then I remembered what Peter Levi had written when he jumped on a bus to cross Afghanistan: 'To descend on a remote city out of the air without a slow arrival is to deprive yourself of any chance of understanding where you are going.' Fitzroy Maclean too: 'You can cross Siberia by jet in a few hours, where a train takes as many days. But it is not at all the same thing.'

Anyway, it wasn't as if the Trans-Siberian Railway was a fast train ride. It could hardly be termed an express, with at least one hundred timetabled stops out of the eight hundred stations between Khabarovsk and Moscow.

Already the railway carriage felt much warmer than it had done the day before. I stood up, letting the jump-seat spring back against the wall, and made my way down the corridor. Directly opposite the lavatory was a cubbyhole for the conductress. Next to this was the most important item on the whole of the Trans-Siberian Rail system: a majestic samovar. We may have fallen out of favour with Intourist after only one day but we were determined not to jeopardise our supply of boiling water. Lea had slipped Ella, the conductress, a couple of chocolate bars. Now I was to be reimbursed with a glass of tea in a polished metal holder, after the fire had been stoked up with extra logs.

I re-emerged from the lavatory to find the corridor full of a dishevelled flotsam of Sundowners wearing hairnets and waving toothbrushes. The stampede for the dining car was underway.

Irene said nothing all morning. *This is what it's all about*, I thought. *I'm experiencing the cold war at first hand*. But how was I expected to liaise between officialdom and the tour group if our Intourist guide had shut up shop?

By mid-afternoon, the fur hat had dried out and it looked less spiky. Irene decided to make a supreme effort towards world peace, and offered Lea some travel sickness pills for Zhenka. After all, iron curtain or no iron curtain, we were to spend the next seven days together in an area smaller than a sputnik. There was frost enough outside.

Early in the evening rumours reached us of a fault in the complicated heating system of the dining car, eight carriages up-train. Irene told us that the problem was too technical for a satisfactory translation. However, closer investigation by Big Ron revealed that the attendants responsible had simply not shovelled enough coal on board at the last pick-up point. Whatever the cause, we were advised to wear plenty for our next meal, and gloves too, to prevent the cutlery sticking to our hands like the metal door handles between carriages did.

Outside, the temperature was down to minus 22 degrees.

Our train crawled into Irkutsk at 7.30 a.m. on the second day of December, 1975. Lea had been awake since six. She told me that one of the passengers had spoken to her in the corridor about a medical problem that needed treatment.

Charlie was in his late forties. He worked as a telegraph engineer in the Northern Territory, and lived with his mother. This was his big trip – the first time he'd left Australia, or his mother – and he was grabbing life by the throat.

Everyone liked Charlie. Like Big Ron, he was a good mixer. The compartment they shared was the noisiest on the coach.

'He looked worried,' Lea went on. 'Not at all like himself. I think you should go and see him.'

I decided to wait until we reached our hotel. Irene had lots of information for me to pass on to the others. We were to spend a whole day off the train at Irkutsk, and catch another one the following morning. It was still dark outside and the temperature was minus 26 degrees when we made our way to the waiting bus that would take us to the hotel. I sat on an empty seat next to Charlie and asked how he was.

'I could do with seeing a doctor, Kelvin,' Charlie whispered. 'I got drinking with some GIs when we were in Bangkok and they took me to the Starlight Hotel where they were staying. They ordered Thai girls like takeaways. They were beautiful, but I think

I may have caught something. Shit, Kelvin … I never *saw* a girl in the buff before, much less slept with one.'

'It'll be alright,' I said. 'We can sort something out with Irene, here in Irkutsk. I'll have a word with her as soon as we get to the hotel.'

The Angara Hotel was a quarter of a mile from the river where it got its name. Irene came to our room.

'Irene, there is one small matter.'

'Oh?'

'We have a bit of a problem …' I hesitated.

'Problem, what is this problem?'

'Charlie has developed certain symptoms of a delicate nature that may require clinical treatment …' Again I dithered. My mouth was dry and my voice sounded as if my tongue was trying to disown it. 'He did something he shouldn't have in Bangkok.'

'Banged cock?' Irene looked puzzled but she was getting warm.

'Brothel,' I said, hoping it didn't lead me into a conversation on the merits of Siberian meat dumplings.

Irene raised her eyebrows. So, she'd been right after all. Charlie and his problem were proof of Western decadence.

'He will require doctoring, yes?'

I nodded.

The taxi glided soundlessly over the snow. When we reached Lermotov Street, Irene indicated to the driver where he should pull up. The doctor had on a white coat. Irene said something to him in Russian. Then she turned to me.

'I will translate everything. First the doctor asks why we are here.'

'There is this emission,' I said.

'He has something missing between the legs?' Irene looked alarmed.

'No, that's *o*mission,' I told her.

'Discharge,' butted in Charlie. 'I have this discharge.'

Irene shook her head. 'No, there is no charge, it is free.'

The doctor took control, glancing at his wristwatch as he gave Irene her instructions.

'Show him!' she ordered Charlie severely.

Charlie unzipped his jeans and flopped out his penis. Irene went berserk. 'No, no!' she screamed. 'Behind the screen, go behind the screen and do it! I am not nursing this banged cock of yours!'

In the afternoon, a few of the Sundowners went on the trip to Baikal. The rest tagged along with Irene on what she referred to as a 'shopping spree'.

'I'd hardly call a few jars of pickled mushrooms a shopping spree,' whispered Lea afterwards. 'Personally I find this whole sightseeing experience a bit disorientating. For instance, I can't tell whether we're in a museum or a department store because everything's displayed in the same glass-fronted vitrines. Even those scary-looking mushrooms of Irene's – which I definitely think belong in a museum.'

'Why are we whispering?' I asked.

'Everyone whispers in Russia, haven't you noticed? Even the drunks.'

Lea was right. There was this deathly silence. I'd put it down to the snow muffling the sounds. But the quiet trailed indoors after you like a fur trapper.

The temperature fell drastically. Outside it was minus 50 degrees when we woke, and only a fraction above freezing in the dining car. Between carriages was the coldest part of the train.

We passed through bleak coalfields that stretched forever. We trundled across long suspension bridges where photographs were forbidden. I remained at my post – glued to the jump-seat. There were not many people out there. None that I could see anyway, just hints of them: bridges, smoke, tracks left in the snow by fur boots or skis. A pram filled with coal on an empty platform where we didn't stop. And statues; I saw more statues than people. But they were all statues of the same man. Now and then, we skirted the graveyards of disused steam locomotives buried in mounds of snow and ice.

In the days when there was no railway, a dirt road linked Moscow and St Petersburg with eastern Siberia, and eventually the Pacific

Ocean. It was known as the Trakt, and I wondered if it still existed. But I had no map of Siberia and could find no one who would tell me.

'Do you realise,' I said to Lea, 'that for the past two years, and probably much longer, maps have been our daily reading matter. Now I really do feel lost without one.'

'But you can't get lost, can you?' she laughed. 'Not physically lost, like you used to when you were running. The map has become like a security blanket for you. A grown-up version of Zhenka's "pinky". Without one you can't be sure you exist.'

A day later, I was sitting alone in the dining car of the train, peering into an untouched bowl of mysterious grey gruel, when a Canadian girl, Jane, asked if she could join me.

'What's it feel like?' she said.

I prodded the floating bits with a fork.

'No, not that,' she laughed. 'To have run across the world. Much further than this long train ride even, through wild places like Iran and Afghanistan!'

'That's one of the reasons I came on the Trans-Siberian Railway,' I told her. 'To try and find out what it felt like.'

'And have you?'

'No, not yet, but I'm still looking.'

'I know. I've watched you in the corridor day after day – just staring out into the landscape. But it's all trees and snow to me. Besides, we're flashing through so quickly.'

'That's right,' I nodded, 'quickly, quickly.' And I laughed to myself because I'd remembered an Indian voice hurrying us along on the Grand Trunk Road to Delhi. 'But it is that short span of time that throws me. Take this stretch for instance. It's about two thousand miles from Novosibirsk to Moscow. We left yesterday, and we're due to arrive tomorrow. That's only two and a half days to cover two thousand miles. To cross those countries you mentioned earlier – Iran and Afghanistan – involves a similar distance, perhaps only three hundred miles more, and yet it took us over three months.'

'Is that what you write in your notebook?'

'Partly.'

I glanced at the small crumpled notebook on the table in front of me. I'd carried it with me on the journey as far back as Europe, writing when I was too tired to run, or when I'd been forced to walk for some other reason, such as illness or a sprained ankle. I'd jotted things down wherever we'd been and now, months on, it made muddled reading.

Jane reached across the white starched tablecloth for her glass of tea. 'Look at this,' she said, pointing to the embossed decorations around the handle of the ornate metal container. 'Sputniks with cosmonauts hurtling through space!'

'I wonder if they came back to earth with a bump?'

She laughed. 'I bet they did. And then they were put on a train to Siberia to reflect upon their time in space.'

'Better get back to my corridor,' I said, folding shut the notebook. As I picked it up, an aerogramme fell onto the table. The letter had reached me at Faulconbridge a few days after our metal trunk of belongings had been collected for delivery to the docks. The aerogramme was addressed to me c/o the British Embassy in Sydney and they had kindly redirected it.

'This letter,' I said to Jane. 'A boy glimpses two men running along his stretch of road, and then they are gone. But he keeps the memory of it. And that will blur in time of course, even though he has the yellowing newsprint. You can read it if you like.'

My dear brother Kalwin and sister Mrs Kalwin,
I pray for you that may Allah (God) complete your journey safely. Do you remember this sentence: "My sister, do you want a dog?" Perhaps you remember me with the help of this sentence. I met you on 28 December, 1974 at 9.00 a.m. in Pakistan between the city Peshawar and Rawalpindi, when you have completed about 5,900 miles of your journey. I am a student at college. In December I read in the two newspapers of my country, *The Pakistan Times* and *The Daily Journal*, that two travellers are travelling the distance between London

and Sydney on foot. I became very surprised and I cut off the piece of paper for memorial. That piece of paper is still kept in my file. My home is situated near the G.T. Road. I often walk along the road under the shadows of the trees and learn my lessons and enjoy the road.

When I saw a van standing beside the road I came near it and a girl was getting something from the trolley. After some time the two persons (men) passed running near the van. I asked your driver why are the men running. He told me that they are travellers. Then I understood the whole thing. I saw your blue-eyed boy. I had wanted to give you a beautiful little white dog as a gift. But my sister Mrs Kalwin said "No, we have not any place to keep it." I calculated your date of arrival according to the newspaper and now I am writing a letter to you.

I often tell your adventure to my friends and show the piece of paper as a proof. Please answer me soon and tell me that you have reached safety.

Your Brother, Mohammad Usman.

'It's a marvellous letter,' said Jane.

We both looked out of the carriage window at the white unmarked steppe. The train was approaching a large stone obelisk.

'We're leaving Asia!' cried Jane excitedly. 'That's the boundary stone. Irene told me. It says Europe on the other side – see?' She rushed from the dining car to pass on the information to her friends.

I put away my aerogramme and the notebook. Then I strained my eyes to find some colour in the monochrome landscape beyond the smudgy window. There was deep snow in Europe too. It reminded me of a cold winter when I'd helped my grandfather build a snowman in the backyard. When we'd finished, it was so big you could hardly squeeze past to get to the lavatory. I had picked two lumps of coal out of a tin bath in the shed and sunk them in the snowman's head for eyes.

'Don't go losing any coal, young Kel,' Grandfather had shouted. I wondered now what he would have made of it, this journey on foot, with those eyes of his, orphaned among stars. I can't recall him believing in much, only that he was a man passing through. And that he always spoke to me as if he could see. When I sat on his bruised knees and told him I was going to be a runner, he asked me where I would run to.

Perhaps it wasn't the endurance that got handed down. Perhaps he just gave me a double helping of curiosity.

Postscript

Keith Bartlam pursued his chosen vocation as a schoolteacher, before renouncing all worldly possessions to become a sannyasi at an ashram in Poona. Here, he was given a new name by Bhagwan Shree Rajneesh (the guru who owned 93 Rolls-Royces), instructed to wear orange or red, and to leave his mind and shoes outside. In his quest for enlightenment Keith also stayed at Rajneeshpuram, the guru's ranch commune in Oregon. Ten years ago he told me he was setting up an old folks home for hippies somewhere near Bristol. I have not seen him since.

Ever reluctant to hang up his spikes, Baz still runs and continues to win races. On his return to England he became the Midlands AAA 10,000-metre track champion. Later, he met and married Jenny and they moved to Cornwall where he now works as a postman in Penzance. They have visited South Africa and India, and once spent six months touring Australia where Baz crossed the Nullarbor for a third time – towing a caravan on this occasion. He remains an ebullient and intrepid twitcher.

Chris embarked on a career in computers and now has his own consultancy business. He married Debbie and they live in a small Staffordshire village called Standon Bowers. He too returned to India for a holiday, and has also travelled to Egypt and Tunisia.

Lea took up nursing and we lived in a converted cowshed on the edge of the Peak District, where Zhenka attended a village school. Several years after our homecoming, we separated. Lea later cycled across Europe with Mick, her new partner. Then they immigrated to Australia and settled in an outback town called Alpha in the isolated heart of Queensland.

When Zhenka left school he went to live in Stoke and became the lead singer in a rock band. He has two children of his own now: Ryan and Natasha. The journeys Zhenka has since undertaken – to the Egyptian tombs and the Aztec ruins on the Inca trail – reflect his desire to cross boundaries of an altogether different kind; hence his ongoing commitment to the study of spiritualism.

In 1983 I enrolled at art college and met Jo Baker, a fellow student who later moved in with me. Three years on we lugged a scuffed suitcase full of collages around the art galleries of Amsterdam to secure our first overseas exhibitions. Shows in London followed. Peter Blake, the pop artist who designed the *Sergeant Pepper* album cover, was an early collector. Once, we took our work to New York, sold a painting each, and bought tickets on a Greyhound bus heading for New Mexico. Jo and I parted in 1991.

The next year I got to know another artist: Dooze Storey. We lived in St Ives, Cornwall, in a fisherman's cottage that once belonged to the naive painter Alfred Wallis, whose pictures hang in the Tate. During the winter of 1996, Dooze and I were invited to exhibit our paintings in Poland. My first major show took place at the State Gallery of Art in Sopot, on the shores of a frozen Baltic, whilst Dooze held a one-woman exhibition in the adjoining city of Gdansk.

On our return to England we occupied the topmost loft of an old furniture-maker's in the East End of London. Artists throughout Europe were converging on the capital to convert disused warehouses into studios. Some, like Tracey Emin, were already on the brink of pop star notoriety. Others such as ourselves were desperately short of buyers. One day, we stashed all our unsold paintings in the basement of a bookshop at Spitalfields Market, acquired a second-hand Gas Board van, and took off for the Mediterranean.

We thought we had bought a windmill on the edge of a medieval village overlooked by a ruined castle, but the local *maire* stepped in and vetoed our plans. Instead, we found an empty shepherd's hut to live in that had no water, electricity or neighbours.

In the year 2000, Dooze gave birth to a baby boy. We named him Ruben.

For a current catalogue and a full listing of Summersdale travel books, visit our website:

www. summersdale.com